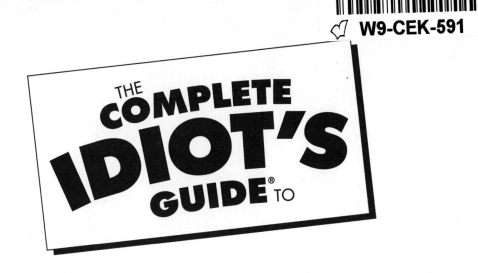

Investing

Third Edition

*by Edward T. Koch, Debra DeSalvo,
and Joshua A. Kennon.*

ALPHA

A member of Penguin Group (USA) Inc.

"Commit thy works unto the Lord, and thy thoughts shall be established."—Proverbs 16:3
This book is dedicated to God the Father, Son, and Holy Spirit. May it be the first of many.

ALPHA BOOKS

Published by the Penguin Group

Penguin Group (USA) Inc., 375 Hudson Street, New York, New York 10014, U.S.A.

Penguin Group (Canada), 10 Alcorn Avenue, Toronto, Ontario, Canada M4V 3B2 (a division of Pearson Penguin Canada Inc.)

Penguin Books Ltd, 80 Strand, London WC2R 0RL, England

Penguin Ireland, 25 St Stephen's Green, Dublin 2, Ireland (a division of Penguin Books Ltd)

Penguin Group (Australia), 250 Camberwell Road, Camberwell, Victoria 3124, Australia (a division of Pearson Australia Group Pty Ltd)

Penguin Books India Pvt Ltd, 11 Community Centre, Panchsheel Park, New Delhi—110 017, India

Penguin Group (NZ), cnr Airborne and Rosedale Roads, Albany, Auckland 1310, New Zealand (a division of Pearson New Zealand Ltd)

Penguin Books (South Africa) (Pty) Ltd, 24 Sturdee Avenue, Rosebank, Johannesburg 2196, South Africa

Penguin Books Ltd, Registered Offices: 80 Strand, London WC2R 0RL, England

International Standard Book Number: 1-59257-480-7
Library of Congress Catalog Card Number: 2005933834

08   8   7   6

Interpretation of the printing code: The rightmost number of the first series of numbers is the year of the book's printing; the rightmost number of the second series of numbers is the number of the book's printing. For example, a printing code of 05-1 shows that the first printing occurred in 2005.

Printed in the United States of America

Note: This publication contains the opinions and ideas of its authors. It is intended to provide helpful and informative material on the subject matter covered. It is sold with the understanding that the authors and publisher are not engaged in rendering professional services in the book. If the reader requires personal assistance or advice, a competent professional should be consulted.

The authors and publisher specifically disclaim any responsibility for any liability, loss, or risk, personal or otherwise, which is incurred as a consequence, directly or indirectly, of the use and application of any of the contents of this book.

Most Alpha books are available at special quantity discounts for bulk purchases for sales promotions, premiums, fundraising, or educational use. Special books, or book excerpts, can also be created to fit specific needs.

For details, write: Special Markets, Alpha Books, 375 Hudson Street, New York, NY 10014.

Publisher: *Marie Butler-Knight*
Editorial Director: *Mike Sanders*
Senior Managing Editor: *Jennifer Bowles*
Acquisitions Editor: *Tom Stevens*
Development Editor: *Ginny Bess Munroe*
Production Editor: *Megan Douglass*
Copy Editor: *Ross Patty*

Cartoonist: *Jody Schaeffer*
Book Designer: *Trina Wurst*
Cover Designer: *Bill Thomas*
Indexer: *Angie Bess*
Layout: *Ayanna Lacey*
Proofreading: *Mary Hunt*

Contents at a Glance

Contents

Appendixes

Foreword

Blame it on Gerald Ford. On September 2, 1974, less than a month after he had assumed office following Richard Nixon's resignation, President Ford signed the Employee Retirement Income Security Act into law. Although the primary goal of ERISA was to increase the security of traditional pensions, one of its least debated provisions was to have an unexpectedly profound effect on the way Americans prepare for their financial futures—because ERISA was the legislation that established Individual Retirement Accounts, the innovation that allowed us to save for our golden years and save on taxes at the same time.

IRAs were targeted at what was believed to be a relatively small proportion of the population, namely those individuals who weren't covered by a pension plan. It didn't take long though for companies to realize that it was a whole lot cheaper to let their workers "self-direct" their own retirement accounts than to guarantee them an income for life, and that small proportion of the population grew very large indeed.

So thirty years ago it may have been reasonable to leave your savings for a down payment or tuition at the bank and rely on the government and your employer to manage the funding of life after work. Today, however, Americans are expected to plan for their own financial security. You're the one who has to understand the differences between an REIT and an ETF, between a lump sum payout and an annuity. And if proposed legislation is passed, you may even be managing a portion of your own Social Security account.

It's a huge responsibility, especially if your vision is to reach your goals rather than just get by. You'll need to make thousands of decisions about your finances over your lifetime, but how can you be sure that you're making informed choices and not just falling for the latest financial industry sales pitch?

This third edition of *The Complete Idiot's Guide to Investing* is an essential reference manual: clear, comprehensive, and objective. You'll find definitions to help you decipher the jargon that somehow invades every investment communication. No need to scratch your head the next time your co-worker mentions "ticker symbols" or "FICO scores." You'll get explanations of key financial concepts; for instance, you'll see why time really is money. And you'll find concrete advice on managing your money in a complex world: how to start a savings plan; how to balance your priorities; how to make sure that the level of risk in your portfolio matches your objectives and personality; and how to avoid the most expensive—yet all too common—mistakes.

Maybe you want to start making your own investment decisions, rather than reacting to the latest tip from your brother-in-law. Or you might want to continue using a financial advisor, but be better able to evaluate whether you should in fact jump when he calls. Or maybe you just want to join in that water cooler conversation the next time the topic turns to investments. *The Complete Idiot's Guide to Investing* will give you the knowledge base you need to ask intelligent questions and, just as critically, evaluate the answers you might get. You've just taken your first step toward financial success.

Theresa Hamacher

—Theresa Hamacher, CFA, is the former Chief Investment Officer (CIO) for Pioneer Investment Management USA in Boston, MA, where she supervised a team of over 50 investment professionals managing more than $15 billion in global equity and fixed income assets for mutual fund and institutional clients. Previously, she was the CIO for Prudential Mutual Funds in Newark, NJ. She is a Chartered Financial Analyst and is working on a book about retirement investing in America.

Introduction

Even though this book is called *The Complete Idiot's Guide to Investing, Third Edition,* we wrote it for smart people—people with the common sense to know that investing can't be all that difficult. After all, lots of people do it very successfully. You may even have a sneaking suspicion that investing is the key to making dreams come true. Guess what? You're 100 percent correct!

You may have tried to tackle investing before and had a bad experience with a blow-hard financial advisor or a tedious, confusing book. If you threw up your hands in frustration and said "Forget it!" but can't get rid of the nagging feeling that you're missing out on something very important, don't despair. We wrote this book for you.

This book assumes you know less than nothing about investing, but doesn't patronize you by telling you what to do. Instead, we offer you a step-by-step guide so that you can figure out exactly what investment strategies will work for your situation:

- How much you need to save to put the kids through college *and* retire happily

- How much risk you can take on and still sleep at night

- How to create a balanced portfolio of investments tailored to your financial goals

- How to manage your investments from year to year and still roll with life's changes

Questionnaires, worksheets, dreadful jokes—they're all in here. It's best to start at the beginning and work through to the end, but feel free to skip around until you get comfortable. Just remember that you'll find everything you need to know in this book to become someone who can make rational, disciplined investing decisions. Here's the gist ....

Part 1, "What Does 'Financial Security' Mean to You?" helps you figure out exactly that, because there's no point in investing without specific goals. You'll also take a risk tolerance questionnaire and create your own income statement and balance sheet. You'll also learn several basic time value of money formulas you can use to answer questions such as, "If I want to have $100,000 in 5 years and I can earn a 10 percent return, how much do I need to invest annually?"

Part 2, "Creating a Plan," is based on the premise that you have to know what you've got before you can get any more. Here, you'll take a close look at your retirement needs, your debt and credit situation, and what it will take to send you—or your child—to college.

Part 3, "Investing 101," is a primer in the basics. Everything you ever wanted to know but felt too stupid to ask, from what they're really up to on Wall Street to how to pick a mutual fund.

Part 4, "Basic Financial Statement Analysis," will provide a tutorial on using the income statement, balance sheet, statement of cash flows, and footnotes to evaluate an investment. By knowing what to look for and what to avoid, you'll empower yourself to make smarter, more intelligent decisions.

Part 5, "Fundamental Investing Strategies," introduces you to Ben Graham's "margin of safety," choosing an asset allocation based upon your goals and objectives, evaluating your investment performance, grading your financial advisors, and lowering your tax bill.

Part 6, "Advanced Investment Strategies," is for readers who want to explore more complicated, alternative investments. It's also a source of answers for questions you may have when you hear words like "option" or "futures contract" bandied about.

In addition, you get a comprehensive glossary with clear, straightforward definitions of investment terms and an appendix with some recommendations for further reading and financial exploration.

One caveat: Although we have made every effort to confirm our data, accidents do happen. Equally important to keep in mind is that tax laws are under constant revision, reinterpretation, and so on. As a result, please double-check with the appropriate sources (e.g., the IRS or your accountant) before undertaking any course of action.

Extras

If you're more a scanner than a reader, you'll appreciate our sidebars. These explain confusing jargon, help you avoid expensive mistakes, and offer super inside strategies. Look for the following boxes:

Crash Alert ___

When dealing with money, mistakes can be costly. This box alerts you to tax issues, legal snarls, and scams, so you can steer clear.

 Investor's Idiom ___

Yes, investing has its own language, but it's not hard to learn. Peek in this box for clear, succinct explanations of any italicized terms.

Super Strategies

These boxes outline super-smart investing strategies you can apply right away to improve your finances. Hint: Some of these strategies appear only in the box, not in the text, so don't pass

 **Fiscal Facts** ___

These little boxes contain just-for-fun facts about the financial world. Great for cocktail party chatter.

Acknowledgments

Joshua would like to thank his family, notably Mark and Tammy for their unwavering love and support. I'm proud to call you not just my parents, but my friends. To Caleb, who spent countless hours talking to me from Qatar in the middle of the night as I worked on this project; it kept me sane. I'm proud of the man you've become. To Kelsey, for countless games of Monopoly, Clue, and enduring endless stories about Warren, I pray you accomplish everything you desire in life. To Harley, who for years never hesitated to tell me I would become the man I wanted to be (SRF); may your portfolio grow with each passing day. To Donna, for her belief in me and always being there; when I'm sitting at my desk reading annual reports until 2 A.M., it's a great source of comfort knowing I can call. To Ruby, for her unconditional love; one of my most treasured memories is sitting with you, drinking coffee in the mornings as a child. Decades later, the china is gold-rimmed and the beans gourmet, but the company is just as sweet.

Joshua would also like to thank Molly Wright for her wisdom, patience, understanding, love, and faith; I'm a better man because you are in my life. To Aaron Green, for his forbearance, humor, endless pots of coffee, and constant reassurance; your strength and ability to hold it together have enabled me to accomplish things that otherwise would not have been possible.

Finally, to everyone else who has made the journey more pleasant and helped me along the way—Ashly Vallimont, Jocelyn Nordstrom, Laura Hubbard, Ellary Draper, Karen Ashe, Mat Williams, James Byrne, Eric Parker, Katie Waldo, Diana Crane, Jill Brown, Chris VanHoozer, Tony Dickson, Anne Marie DuWan, Dr. Mordechai Rozanski, Dr. Barton Luedeke, Kirk Sibley, Millicent Daugherty, Elem Eley, Joseph Woodhull, and the folks at both the NJM Insurance Group and About.com.

Ed would like to thank his former associates at FleetBoston Financial. Those who came through at "crunch time" include Frances McPartland, Charlie Yue, John Bolton, Donna Todaro, Eddie Aydin, Christine Flynn, and Ben Campbell of the Columbia Management Group, and Jane Higgins of the Private Clients Group. Also, a special thanks from Ed to Skip and Elaine Howland: best friends and major support for so many years.

Ed would also like to thank his family. His wife Joan, for her understanding and support when deadlines were nigh. To his daughter, Emily, and to his son, John, who fill him with pride. And last but not least, to the newest apples of "Booba's" eye: Henry, Oliver, and Ella.

Trademarks

Part 1

What Does "Financial Security" Mean to You?

Investing is really very simple—it's about putting your money to work for you over time. The longer your money is parked in an investment, the more time it has to grow … and grow … and grow!

But what are you growing it for? Before you choose investments, you need to identify your investment objectives. Are you saving to buy a home? To put kids through school? For retirement? Or all three? How much time do you have to reach those goals?

Next, you need to figure out how much risk you're willing to take with your hard-earned cash to try to meet those objectives. Finally, you need to take a look at what you've already got—and what you owe.

There's no point in putting yourself into some cookie-cutter investment plan. To invest really well, you must know yourself really well. In this part, we're going to explore the dark cave that is your financial psyche.

Put Your Money to Work for You

In This Chapter

- How investing will put your money to work for you
- Recent changes in the regulatory environment
- The relationship between time, risk, and your sanity
- Thinking big when starting small
- Maintaining perspective

When John D. Rockefeller was a teen during the mid-1800s, he lent $50 to a neighboring farmer. A year later, the farmer paid him back the $50 plus $3.50 interest on the loan. The week before, Rockefeller had earned a measly $1.12 after 30 hours of backbreaking work hoeing potatoes for another neighbor. "From that time on," Rockefeller wrote in his autobiography, *Random Reminiscences*, "I was determined to make money work for me."

Putting your money to work for you is the essence of investing—and anyone can learn to do it well. Think for a moment about what you envision a successful investor to look like. Maybe you picture someone in a power suit, up at the crack of dawn checking stock quotes in *The Wall Street Journal* before he or she has even had coffee. A real mover and shaker.

Well, toss that picture right out of your head and take a walk over to the closest mirror. See that good-lookin' person looking back at you? That's what a successful investor looks like. It's anybody. It certainly could be you.

"But where am I going to get the money I need to start investing?" you may be thinking. That's simple: any dollar you aren't using to pay bills is money you can invest. Luckily, you have a lot more investment options than young Rockefeller did. On the other hand, separating the wheat from the chaff is going to be a little more complicated for you than it was for our boy on the farm. Before you start threshing your investment opportunities, you'll need to lay a little groundwork.

Become an Educated Investor, Not Just a Consumer

Today, there are a lot of educated consumers, but not many educated investors. The stock market's unusually strong performance during the 1990s was splashed across the covers of financial magazines, convincing individual investors to "come on in, the water's fine!" All the raving about how spectacularly the stock market performed created a new class of investing consumers who jumped into the market feet first.

Fiscal Facts

The word millionaire is believed to have first come into use in Paris around 1720. A number of French noblemen invested in shares of The Mississippi Company and became fabulously (temporarily) wealthy. They were called "millionaires." The Mississippi Company was a contemporary of the equally and initially profitable South Sea Company in England … and both bubbles burst!

These are the same investors who panicked and dumped their stock holdings—collectively losing billions—when the market went south in 2002 due to revelations that some important and heretofore respectable corporations were cooking the books. Truth is, the stream of accounting scandals was a direct result of the unbridled exuberance of the market during the 1990s, when the stock of many Internet-based companies (the shiny new "dotcoms") took off like rockets despite the fact that many of these "businesses" were unprofitable.

Investing in a Post-Bubble World

Several years after the fallout of the Internet bubble, Wall Street has changed for the better. In the wake of Worldcom and Enron, the regulatory environment has significantly strengthened thanks to several key developments, including the following:

- Congress passed the Sarbanes-Oxley Act of 2002. This legislation requires a company to formally document the internal controls it has in place to prevent inaccurate accounting (both honest and dishonest). It also requires CEOs and CFOs to personally guarantee they have reviewed the financial statements and that they are not aware of *material* misstatement or fraud.

Investor's Idiom

A rule of thumb is that information is considered **material** if it would have changed reported net income or shareholders' equity by 5+ percent, or if disclosure would have caused a reasonable investor to increase or decrease his holdings.

- The New York State Attorney General's Office has leveled the playing field in everything from mutual funds to insurance brokerage services by aggressively pursuing companies and individuals it believes engaged in questionable or fraudulent practices.

- The Financial Accounting Standards Board (FASB), the nation's highest accounting authority, is set to begin requiring corporations to expense stock options awarded to employees. Formerly, this very real compensation expense was buried in the footnotes where only experienced investors and analysts were likely to tread.

What does all of this mean for you? In theory, it is going to be difficult for companies to manage their numbers in the next few years. We know from history, however, that it is only a matter of time before accounting shenanigans arise yet again. The good news: you can protect yourself through education. By the time you reach the end of this book, you will have an understanding of how to build a portfolio that is suited for your life circumstances, enabling you to weather even the toughest financial storms.

Time, Risk, and Your Sanity

Risk is defined as the potential for permanent loss of *capital*. One of the biggest influences upon the amount of risk involved in any investment is the amount of time you are financially and emotionally able to hold an investment. Let's take a look at how this time and risk relationship works in the stock market.

You'll learn in Chapter 11 that common stock represents ownership in a company. People who own *stock* are known as shareholders because they are entitled to a "share" of the profit (or loss).

Investor's Idiom

In the business world, **capital** refers to assets (cash, stocks, bonds, machinery, inventory, etc.) that generate income.

There are many reasons a corporation may decide to issue stock. Most often, management and the existing owners want to raise capital in order to grow the business. The money raised is used to build factories, create new divisions, or fund other major undertakings designed to increase the overall size and profitability of the firm. This is known as *equity financing* because the company is literally selling equity (ownership).

History has proven there is no better way to increase your wealth over the long-term than by owning businesses. The ride, however, can be rather bumpy. Here's a real, extreme example from the stock market of the interrelationship between time, risk, and your sanity.

Assume it is the end of October 1987 and you are heavily invested in stocks. You've witnessed the following sickening drops in the stock market:

◆ In one day, October 19, 1987, the Dow Jones Industrial Average fell 22.61 percent.

◆ Within 10 days, the market had fallen 34 percent.

◆ By the end of October, the market was down 21.5 percent.

Investor's Idiom

When you own **stock**, you own a fraction of the company that issued it. Like any owner, you are entitled to a share of the company's profit or loss.

If your time frame was only a few months, you were one unhappy camper. Putting your family's Christmas money into the stock market in September would have been a lousy idea because you didn't have time to recover from the crash.

But what if you were in the stock market for the long haul? Let's expand the time frame. The Dow began 1987 at 1,927. At the end of 1996, ten years later, it closed at 6,561. Despite significant volatility over the course of the decade, you would have more than tripled your wealth at a compound annual growth rate of approximately 13 percent per year. What does all this mean? Simply, risk is reduced as time is added. Here is the relationship between time, risk, and return.

Crash Alert

The single most important thing you can do for yourself as an investor is to develop a long-term horizon. This will inoculate you against persuasive pitches to buy the latest hot investment and prevent you from selling based on bits of news and rumors. "Just how long is long-term?" you ask. Think ten years or more.

In other words, the later you start investing, the less risk you can afford to take. If you're 60 and hope to retire at 65, and you do some calculations on the back of an envelope and realize you'll be $50,000 short of income when you retire, you shouldn't turn to the stock market because you aren't giving yourself enough time to ride out the risk. If you start to invest for retirement at a young age, on the other hand, you can put a high percentage of your savings in the stock market because you have time to ride out the highs and lows. A good rule of thumb is to give your investments at least 10 years to ride out stock market volatility.

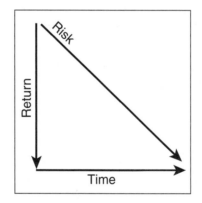

Given a decent timeframe, though, stocks have historically performed quite well. Here's the data going back to 1926, when the forerunner to the *Standard & Poor's 500*, the Standard & Poor's 90, was first tabulated:

Compound Annual Return 1926—2004	
Standard & Poor's 500 Stock Index	+10.46%
Long-Term Government Bonds Index	+ 5.40%
U.S. Treasury Bills Index	+ 3.70%
Inflation (Consumer Price Index)	+ 3.00%

(*Source:* Ibbotson Associates, Inc. Stocks, Bonds, Bills and Inflation® 2004 Yearbook. *All rights reserved. Used with permission.*)

Investor's Idiom

The **S&P 500** is a list of five hundred stocks selected by the folks at Standard and Poors for size, industry, and liquidity. This list, known as an index, is used on Wall Street as a broad measure of stock performance.

As you can see, the total return for stocks over the past 78 years was nearly 2× that of risk-free government bonds and 3× the inflation rate. Stocks are clearly worth the risk if you can afford to hold them for ten years or longer.

Every investing goal will have a different timeframe based upon your personal goals. You might want to buy your first house in five years, for example, in which case your savings would need to be in investments that don't fluctuate significantly. Perhaps you just got married, and, although there might not be a child on the scene for a couple years, you want to begin a 20-year savings plan for his or her college education. Under these circumstances, your investment choices are much broader.

In general, the less time you have to achieve your goal, the greater the need to insist upon safety of principal. We'll talk more about the importance of aligning your investment choices with your timeframe in Chapter 4.

Do Not Despise the Day of Small Beginnings

One of the biggest mental obstacles people confront in the quest to build wealth is the misconception that it is pointless to try unless you can put away large sums of money. As you'll learn in Chapter 2, this is simply not true; empires can be built on tiny amounts given enough time and the right rate of compounding.

It is important for you to realize that very few people enter the investment process with a clean slate. Some come to the table with mortgage payments and student loans; others are drowning in credit card debt. If this describes you, don't despair. It doesn't take a high IQ, prescient insight, luck, or the ability to discern macroeconomic trends to build extraordinary wealth. The only traits necessary are discipline, patience, a desire to avoid large mistakes, and a willingness to stick to your guns when you believe the market has lost its mind. By providing a proper mental framework, this book can help you begin turning your financial ship around, regardless of your current situation.

The Big Picture: Keep Things in Perspective

Before we embark on our journey into that crazy place known as Wall Street, there are four things you should keep in mind:

♦ If you feel overwhelmed, remember that there was a point in everyone's life—even those on the Forbes list—when they didn't know the difference between a dividend and a doughnut. All it takes is a willingness to learn. By picking up this book, you've already taken the first step.

♦ Always keep perspective. Money is never an end unto itself; it is merely the means that allows us to accomplish our bigger, more important goals such as starting a family, attending college, purchasing a house, taking vacations, and retiring in comfort.

♦ There are no cookie-cutter investing solutions. The ideal portfolio for you is going to depend upon a myriad of factors including your personal resources, the timeframe involved, your risk tolerance, and, in some cases, your personal prejudices (for example, you may pass on an attractive tobacco stock because you have qualms about investing in that sort of enterprise).

♦ Have fun! There is no greater feeling of satisfaction than when you accomplish a goal or know you made an intelligent decision. Once you learn the ground rules, building wealth becomes a self-sustaining process requiring little more than the avoidance of big mistakes.

The Least You Need to Know

♦ Although the regulatory environment on Wall Street is much improved, the first line of defense against financial disaster is a portfolio tailored to your individual needs and objectives.

♦ Common stock represents fractional ownership in a business.

♦ Riskier investments, such as stocks, can make you a lot of money, but only if you have time to ride out the ups and downs.

♦ The later you start investing, the less risk you can afford to take.

♦ When building wealth, discipline and patience are more important than a high IQ.

2

The Miracle of Compounding

In This Chapter

- ◆ The power of compound interest
- ◆ The importance of beginning early
- ◆ Calculating the present and future values of a lump sum
- ◆ Calculating the present and future values of an annuity
- ◆ Valuing a perpetuity

Albert Einstein, Nobel Prize winner and father of relativity theory, once remarked that compound interest was the most powerful force in the Universe. Al knew that every time you invest a dollar, it generates interest. After a while, you earn interest on your interest. In a few years, a virtuous cycle is born, resulting in you sipping drinks on a beach in Tahiti. In this chapter, you'll learn to master the math of compounding, improving both your financial health and your ability to impress your less fiscally-savvy friends!

How Compounding Makes the Difference

Compounding is affected by three variables:

- **The Amount You Invest:** It's a simple premise: The more money you invest, the greater the eventual value of your *portfolio*. Investing an extra $50 per month can increase your wealth by hundreds of thousands of dollars given enough time.

- **The Rate of Return You Earn:** You may not think there is a significant difference between a 10 percent and a 12 percent return. Over the long-run, however, a seemingly-unimportant percentage point or two can result in breathtaking disparities.

Investor's Idiom

A **portfolio** is a term used to describe a collection of assets. A portfolio can contain stocks, bonds, mutual funds, oil, gold, baseball cards, fine art, or anything else of value.

For example, two 20-year-olds, Jocelyn and Ashly, invest $5,000 each year until they reach retirement at age 65. The first earns a 10 percent return, the second 12 percent. In the end, Jocelyn will retire with $3.6 million. Ashly, on the other hand, will retire with $6.8 million, or nearly twice as much!

Crash Alert

You'll learn in later chapters that the rate of return you earn is largely dependent upon the amount of time you have to invest. If there is a chance you will need the money within the next few years, you will necessarily want to accept a lower rate of return in exchange for safety of principal. Otherwise, you could be forced to sell the investment in a down market, losing a substantial chunk of your capital.

- **The Length of Time You Allow the Money to Compound:** The longer your money is allowed to compound, the stronger the interest-upon-interest cycle becomes.

  Need proof? If you started investing $10,000 per year when you were 25, earning a 12 percent return, you would retire with $7.67 million. If you waited just ten years and began the same investing program at 35, you would retire with only $2.41 million.

  "Don't worry—I'll just contribute more when I'm 30," you say. Good luck! To end up with the same amount, you would have to save $31,782 annually instead of $10,000!

What Is the Time Value of Money?

If you were offered $1,000 today or $1,000 one year from now, which would you choose? Most everyone would opt for the money today because it could be immediately spent or invested. This concept—that cash today is more valuable than cash tomorrow—is known as the *time value of money* (TVM). It is the basis of finance; once you are aware of its implications, it can drastically change the way you think about capital.

During the remainder of the chapter, you'll learn the TVM formulas you need to answer questions such as, "If I want to have $10,000 in five years and can earn 6 percent on my money, how much should I invest as a lump-sum today?" and "If I save $5,000 per year for the next 10 years and earn 8 percent on my money, how much will my nest egg be worth at the end of the period?" Not only can you change your life forever with this knowledge, you'll be able to impress people at cocktail parties.

The Future Value of a Single Amount

Every time you spend a dollar, you are also spending all of the investment income that it could have generated from now until doomsday. One of the keys to financial success is to know the true economic cost of every decision you make.

Here's an example: your friends invite you to dinner and a movie. You expect the evening to cost approximately $50. "No problem." You think, "It's only $50 bucks, right?" Wrong. The economic cost of a night on the town depends upon two things: the number of years you can invest the money without touching it and the after-tax rate of return you could earn.

Investor's Idiom

The future value of a single amount formula answers the question, "How much would a lump sum investment grow to in X years if I could invest it at a rate of return of Y percent?"

Thankfully, there's a formula to help you decide if the experience is worth the expense. It's called the *future value of a single amount.*

$$FV = PV (1 + i)^n$$

FV (Future Value): What the investment will be worth in the future.

PV (Present Value): The amount you are investing today ($50).

I (Interest Rate): The after-tax return you expect to earn on your investment.

N (Number of Periods): The number of years you expect to have the money invested without touching it.

Fiscal Facts _____

Billionaire investor Warren Buffett knows a thing or two about the power of compounding. Buffett's holding company, Berkshire Hathaway, has risen from $19 per share in 1965 to $90,000 per share in 2005 thanks to the businesslike approach to selecting investments the "Oracle of Omaha" employs.

Assume you are only 30 years old and will invest the money for 35 years until retirement at 65. You plan on placing all of your funds in stocks and expect to earn an after-tax return of 12 percent (you'll learn about historical rates of return for different types of assets in the next chapter). Now that you're armed with the info you need, simply plug it into the formula:

$$FV = \$50 \ (1+.12)^{35}$$

$$FV = \$50 \ (1.12)^{35}$$

$$FV = \$50 \ (52.79962)$$

$$FV = \$2,639.98$$

Your eyes aren't playing tricks on you—by choosing to spend the $50 instead of investing it, you have given up $2,639.98 in future wealth! Adjust the formula for someone who is 20 years old (by changing "n" to 45) and the result is an astounding $8,199.38! For someone ten years away from retirement, the cost is still a whopping $155.29.

An Easy Way to Figure the Future Value of a Single Sum

If you're in a hurry and need to calculate the future value of a single sum, you can turn to this handy-dandy chart. It has its limitations (the results aren't as precise and you can't figure out half-percentage points, for example, which you learned earlier can make a substantial difference over time) but these numbers should serve as an easy-to-use shortcut.

Future Value of a Single Amount ($1 Compounded)

Rate Years	2%	3%	4%	5%	6%	7%	8%	9%	10%	11%	12%
1	1.020	1.030	1.040	1.050	1.060	1.070	1.080	1.090	1.100	1.110	1.120
2	1.040	1.061	1.082	1.102	1.124	1.145	1.166	1.188	1.210	1.232	1.254
3	1.061	1.093	1.125	1.158	1.191	1.225	1.260	1.295	1.331	1.368	1.405
4	1.082	1.126	1.170	1.216	1.262	1.311	1.360	1.412	1.464	1.518	1.574
5	1.104	1.159	1.217	1.276	1.338	1.403	1.469	1.539	1.611	1.685	1.762
6	1.126	1.194	1.265	1.340	1.419	1.501	1.587	1.677	1.772	1.870	1.974
7	1.149	1.230	1.316	1.407	1.504	1.606	1.714	1.828	1.949	2.076	2.211
8	1.172	1.267	1.369	1.477	1.594	1.718	1.851	1.993	2.144	2.305	2.476
9	1.195	1.305	1.423	1.551	1.689	1.838	1.999	2.172	2.358	2.558	2.773
10	1.219	1.344	1.480	1.629	1.791	1.967	2.159	2.367	2.594	2.839	3.106
11	1.243	1.384	1.539	1.710	1.898	2.105	2.332	2.580	2.853	3.152	3.479
12	1.268	1.426	1.601	1.796	2.012	2.252	2.518	2.813	3.138	3.498	3.896
13	1.294	1.469	1.665	1.886	2.133	2.410	2.720	3.066	3.452	3.883	4.363
14	1.319	1.513	1.732	1.980	2.261	2.579	2.937	3.342	3.797	4.310	4.887
15	1.346	1.558	1.801	2.079	2.397	2.759	3.172	3.642	4.177	4.785	5.474
16	1.373	1.605	1.873	2.183	2.540	2.952	3.426	3.970	4.595	5.311	6.130
17	1.400	1.653	1.948	2.292	2.693	3.159	3.700	4.328	5.054	5.895	6.866
18	1.428	1.702	2.026	2.407	2.854	3.380	3.996	4.717	5.560	6.543	7.690
19	1.457	1.753	2.107	2.527	3.026	3.616	4.316	5.142	6.116	7.263	8.613
20	1.486	1.806	2.191	2.653	3.207	3.870	4.661	5.604	6.727	8.062	9.646
21	1.516	1.860	2.279	2.786	3.399	4.140	5.034	6.109	7.400	8.949	10.804
22	1.546	1.916	2.370	2.925	3.603	4.430	5.436	6.658	8.140	9.933	12.100
23	1.577	1.974	2.465	3.071	3.820	4.740	5.871	7.258	8.954	11.026	13.552
24	1.608	2.033	2.563	3.225	4.049	5.072	6.341	7.911	9.850	12.239	15.178
25	1.641	2.094	2.666	3.386	4.292	5.427	6.848	8.623	10.834	13.585	17.000
30	1.811	2.427	3.243	4.322	5.743	7.612	10.062	13.267	17.449	22.892	29.960
40	2.208	3.262	4.801	7.040	10.285	14.974	21.724	31.408	45.258	64.999	93.049

(1) To find the future value, take a given rate, go down column to correct year; multiply this by your actual number; e.g., $28,000 growing at 5% for 5 years: $28,000 x 1.276 = $35,728.

(2) Can also be used for inflation adjustments; e.g., what does $5,000 have to grow to in 7 years to offset 3% inflation? $5,000 × 1.230 = $6,150.

Present Value of a Single Amount

Your daughter is currently three years old. You expect her education to cost $100,000 when she leaves for school in fifteen years. You want to invest a single, lump sum today that will be sufficient to pay the bill when the time comes. You know you can earn a 6 percent after-tax return. How much should you invest?

Thanks to the *present value of a single amount* formula, you can answer this question in a matter of seconds!

$$PV = FV \div (1 + i)^n$$

The variables are the same as in our previous formula (this is one case of powerful math being very simple!). Go ahead—plug in the data to solve your quandary.

Investor's Idiom

The **present value of a single amount** formula answers the question, "How much do I have to invest today as a lump sum in order for it to grow into X amount in Y years if I could invest it at a rate of return of Z percent?"

$$PV = FV \div (1 + i)^n$$

$$PV = \$100,000 \div (1.06)^{15}$$

$$PV = \$100,000 \div 2.396558$$

$$PV = \$41,727$$

The answer, $41,727, is the amount of money you need to invest today in order to meet your goal. Don't have that kind of cash sitting around the house? You'll have to figure out how to increase the rate of return and (or) the length of time.

An Easy Way to Figure the Present Value of a Single Sum

Mathematicians, the clever folks they are, devised a chart for the present value of a single sum. Again, the results aren't as precise as doing the calculation by hand but for those of you who want to do TVM calculations on the fly, this should prove useful.

Present Value of a Single Amount ($1 Discounted)

Rate Years	2%	3%	4%	5%	6%	7%	8%	9%	10%	11%	12%
1	.980	.971	.962	.952	.943	.935	.926	.917	.909	.901	.893
2	.961	.943	.925	.907	.890	.873	.857	.842	.826	.812	.797
3	.942	.915	.889	.864	.840	.816	.794	.772	.751	.731	.712
4	.924	.888	.855	.823	.792	.763	.735	.708	.683	.659	.636
5	.906	.863	.822	.784	.747	.713	.681	.650	.621	.593	.567
6	.888	.837	.790	.746	.705	.666	.630	.596	.564	.535	.507
7	.871	.813	.760	.711	.665	.623	.583	.547	.513	.482	.452
8	.853	.789	.731	.677	.627	.582	.540	.502	.467	.434	.404
9	.837	.766	.703	.645	.592	.544	.500	.460	.424	.391	.361
10	.820	.744	.676	.614	.558	.508	.463	.422	.386	.352	.322
11	.804	.722	.650	.585	.527	.475	.429	.388	.350	.317	.287
12	.789	.701	.625	.557	.497	.444	.397	.356	.319	.286	.257
13	.773	.861	.601	.530	.469	.415	.368	.326	.290	.258	.229
14	.758	.661	.577	.505	.442	.388	.340	.299	.263	.232	.205
15	.743	.642	.555	.481	.417	.362	.315	.275	.239	.209	.183
16	.728	.623	.534	.458	.394	.339	.292	.252	.218	.188	.163
17	.714	.605	.513	.436	.371	.317	.270	.231	.198	.170	.146
18	.700	.587	.494	.416	.350	.296	.250	.212	.180	.153	.130
19	.686	.570	.475	.396	.331	.277	.232	.194	.164	.138	.116
20	.673	.554	.456	.377	.312	.258	.215	.178	.149	.124	.104
21	.660	.538	.439	.359	.294	.242	.199	.164	.135	.112	.093
22	.647	.522	.422	.342	.278	.226	.184	.150	.123	.101	.083
23	.634	.507	.406	.326	.262	.211	.170	.138	.112	.091	.074
24	.622	.492	.390	.310	.247	.197	.158	.126	.102	.082	.066
25	.610	.478	.375	.295	.233	.184	.146	.116	.092	.074	.059
30	.552	.412	.308	.231	.174	.131	.099	.075	.057	.044	.033
40	.453	.307	.208	.142	.097	.067	.046	.032	.022	.015	.011

(1) To find the present value of a single sum, take a given rate, go down column to correct year; multiply this by your actual number; e.g., $28,000 discounted at 5% for 5 years: $28,000 x .784 = $21,952.

Investor's Idiom

An **annuity** is a series of cash flows identical in amount and frequency.

Future Value of an Annuity

You've seen the light. You understand the power of compounding interest and decided to cut expenses to come up with $10,000 in extra investment cash each year. You know you can earn an after-tax return of 8.5 percent per annum and don't plan on retiring for another 20 years. Just how large will your nest egg have grown by the time you're ready to stop working?

To answer that question, you turn to our third formula: the *future value of an annuity*.

Future Value of an Annuity

$$FVA = pmt \left(\frac{1 - (1 + i)^n}{i} \right)$$

(Future Value of an Annuity): The ultimate value of your nest egg if you invest the same amount of cash annually

PMT (Payment): The amount of each annual investment.

I (Interest Rate): The after-tax return you expect to earn on your investment.

N (Number of Periods): The number of years you expect to have the money invested without touching it.

Once again, masterfully do the math on your calculator:

Solving for the Future Value of an Annuity

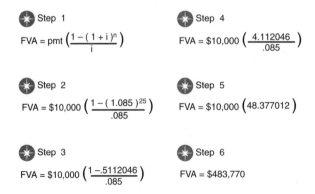

Step 1

$$FVA = pmt \left(\frac{1 - (1 + i)^n}{i} \right)$$

Step 2

$$FVA = \$10,000 \left(\frac{1 - (1.085)^{25}}{.085} \right)$$

Step 3

$$FVA = \$10,000 \left(\frac{1 - .5112046}{.085} \right)$$

Step 4

$$FVA = \$10,000 \left(\frac{4.112046}{.085} \right)$$

Step 5

$$FVA = \$10,000 \left(48.377012 \right)$$

Step 6

$$FVA = \$483,770$$

Investor's Idiom

The **future value of an annuity** formula answers the question, "How much money will I have if I invest a set, regular amount of X annually for Y years and earn a rate of return of Z percent?"

In other words, when you punch out for the last time, the $200,000 you've invested will have grown to $483,770, a 2.4-fold increase.

An Easy Way to Figure the Future Value of an Annuity

For the quantitatively challenged, we once again offer thee a chart:

Future Value of an Annuity ($1 Invested & Compounded Annually)

Rate Years	2%	3%	4%	5%	6%	7%	8%	9%	10%	11%	12%
1	1.000	1.000	1.000	1.000	1.000	1.000	1.000	1.000	1.000	1.000	1.000
2	2.020	2.030	2.040	2.050	2.060	2.070	2.080	2.090	2.100	2.110	2.120
3	3.060	3.091	3.122	3.152	3.184	3.215	3.246	3.278	3.310	3.342	3.374
4	4.122	4.184	4.246	4.310	4.375	4.440	4.506	4.573	4.641	4.710	4.779
5	5.204	5.309	5.416	5.526	5.637	5.751	5.867	5.985	6.105	6.228	6.353
6	6.308	6.468	6.633	6.802	6.975	7.153	7.336	7.523	7.716	7.913	8.115
7	7.434	7.662	7.898	8.142	8.394	8.654	8.923	9.200	9.487	9.783	10.089
8	8.583	8.892	9.214	9.549	9.897	10.260	10.637	11.028	11.436	11.859	12.300
9	9.755	10.159	10.583	11.027	11.491	11.978	12.488	13.021	13.579	14.164	14.776
10	10.950	11.464	12.006	12.578	13.181	13.816	14.487	15.193	15.937	16.722	17.549
11	12.169	12.808	13.486	14.207	14.972	15.784	16.645	17.560	18.531	19.561	20.655
12	13.412	14.192	15.026	15.917	16.870	17.888	18.977	20.141	21.384	22.713	24.133
13	14.680	15.618	16.627	17.713	18.882	20.141	21.495	22.953	24.523	26.211	28.029
14	15.974	17.086	18.292	19.598	21.015	22.550	24.215	26.019	27.975	30.095	32.392
15	17.293	18.599	20.023	21.578	23.276	25.129	27.152	29.361	31.772	34.405	37.280
16	18.639	20.157	21.824	23.657	25.672	27.888	30.324	33.003	35.949	39.190	42.753
17	20.012	21.761	23.697	25.840	28.213	30.840	33.750	36.973	40.544	44.500	48.883

continues

Future Value of an Annuity ($1 Invested & Compounded Annually)
(continued)

Rate Years	2%	3%	4%	5%	6%	7%	8%	9%	10%	11%	12%
18	21.412	23.414	25.645	28.132	30.905	33.999	37.450	41.301	45.599	50.396	55.749
19	22.840	25.117	27.671	30.539	33.760	37.379	41.446	46.018	51.158	56.939	64.439
20	24.297	26.870	29.778	33.066	36.785	40.995	45.762	51.159	57.274	64.202	72.052
21	25.783	28.676	31.969	35.719	39.992	44.865	50.422	56.764	64.002	72.264	81.698
22	27.299	30.536	34.248	38.505	43.392	49.005	55.456	62.872	71.402	81.213	92.502
23	28.845	32.452	36.618	41.430	46.995	53.435	60.893	69.531	79.542	91.147	104.602
24	30.421	34.426	39.082	44.501	50.815	58.176	66.764	76.789	88.496	102.173	118.154
25	32.030	36.459	41.645	47.726	54.864	63.248	73.105	84.699	98.346	114.412	133.333
30	40.567	47.575	56.084	66.438	79.057	94.459	113.282	136.305	164.491	199.018	241.330
40	60.401	75.400	95.024	120.797	154.758	199.630	295.052	337.872	442.580	581.812	767.080

(1) To find the future value of an annuity, take a given rate, go down column to correct year; multiply this by the amount you are investing annually; e.g., $10,000 invested each year at 5% for 10 years: $10,000 x 12.578 = $125,780.

Present Value of an Annuity

One night, as you sit at home reading yet another financial treatise (hey, we authors can dream!), you get a call from a good friend, Aaron; a rather dapper fellow with a penchant for high-quality suits, fine wine, and expensive houses. Unlike you, the consummate investor, he prefers to spend his money rather than compound it.

Fiscal Facts

You often hear of lottery winners taking a cash payment instead of the bigger, reported prize. In almost every case, this makes financial sense (playing the lottery, however, does not). The reason is simple: the lump-sum option is simply the present value of the annuity. If the winner actually bothered to calculate the implied interest rate, he would likely conclude he could earn a higher rate of return by working with a reputable investment advisor.

"Friend," he says to you, "I found the most extraordinary vacation home in Switzerland. You know I despise debt, so I was thinking that instead of going to the bank and mortgaging those apartment buildings I own. I could sell you the right to receive all of the rental income they generate for the next five years; on average, this amounts to $50,000 per annum. Are you interested?"

What is the value of the annuity (the $50,000 stream of cash flow each year for five years) to you? That depends upon your required rate of return. Assume for our example that you, being the budding financier that you are, won't invest unless you earn at least 12 percent on your money. The formula that will help you answer the question is known as the *present value of an annuity*.

You know the drill—plug the data into the formula, whip out your calculator, and prepare to be amazed at your own financial prowess.

Present Value of an Annuity

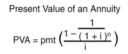

$$PVA = pmt \left(\frac{1 - \frac{1}{(1+i)^n}}{i} \right)$$

The answer, $180,239, is the maximum amount you can pay for the annuity and still earn your 12 percent rate of return.

Solving for Present Value of an Annuity

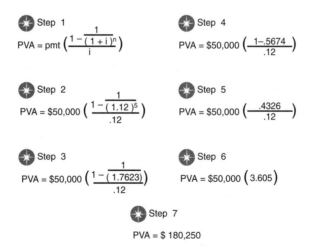

Step 1
$$PVA = pmt \left(\frac{1 - \frac{1}{(1+i)^n}}{i} \right)$$

Step 2
$$PVA = \$50,000 \left(\frac{1 - \frac{1}{(1.12)^5}}{.12} \right)$$

Step 3
$$PVA = \$50,000 \left(\frac{1 - \frac{1}{(1.7623)}}{.12} \right)$$

Step 4
$$PVA = \$50,000 \left(\frac{1 - .5674}{.12} \right)$$

Step 5
$$PVA = \$50,000 \left(\frac{.4326}{.12} \right)$$

Step 6
$$PVA = \$50,000 \left(3.605 \right)$$

Step 7
$$PVA = \$ 180,250$$

An Easy Way to Figure the Present Value of an Annuity

Okay, okay ...for those of you who skipped the formula and went straight for the chart, here it is. We aim to please.

Present Value of an Annuity ($1 Received and Discounted Annually)

Rate Years	2%	3%	4%	5%	6%	7%	8%	9%	10%	11%	12%
1	.980	.971	.962	.952	.943	.935	.926	.917	.909	.901	.893
2	1.942	1.913	1.886	1.859	1.833	1.808	1.3783	1.759	1.736	1.713	1.690
3	2.884	2.829	2.775	2.723	2.673	2.624	2.577	2.531	2.487	2.444	2.402
4	3.808	3.717	3.630	3.546	3.465	3.387	3.312	3.240	3.170	3.102	3.037
5	4.713	4.580	4.452	4.329	4.212	4.100	3.993	3.890	3.791	3.696	3.605
6	5.601	5.417	5.242	5.076	4.917	4.767	5.623	4.486	4.355	4.231	4.111
7	6.472	6.230	6.002	5.786	5.582	5.389	5.206	5.033	4.868	4.712	4.564
8	7.326	7.020	6.733	6.463	6.210	5.971	5.747	5.535	5.335	5.146	4.968
9	8.162	7.786	7.435	7.108	6.802	6.515	6.247	5.995	5.759	5.537	5.328
10	8.983	8.530	8.111	7.722	7.360	7.024	6.710	6.418	6.145	5.889	5.650
11	9.787	9.253	8.760	8.306	7.887	7.499	7.139	6.805	6.495	6.207	5.938
12	10.575	9.954	9.385	8.863	8.384	7.943	7.536	7.161	6.814	6.492	6.194
13	11.348	10.635	9.986	9.394	8.853	8.358	7.904	7.487	7.103	6.750	6.424
14	12.106	11.296	10.563	9.899	9.295	8.746	8.244	7.786	7.367	6.982	6.628
15	12.849	11.938	11.118	10.380	9.712	9.108	8.560	8.061	7.606	7.191	6.811
16	13.578	12.561	11.652	10.838	10.106	9.447	8.851	8.313	7.824	7.379	6.974
17	14.292	13.166	12.166	11.274	10.477	9.763	9.122	8.544	8.022	7.549	7.120
18	14.992	13.754	12.659	11.690	10.828	10.059	9.372	8.756	8.201	7.702	7.250
19	15.679	14.324	13.134	12.085	11.158	10.336	9.604	8.950	8.365	7.839	7.366
20	16.352	14.878	13.590	12.462	11.470	10.594	9.818	9.129	8.514	7.963	7.469
21	17.011	15.415	14.029	12.821	11.764	10.836	10.017	9.292	8.649	8.075	7.562
22	17.658	15.937	14.451	13.163	12.042	11.061	10.201	9.442	8.772	8.176	7.645
23	18.292	16.444	14.857	13.489	12.303	11.272	10.371	9.580	8.883	8.266	7.718
24	18.914	16.936	15.247	13.799	12.550	11.469	10.529	9.707	8.985	8.348	7.784
25	19.524	17.413	15.622	14.094	12.783	11.654	10.675	9.823	9.077	8.422	7.843

Rate Years	2%	3%	4%	5%	6%	7%	8%	9%	10%	11%	12%
30	22.397	19.601	17.292	15.373	13.765	12.409	11.258	10.274	9.427	8.694	8.055
40	27.356	23.115	19.793	17.159	15.046	13.332	11.925	10.757	9.779	8.951	8.244

(1) To find the present value of an annuity, take a given rate, go down column to correct year; multiply this by the amount of the annual cash flow; e.g., $10,000 annual cash flow discounted at a required rate of return of 10% for 20 years: $10,000 x 8.514 = $85,140. In other words, if someone offered you a cash flow stream of $10,000 per year for the next 20 years and you insisted on earning at least 10% on your investment, you could not pay more than this amount ($85,140).

To Eternity and Beyond: Determining the Value of a Perpetuity

What if you have an asset that you expect to last forever (or at least a really, really long time)? This formula is the easiest of all:

Value of *Perpetuity* = Cash Flow ÷ Required Rate of Return

You are offered the chance to purchase an asset that generates $500 per year. How much should you pay for it? As you can see from the formula, it depends upon your required rate of return. If you were happy with 5 percent, then your calculation would look something like this:

Value of Perpetuity = $500 ÷ .05

Value of Perpetuity = $10,000

Investor's Idiom

Perpetuity literally means forever. As you'll see in Chapter 13, most preferred stocks are valued as perpetuities because the investor is free to hold them forever.

In other words, $10,000 is the maximum price you could pay and still earn your 5 percent required rate of return.

Endless Choices: TVM Derivations

For each time value of money formula, there are numerous ways to solve for other variables, such as the interest rate. Obviously, we can't cover them all—it would take an entire book to walk you through that many equations! Now that you understand the concept, however, you see that it is not difficult to build your net worth if you act rationally. As we said before, wealth is not the product of luck; it is the natural result of discipline.

Another option is to purchase a financial calculator. Among the best are the BAII Plus Professional by Texas Instruments and the BA10II by Hewlett-Packard. By pressing a few buttons, you can solve complex financial problems that go way beyond the scope of this chapter.

And Now for a Surprise

Right now, at this very moment, you have all the information necessary to value bonds and preferred stock (don't worry if you don't know much about either subject; we'll take care of that in Chapters 12 and 13).

The Least You Need to Know

- The value of your portfolio is determined by three variables: (1) the amount you invest, (2) the rate of return you earn, and (3) the length of time you allow the money to compound.

- The Time Value of Money (TVM) concept tells us that cash today is more valuable than cash tomorrow.

- When you spend a dollar, you are also spending all of the income it could have generated from now until doomsday.

- An annuity is a series of cash flows identical in amount and frequency.

- A perpetuity is an asset that you expect to generate cash forever.

How Do You Really Feel About Risk?

In This Chapter

- ◆ How much risk is too much for you?
- ◆ How to calculate simple return on investment
- ◆ Understanding the relationship between risk and return
- ◆ Getting a grip on your own risk tolerance
- ◆ Evaluating your unique timeframe

Jumped out of any airplanes lately? Or are you the type who white-knuckled it and sucked down three drinks during your last commercial flight?

Whether we perceive a given situation as exciting or terrifying has to do with our tolerance for risk. Many of us like to kid ourselves about how much risk we're willing to accept. We dream of jumping out of a plane or skiing top-speed down a steep slope—but when we find ourselves at the door of that plane or the top of that slope, we wish we had our feet firmly planted on terra firma.

You can chicken out of skydiving or skiing with only your pride to salvage, but if you make investments that require more risk tolerance than you have, you'll be a miserable, sleep-deprived wreck. So the first step before you invest in anything is to analyze and get comfortable with your risk tolerance. The investing world is no place for false bravado.

What Is Return?

In investing, risk is defined as the possibility of permanent loss or impairment of capital. When you invest in something, you decide to do so because you expect to receive more money in the future than you invested today. The difference between the amount you put in and the total amount you receive at the end of the investment period is your *return*. You're going to learn how to calculate return in several ways in Chapter 22. For now, let's cover the basics.

Return on investment (ROI) is also called rate of return. It's typically expressed as a percentage of the original investment. Let's say your little brother asks to borrow $500 to buy an old car that he intends to fix up and resell. When he sells the car for $1,000, he gives you back your $500 and splits the $500 profit with you. You get $500 plus $250, or $750. Because $250 is half of $500, for every dollar you invested, you earned 50¢. Your ROI is 50 percent.

Investor's Idiom

Return is the amount you earn from an investment over a given period of time. Generally, higher returns require the investor to assume greater risk.

Return on investment (ROI), also called rate of return, is expressed as a percentage of your original investment.

What You Made, What You Paid

Here's a formula you can use to calculate the return on any investment:

1. The total you receive at the end of the investment period is your end-of-period wealth (A).

2. Your original investment is called your beginning-of-period wealth (B).

3. If you subtract your beginning-of-period wealth (B) from your end-of-period wealth, you'll get your *return*: A – B.

Now that you've figured out your return, you can easily calculate your ROI. Use the following formula to figure out your return as a percentage of your original investment (B).

$$\frac{[A - B]}{B} \times 100 = ROI$$

Applying the formula to the preceding example, you get:

$$\frac{[\$750 - \$500]}{\$500} \times \$100 = \frac{\$250}{\$500} \times 100 = .50 \times 100 = 50\%$$

An easy way to remember this formula is the following:

What you made (e.g., $250) divided (÷) by what you paid (e.g., $500), times (×) 100.

Fear of Heights: The Higher the Return, the Greater the Risk

When you lent your brother the money to buy that car, you took the risk that a number of things could have gone wrong:

- ♦ He might not have been able to sell the car.
- ♦ The car might have been stolen or vandalized before he sold it.
- ♦ He could have sold it for a disappointing return.

Before lending him the money, you calculated your expected ROI in your head—even if you didn't know that's what you were doing!—and found it sufficient payback for the risk you were accepting. If your brother lives in a neighborhood where cars are stolen every night, maybe you would have decided not to risk your $500. Then again, if he swore to you that he could resell the car for $1,500, making your return $500 instead of $250, maybe you'd have gone for it anyway. After all, a 100 percent return on investment is a pretty sweet deal.

In this case: $\frac{[\$1,000 - \$500]}{500} = \frac{\$500}{500} = 1 \times 100 = 100\%$

Crash Alert

Now that you understand the relationship between risk and return, you'll never be fooled by investments that promise a high return with little or no risk of losing your money. Remember, if something sounds too good to be true, it probably is.

This concept is one of the basic rules of investing: Generally speaking, the higher the rate of return, the greater the risk. Only you can determine how much risk you want to take.

The rate of return from investing in a small business, for example, can be very high. But roughly one out of every seven small businesses fails, so the risk of losing your investment is very high as well. In contrast, the return banks offer on savings accounts is typically very low—3 or 4 percent—but the risk of capital loss is virtually nonexistent.

Super Strategy

Are there exceptions to the higher-returns-require-higher-risk rule? Yes. To take advantage of them, you must have the financial resources to wait out the investment for several years if it treads water or falls further. You must also possess an extensive background in both accounting and finance.

Here's a perfect case study: when Berkshire Hathaway acquired a large stake in the Washington Post Company during the 1970s, the paper was trading at less than 20 percent of its private-market value. The business was in excellent financial condition, had a controlling shareholder (the late Katharine Graham) who allowed management to pursue actions it believed intelligent in the long-run, and possessed a powerful franchise recognized throughout the world.

Today, the stock Berkshire acquired for $10+ million has grown over 17,000 percent to $1.7 billion; a shining example of when *lower* risk results in *higher* returns.

The Tools of the Trade

To control risk, investment professionals use several tactics, which you can apply yourself to your own portfolio of investments.

Before we discuss these tactics, let's look at a basic tenet of investment theory: standard deviation. Don't panic. No need to fear scary flashbacks of the math section of the SAT. It's just a mathematical term that helps to frame the likelihood (or, in quantitative terms, probability) of a given number recurring.

Standard Deviation and a Podunk Potato

Freddie has played third base for the Podunk Potatoes for the past 12 years. His batting average each year has been:

(1) .290	(5) .390	(9) .330
(2) .380	(6) .320	(10) .340
(3) .300	(7) .270	(11) .350
(4) .310	(8) .370	(12) .370

What will he bat in his thirteenth year? Let's look at his average. To calculate the average of any group of figures, simply add them together and divide by the number of figures—12, in this case.

Freddie's average is .335. But maybe in years two and five, Freddie got lucky and his batting average was boosted by a stew of easy pitches.

And, let's say he was bothered by injuries in years one and seven, when his scores were particularly unattractive. These aren't normal situations, so why don't we just throw out those four years? This is similar to what figure skating and gymnastics judges do when scoring a routine—they throw out the highest and lowest scores. This is also what financial analysts do when they are trying to find a pattern in a bunch of numbers. They disregard the very highest and the very lowest numbers. Analysts usually dump about a third of the numbers they are given, which is what we're doing in this case by getting rid of four out of twelve of Freddie's batting averages.

If we get rid of years one, two, five, and seven, Freddie's lowest score turns out to be the .300 he batted in year three. His highest score becomes the .370 he batted in year twelve. The difference between those two years, or the spread, is:

$$.370 - .300 = .07$$

So we could think of Freddie as someone who tends to bat between .300 and .370. If we divide that .07 difference in half, we could say that Freddie bats his average of .335 plus or minus .035. That "plus or minus .035" is called the first level standard deviation. It gives you a pretty clear picture of Freddie's potential future performance. His batting average in a given year can deviate up or down from the overall average by .035.

Deviant Behavior

We can follow the same procedure with the stock market by looking at the annual returns as far back as we want to go. Let's assume that for a single year, the stock market returned 12 percent with a standard deviation of plus or minus 15. This would mean that stocks returned between +27 percent (12 + 15) and -3 percent (12 − 15) that year.

Fiscal Facts

A huge amount of wealth is invested in the stock market. It is estimated that of the $33 trillion in world-wide capitalization, 50 percent, or $16.5 trillion, is capitalized in the United States. (Source: *Ibbotson Associates, Inc. Stocks, Bonds, Bills and Inflation* © 2004 Yearbook.)

That same year, bonds returned 5 percent and money market instruments returned 3 percent. Well, if the stock you were holding was at the low end of the stock market return, you would've actually lost -3 percent and probably would've been happier with your money parked in bonds or even in a savings account.

What's interesting, though, is that when we look at stock market returns over a 20-year period, the standard deviation really comes down from +/-15 to closer to +/-3. This means stock investors who stay in the market for 20 years could expect returns of 12 percent +/-3. The low would be 12 percent − 3, or 9 percent. The high would be 12 percent + 3, or 15 percent. This means that, for investors with a 20-year time horizon, stocks have historically performed very well. Also, for each and every 20-year period, stocks have returned more than bonds. Over time the returns from stocks smooth out and the deviation drops.

Basically, the longer you hold a high-risk investment like stock, the smaller the standard deviation will become. Over time all the fluctuations matter less and less. What matters is how the investment performs over the long run, not the short term. Historically, stocks have been very volatile over short periods, but have performed very well over 10–20 year horizons.

Therefore, we can say that the standard deviation (risk) of the highest-risk/highest-return investment declines as the timeframe increases. This is a key concept in investment theory and, for your purposes, asset allocation, which we discuss in Chapter 21.

How does this all apply to you? Once you understand how time, risk, and return interact, you can begin to think about how to allocate your investment assets. Simply put, if your timeframe is short, you shouldn't own much common stock. If you have a long timeframe, you should have a substantial portion of your assets allocated to stock, because over time the ups and downs in the stock market—as represented by the standard deviation—tend to neutralize each other.

The Four Broad Asset Classes

There are four broad classes of assets from which you can choose when you build your portfolio:

- **Equities:** As you learned in Chapter 1, common stock represents ownership in a company. Corporations sell ownership in the form of stock to raise capital. This is called equity financing.

  As an owner, you are entitled to the fruits of the company's success: higher cash dividends and, ultimately, a higher stock price. On the other hand, you are vulnerable to the costs of failure: a reduction in (or even elimination of) the cash dividend and a lower (perhaps substantially lower) stock price. Equities offer the highest long-term returns but are subject to considerable short-term volatility.

- **Fixed Income:** Bonds, on the other hand, are a form of debt financing. When you buy a bond you are lending money for a specified length of time to the bond issuer in exchange for periodic interest payments. Many new investors are unaware that bonds with long maturities can fluctuate just as wildly as common stock and, in some cases, possess a slight (but very real) inflation wipe-out risk. We'll get into that—and other cheery considerations for fixed-income investing—in Chapter 12.

- **Money Market Instruments:** Money market instruments pay rates that vary from day to day, week to week, or month to month. They are very *liquid*. This means they can be converted to cash easily and quickly. A savings account can be cashed in any day for the same price you paid. Treasury bills can be sold within 24 hours. The purpose of money market instruments is to provide instant (or close-to-instant) liquidity in your portfolio.

- **Real Estate:** Real estate can be a very attractive investment if purchased intelligently. As an investor, you are most likely to acquire property by purchasing shares of Real Estate Investment Trusts, or REITs. We'll dive into that topic in Chapter 15.

Investor's Idiom

An investment is considered **liquid** if it can be converted into cash quickly and easily. Money market instruments offer liquidity because they can be converted to cash right away, generally within 24 hours, whereas some types of investments penalize you for liquidating them before a certain time, such as a retirement IRA.

Variety Is the Spice of Life

What's life without a little diversity? Well, in the world of investing, diversity can mean the difference between taking off or crashing and burning. *Diversification* is another method investment pros use to increase your portfolio's ability to handle greater risk—and thereby earn greater returns.

Investor's Idiom

Diversification is a method of decreasing risk by increasing the variety of assets in a portfolio. If you own lots of different stocks, for example, your whole portfolio won't tank if one company goes bankrupt.

The more stocks you add to your portfolio, the closer your long-terms will be to the market average of a benchmark such as the S&P 500. The reason for increasing your number of stock holdings is to help minimize event risk. This is the risk that one event could really damage the value of a stock you own.

In 1997, while the S&P 500 was up 33 percent, McDonald's stock rose only 6 percent. Why? Well, the Arch Deluxe didn't exactly fly off the grill, if you recall. There was also some media flap about the quality of your average McDonald's meal. So if you had all your money in McDonald's stock, you were probably too queasy to eat a dozen Arch Deluxes for the sake of saving your investment. On the other hand, in the first six months of 1998, the S&P was up almost 18 percent, but McDonald's stock price skyrocketed 50 percent. Why? McDonald's went on a campaign to solve its problems—dumping the loser burger and running some popular specials, like its Beanie Baby giveaway. Now here's what's really interesting—over that year and half, the returns for the S&P 500 and for McDonald's stock are very close. The S&P 500 didn't perform as spectacularly as McDonald's did in the first six months of 1998, but neither did it drop as dizzyingly in 1997. This is the value of diversification—over time it may dampen the highs, but it cushions the lows. We'll discuss ways to diversify in Chapter 21.

Quiz Thyself to Know Thyself: Risk Tolerance Quiz

The key to successful investing is to determine how much risk you can handle, taking into consideration:

- ◆ Your future obligations, such as children, a mortgage, or a business.

- ◆ Your liquidity constraints. If you don't have health insurance and you break your leg, for example, you'll need cash to cover the medical bills.

◆ Your growth requirements, such as the standard of living you want to maintain when you retire. Social Security probably won't do it for you, so you'll need some investments that really grow, such as stocks.

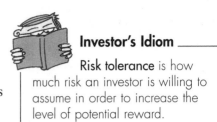

◆ Your investment objectives (which we'll delve into in the next chapter).

◆ Your investment philosophy; in other words, how willing are you to take risk?

But how do you know whether you can ride out the bumps and take the lumps that long-term investors in high-risk, high-return investments like stocks have to tolerate? How do you know your *risk tolerance* level? To complete the quiz, make a checkmark next to the statement that best describes your feelings. To score the quiz, simply add up the numbers next to your checkmarks. Then look up your score on our handy Risk Chart.

A. Return on Investment

___1. I'm willing to sacrifice return in order to receive a minimum assured rate of return.

___2. I'm much more concerned with getting solid, consistent results on my investments than superior investment returns.

___3. Hey, you've got to be in it to win it! I can accept fluctuating year-by-year returns in order to achieve higher total returns over time.

B. Capital

___1. Although I may not get as much income right now from my investment, I'm interested in preserving what capital I have and don't want to see the market value of my securities decrease. When it comes to my future, I like to play it safe.

___2. Show me the money. Current income is more important than capital preservation.

___3. Sure, I'm interested in preserving my capital, but I can take some decrease of market value to increase the income I'm earning on my investments right now.

C. Growth Risk

___1. Even looking at dice gives me the willies! I am definitely not much of a gambler. I'm more concerned in preserving the value of my current assets than in investing in riskier securities that have the potential to increase in value at a later time.

___2. Growth of my assets in the future is as important to me as preserving the value of my current assets.

___3. I am more concerned with providing greater future growth than playing it safe now and preserving my current assets.

D. Growth Risk

___1. Keeping risk very low is more important for me than taking a chance in order to achieve superior investment returns.

___2. Hey, there's chance in everything. Some market risk is inevitable in order to get the growth I deem necessary from my investments.

___3. The final result is more important than how I got there. If I have to risk several bad years to meet my goal, that's okay.

E. Knowledge of Future Liabilities

___1. I feel I can make a fairly accurate prediction of what my future liabilities will be.

___2. Well, I may not have a crystal ball, but I think I can accurately predict some of my future liabilities. Other possible liabilities are subject to rough estimates.

___3. Do I look like a fortune teller? I'm relatively uncertain about what my future liabilities will be.

F. Diversification

___1. I don't like to put my eggs in one (or two) baskets. I believe in keeping my investment portfolio well diversified.

___2. I don't like complications. I think it's best to keep the investment process simple. I utilize a level of diversification that leaves me comfortable but still provides the ability for me to take advantage of opportunities I find especially attractive.

___3. You don't get to be a billionaire by playing it safe. The final result is more important than how it was derived. Diversification is not a major issue for me.

G. Blue Chip Companies

___1. The *blue chip* (high quality) stocks of solid, mature companies give me the perfect combination of current income and stability. I don't need to have extraordinary growth on my investments to be satisfied.

Investor's Idiom

The term **blue chip**, a phrase used to describe the shares of high-quality, well-established companies, is derived from the fact that the chip with the highest value in nineteenth-century poker games was—you guessed it—blue.

___2. Blue chip companies are great, but I don't necessarily need to be that conservative with my investments. The stocks of solid companies in growing businesses will give very good results with a level of risk I can tolerate.

___3. Entrepreneurship is where you find the action! The stocks of small companies may be more volatile, but I prefer them because they reward me with the highest long-term rates of return.

H. Rates of Return

Given the choice of the following three investments identical in every other respective, I would choose:

___1. Investment 1: 100 percent chance of a 5 percent rate of return per year over the next five years.

___2. Investment 2: 75 percent chance of a 10 percent rate of return per year, 25 percent chance of a 4 percent rate of return per year over the next five years.

___3. Investment 3: 50 percent chance of a 20 percent rate of return per year, 50 percent chance of a 0 percent rate of return per year over the next five years.

I. Short-Term Investments

Use the following graph to answer the question.

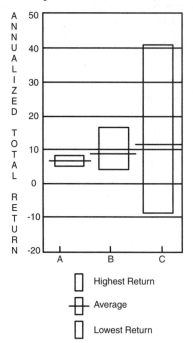

Range of Total Returns: 1-Year Periods

Assuming the expected rate of inflation over the next year is 4 percent, which investment option would you choose for a one-year time horizon?

___1. Investment A would be the most appropriate of the three alternatives for my needs.

___2. Investment B would be the most appropriate of the three alternatives for my needs.

___3. Investment C would be the most appropriate of the three alternatives for my needs.

Calculate Your Score:

Your Risk Tolerance Rating

Point Total	Risk Level
9–14	Low
15–21	Medium
22–27	High

Got the Time? Take the Time Horizon Quiz

Are we done? Can you go to sleep now? Not quite. We haven't addressed timeframe.

Each of us has our own attitude toward time, and before you invest a dime, you need to determine yours. Believe it or not, though, almost everybody is a short-term, medium-term, and long-term investor simultaneously. How so? You might be saving for retirement, investing to send your kids to college, *and* saving for a vacation all at once. Each of these savings plans has its own time horizon; that is, each has a limit as to how much time is needed to reach the intended goal. How do you figure out what this time horizon is? Well, sometimes you may find that your investment priorities conflict. The manner in which you most consistently opt to resolve those conflicts indicates your true investment time horizon. Take the following quiz and check your results on the scale. This is extremely important because it will determine your investment objectives, which we are going to discuss in the next chapter. Again, simply add up the numbers next to each question and find where you fall on the Timeframe Chart:

A. Time and Investments

Considering time to be the most important factor distinguishing the three investments shown on the following chart, determine which one you would choose:

____1. Investment A would be most appropriate for my needs.

____2. Investment B would be most appropriate for my needs.

____3. Investment C would be most appropriate for my needs.

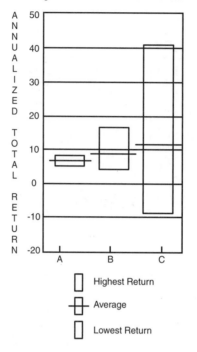

Range of Total Returns: 1-Year Periods

Highest Return

Average

Lowest Return

B. Time and Investments

____1. It is most important to grow assets in an investment fund in the next one to two years.

____2. It is most important to grow assets in an investment fund in the next five years.

____3. It is most important to grow assets in an investment fund in the next ten years or longer.

C. Short Term Versus Long Term

____1. I'm not one to jump to conclusions. I don't feel it's necessary to make decisions based on individual *quarterly* rates of return. However, four consecutive disappointing quarters might cause me to rethink my investment strategy.

____2. I do not make decisions based on one year of investment returns. However, two consecutive disappointing years or a disappointing five-year period may weaken my confidence in my current investment strategy.

___3. I know that good things are worth the wait. Ten years is my preferred barometer for measuring investment results.

Investor's Idiom

In the investment world, the year is divided into four three-month **quarters**. Companies are required to report their financial performance to stockholders every quarter. The quarterly **rate of return** is the return on investment for one quarter, as opposed to **annual return**, which is an investment's return over one year. Companies and mutual funds report results both quarterly and annually.

D. Short Term Versus Long Term

___1. My concerns lie in the here and now. I am most interested in maintaining my current financial position.

___2. I've done fairly well over the past five years. Why not continue in that progress over the next five years?

___3. Time is on my side. My financial position has barely started to reach its potential. I look forward to significant growth.

E. Safety Versus Risk

___1. Safety first, I always say. If I can get high yields from bonds, I will forgo the future potential for gains in stocks.

___2. I don't need to totally play it safe, but I would be willing to accept lower levels of growth over a period of five years in order to hold on to consistent year-to-year returns.

___3. You've got to take the bad with the good. I'm willing to accept several years of negative returns in order to provide greater total returns over a period between five and ten years.

F. Lump Sum Versus Long-Term Worth

Given a choice between receiving $100,000 this year or $300,000 10 years from today (note the implicit rate of return is 11.61%, a very attractive rate):

___1. I would accept $100,000 this year.

___2. I would consider both offers to be equally attractive.

___3. I would accept $300,000 10 years from today.

Check Your Score:

Your Time Horizon Score

Point Total	Time Frame
6–9	Short (0–2 yrs.)
10–13	Intermediate (2–10 yrs.)
14–18	Long (over 10 yrs.)

If you had any difficulty getting through these quizzes, don't panic. You're just going with your gut reaction right now. In fact, for those who are intimidated, we recommend that you return to them after you've read a few more chapters and feel more confident. Once you've completed these quizzes, you should have a much clearer picture of your timeframe and how you really feel about risk.

The Least You Need to Know

◆ Return on investment is the profit you made, expressed as a percentage of your original cost basis.

◆ Generally speaking, the higher the potential return on an investment, the greater the risk.

◆ To reduce risk, you can increase both the time you give your investments to perform and the diversification of your portfolio.

◆ There are four broad asset classes, each with its own risk profile: equities, fixed income, money market instruments, and real estate.

◆ Money market instruments offer the highest liquidity of all the asset classes; that is, they can be easily and quickly converted into cash.

Chapter 4

Selecting Your Investing Objectives and Style

In this Chapter

- Determining which investment objectives are appropriate for each of your life goals
- Protecting your assets through capital preservation
- Using your money to generate current income
- Investing to build wealth
- The perils of speculation
- The value vs. growth debate

Whether or not you realize it, every time you invest, you are attempting to meet one of four different objectives. The key to success is to clearly identify from the outset *which* objective you are seeking. By staying focused, you'll save yourself time and energy that could be devoted to more productive (and enjoyable) things.

Investing Objectives

Just what are these four cornerstones of investing? We thought you'd never ask!

- **Capital Preservation:** Protecting and maintaining the purchasing power of your assets in real, inflation-adjusted terms.

- **Current Income:** Investing your assets in a way that causes them to generate dividend and interest income upon which you can live.

- **Capital Appreciation:** Investing your capital for long-term appreciation and wealth building.

- **Speculation:** Any capital commitment not based upon analysis of quantitative facts, that goes against the statistical probability of an event, or utilizes a large, imprudent amount of leverage in order to amplify returns is speculative.

Investor's Idiom

Three months after the September 11 terrorist attacks, the Series EE savings bond was renamed the **Patriot Bond.** You learn all about the characteristics of savings bonds in Chapters 9 and 12.

As you'll see throughout this chapter, your investment objectives depend upon your specific goals. In fact, it is likely you will use a combination of all four throughout your life; possibly simultaneously. Those approaching retirement after 40 years of employment are going to want both capital preservation *and* current income, for example, while a wet-behind-the-ears college graduate is interested in building wealth.

Now for the cool part: remember those asset classes we talked about in Chapter 3 (equities, fixed income, money market instruments, and real estate)? Each asset class has different characteristics that make them appealing to specific objectives on our list. You already know this intuitively; it would make very little sense for our growth-oriented college grad to invest all of her money in *Patriot Bonds* earning a couple of percentage points for the next 40+ years! For now, let's dive into the nitty-gritty and uncover the differences between capital preservation, current income, capital appreciation, and speculation.

Keeping What You Have: Investing for Capital Preservation

You've worked hard for your money and now you want to protect it. Perhaps you're saving to put a down payment on a house or send a child to college in the next few years. Maybe you're a widow or retired. Regardless, you don't have the luxury of risking any portion of your principal—you need your money to be there, intact, at a moment's notice.

Sound familiar? If so, your investing objective is capital preservation. In exchange for absolute safety, you're willing to accept the lowest returns in the investment world. To achieve this, you will only invest in money market instruments such as savings accounts, money market funds, treasuries, and short-term investment-grade bonds. You want to avoid common and preferred stock, bonds with maturities in excess of one year or with a noninvestment grade rating, and real estate. Don't know what that means? Don't worry—we'll cover it later.

Crash Alert

If your investing objective is capital preservation, the biggest mistake you can make is to reach for a little extra return by purchasing bonds with maturities in excess of one year. As you'll learn later, the trading value of bonds fluctuate just like stock prices. The further away a bond's maturity, the more sensitive it is to changes in interest rates. If you're not careful, you might be forced to cash out at a substantial loss.

Super Strategy

If there is any chance you will need your money in the next two or three years, your objective should be capital preservation. Why? As you learned in previous chapters, risk decreases as time increases. Even placing your money into a diversified group of stocks could leave you with significant losses—certainly not the outcome you want when you go to withdraw the cash!

Show Me the Money! Investing for Current Income

You have a chunk of capital. Maybe you accumulated it through a lifetime of hard work. Maybe you inherited it from a long-lost relative. Perhaps you got lucky and won the lottery. The point is, you have it and you know enough about the power of compounding to realize spending the principal would be a monumental mistake. Surely there must be a way to construct a portfolio designed to generate current income, money you can use to buy groceries and make the car payment.

Fiscal Facts

Did you know that an investor with $10 million in capital could easily generate $700K per-year in current income without ever touching his original principal? That's around $13,500 per week for the rest of his life!

Welcome to the world of income-oriented investing. Instead of attempting to build your net worth, you are interested in maximizing the amount of cash you spend without touching your original investment. Your portfolio will consist of high-quality, investment-grade bonds with maturities of 5 to 8 years, high-quality common stocks that have at least a 20-year history of paying continuous (or better yet—rising) cash dividends, and real estate via Real Estate Investment Trusts, or REITs (more on those in Chapter 15).

Jack and the Beanstalk: Investing for Capital Appreciation

You have time and you're willing to wait 10, 20, and even 30 or more years to achieve long-term portfolio growth. To accomplish this objective, you're happy to reinvest all of the dividend and interest income generated by your investments. You also make regular contributions to your brokerage and retirement accounts out of your paycheck.

Investor's Idiom

Capital appreciation as an investment *objective* is sometimes called growth. This is different than growth as an investing *style*, which we discuss later in the chapter. The term typically refers to an individual who buys stocks in companies boasting rapid increases in earnings.

Congratulations! Your investment objective is long-term capital appreciation. This is the most popular investing objective for those who are more than 10 years away from retirement, funding a college education, or interested in building wealth (if you sit up at night calculating your future millions with the time value of money formulas you learned in Chapter 2, your investment objective is most likely capital appreciation).

Your portfolio is going to be the most volatile of all, but this doesn't bother you in the slightest because you won't need to access your capital for years. Most of your investments are in common stocks of companies with strong financials and dominant positions in their respective industries.

Bet the Farm

You love the action. Some people play the horses, some people play roulette or poker, some people play the office pool, and you play the stock market. Okay, we all have our vices; admit it to yourself (and your spouse), control it as best you can, and get on with your life. Just don't call what you're doing investing. It's entertainment—pay for it out of your entertainment budget.

Many individuals think they are investing when, in fact, they are merely speculating. How can you tell the difference? Most speculation falls into one of three categories:

- **Lack of Analysis:** Merriam Webster defines speculating as, "to take to be true on the basis of insufficient evidence." If I buy General Motors stock because I recognize the product, yet I have only a cursory knowledge of the underlying business, I am, *ipso facto*, speculating. The stock *may* be a wise investment; because I do not have quantitative data to support my decision, whereas an investment analyst would, it is the equivalent of me throwing a dart at a stock table in *The Wall Street Journal*.

- **Betting Against the Odds:** Any time you bet against reasonable probabilities that can result in permanent capital loss, you are speculating.

Super Strategy

For the risk-loving among you, there is a way to ensure your speculative bets are done on a level playing field. Take the probability of winning and multiply it by the potential after-tax prize. Say, for example, we are playing poker together (five card stud). I offer to pay you $100,000 if you manage to get a royal flush at any point during the night if you pay me an upfront premium of $100. How would you know if this was a fair deal?

First, you would have to research the probability of getting a royal flush while playing five card stud; the odds are 0.000154 percent (or, expressed as a decimal, 0.00000154) for each hand. Assume you expected us to play a total of 200 hands throughout the night. Your odds have increased to 0.0308 percent (or 0.000308). You would multiply the odds—expressed as a decimal—against the potential prize. The answer, $30.80, is the amount you should pay for a "fair bet." In other words, you should consider paying a $100 premium only if the potential prize is larger than $308,000 on an after-tax basis.

◆ **Utilizing Large, Imprudent Amounts of Leverage:** Whenever you borrow large sums of money, you add a significant amount of risk to your investments. For some people, such as a landlord, the risk comes in the form of higher payments and interest expense. History is filled with inexperienced, would-be moguls forced to declare bankruptcy on otherwise profitable properties due to a temporary shortage of tenants.

Fiscal Facts

Graham's treatise, *Security Analysis*, is considered the Bible of value investing; a style which seeks to profit from acquiring undervalued assets. There are currently five separate editions in print with original copies of the classic 1934 edition fetching more than $10,000!

This same principal—relying upon your own resources and not those of others—applies on Wall Street as well as Main Street. A sure-fire way to turn what would be a sound investment into an unprofitable speculation is to trade on margin (money borrowed from a brokerage firm). The reason is simple. Even if you're correct about the investment long-term, your broker can sell assets in your account to protect itself if the value of your portfolio falls. This can make temporary price fluctuations permanent losses, and in some cases trigger capital gains taxes. You can also lose more than you have in your account. Many historians blame the 1929 stock market crash on the excessive use of margin. As a result, the Federal Reserve was given power to set minimum margin maintenance requirements that supersede those established by your financial institution.

Benjamin Graham, famed academic and the "Dean of Wall Street," reminded us that, "speculation is neither illegal, immoral, nor fattening to the pocketbook." To protect the individual from doing something stupid, Graham recommend that you make a clear distinction between your investment operations and your speculative plays. In fact, he went so far as to recommend that you keep two separate accounts to avoid the temptation to bet more than you can afford to lose.

Cheat Sheet

Not sure which investments fit each objective? Use this handy cheat-sheet to help you remember!

	Appropriate Investments	Example
Capital Preservation	Savings account, money market funds, Patriot bonds, certificates of deposit, U.S. treasuries, grade bonds.	Plan to put a down payment on a house; send a child to college in the next three years; short-term investment-emergency fund for unforeseen events such as layoffs or household repairs; a vacation fund.
Income	Stocks of companies with long histories of paying dividends, municipal bonds, investment-grade bonds with maturities between 5 and 8 years, real estate through REITs.	Retired and want cash for living expenses or charitable giving.
Capital Appreciation	Stocks of high-grade companies that are industry leaders with strong financial statements, mutual funds, real estate through REITs.	College graduate building wealth; a person more than ten years from retirement.
Speculation	Shorting stock, trading on margin, purchasing companies you don't understand, playing the ponies.	Entertainment

Dollars for Pennies: The Value Investing Approach

Value investors are folks who like buying $1 worth of assets for only 50¢. As you already learned, this school of investing was started by the Dean himself, Benjamin Graham. The philosophy can be applied in numerous ways. On the extreme end, you have folks like Martin Whitman at Third Avenue Funds who is renowned for his expertise in distressed debt and ability to acquire despised companies for pennies of their value. The more traditional model is the management team at Tweedy, Browne & Company who look for value throughout the world based on the criteria found in *Security Analysis,* such as companies selling for a fraction of their working capital or less than the price the firm would fetch in a private sale by an informed, rational buyer.

Although there are countless variations of the discipline, Ben Graham taught three underlying principles that serve as the guidelines for all value-oriented managers.

1. Weighing Machine vs. Voting Machine

The price of a company in the stock market and the true, or *intrinsic*, value of the firm are separate things. In the short run, they may diverge wildly. In the long-run, however, the market price will almost always come to reflect the underlying business. In Graham's words, "in the short-run, the market is a voting machine, in the long-run, a weighing machine."

Investor's Idiom

Intrinsic value is a term used to describe the investor's estimate of the "real" or "true" value of an investment. We'll talk more about estimating intrinsic value later in the book.

This distinction is crucial to successful value investing. In practical terms, it means never allowing yourself get upset about falling stock prices; indeed, you should be excited about being offered the opportunity to acquire additional ownership in businesses at a lower price!

2. Margin of Safety

Say you're an engineer that's been hired to design a bridge capable of supporting 10,000 lbs. of weight. When you draw up the plans, you're going to make certain the bridge can actually support much more than that—perhaps 15,000 lbs. This 5,000 lbs. buffer is there to protect drivers who may underestimate the weight of their vehicle.

Just like a prudent engineer, Graham believed every investment should have a built-in margin of safety to protect the investor against errors in judgment or changes in the economics of a business. The margin of safety is the difference between your estimate of an investment's intrinsic value and the current price of the asset.

Here's an example: You want to buy shares in Ruby's Furniture Emporium (a fictional company). After careful analysis, you decide the stock is worth $40. You call your broker and get the current quote and discover it is trading at $25 per share, significantly less than your estimate of intrinsic value. The $15 difference is your margin of safety.

Super Strategy

If you're going to insist upon a margin of safety in your investments, make sure the margin is large enough. It isn't sufficient to pay $28 per share for a business you think is worth $30. A general rule of thumb is to buy only assets where the current price is only 2/3 of your estimate of intrinsic value.

---

3. Jeeves, Sell Me a Business!

The market is there to serve you, not instruct you. Graham taught his students to think of it as a manic-depressive fellow named Mr. Market. Every day, he offers you the chance to buy or sell ownership in tens of thousands of businesses. You are free to disregard him and take advantage of his mood swings only when the prices are to your liking. For this reason, you don't mind his wild fluctuations any more than you would if your neighbor knocked on your door and offered to buy your house for half of what it is worth.

This mental construct can provide a guard to protect you against succumbing to manias, panics, bubbles, crashes, corrections, recessions, booms, and busts. If you wake up one morning to find that shares of your favorite company have been cut in half, for example, you can ask yourself, "Is there something to this—is the business worth less due to some change in fortunes, or is Mr. Market offering me a ridiculous price because he has, in typical fashion, overacted?"

Grabbing Onto the Rocket: The Growth Approach

On the other side of the philosophical fence, you have those who believe the only way to beat the market over long periods of time is by buying companies that are growing sales and earnings rapidly. These folks are trying to buy the next Wal-Mart or

Starbucks and many (though not all) believe the price you pay is only a secondary consideration, or in extreme cases, completely irrelevant.

To find growth companies, investors generally start by asking three questions:

1. Expanding Market, Industry, or Product

Does the company operate in an expanding industry? Does it have a product with a dominant market share, yet also have room to significantly expand sales? These are two of the first questions growth-oriented investors ask themselves when evaluating a stock.

2. Commitment to Developing New Products

Does the company's management have the willingness to commit time, money, and other resources to developing new products that can significantly and rapidly increase sales and profits? This question seeks to weed out the Pixars of the world from the Pet Rocks and Hula-Hoops.

Investor's Idiom

Venture capital is money provided to a startup firm by wealthy individuals and entities. In many cases, the investee receives advice on improving operations and access to a network of well-connected individuals that can open doors that would otherwise be closed.

3. Profit Margins

The higher the profit margins, the higher the return on equity, or ROE (you'll discover how to calculate it in Chapter 17). Companies with high returns on equity can generate enough cash internally to fund rapid expansion. This means they won't have to turn to the bank or debt markets for funding.

One criticism of growth-oriented managers is that the approach can degenerate into momentum trading or buying stocks that are shooting up in the market without any regard for the underlying business. This is exactly what led to the Internet bubble of the late 1990's when even respectable, white-gloved, well-heeled investment banking firms hyped stocks of companies that had no chance of survival without endless cash infusions by *venture capitalists*.

Can't We All Be Friends?

There are plenty of people in the middle on the value vs. growth debate. On the value side, these managers talk about paying a fair price for an excellent business; on the growth side, they talk about buying growth at a reasonable price.

This middle ground is where people like Warren Buffett and Philip Fisher meet. Ever the trend-bucking analysts, these men realized the entire debate is for naught because the growth rate of an investment is one of the key factors when valuing an asset. One look at the respective records of these seminal giants and you'll realize they were onto something.

Still, some of you aren't going to be satisfied with the middle ground. What's the final verdict between the two approaches? For many people, growth is more enticing because the opportunity to own high-flying companies that are reaching national prominence is sexier than owning a sewer treatment plant that happened to be cheap. In the end, however, investing is about making money—not getting a warm and fuzzy feeling about the assets you own. The evidence seems to support this by pointing to the value folks who have racked up long-term, market-beating returns for decades—men like Warren Buffett, Charlie Munger, Walter Schloss, Bill Ruane, Wally Weitz, Bill Ruane, and the folks at Tweedy, Browne & Company. If you have been fortunate enough to invest with any of them, you have been richly rewarded.

> **Fiscal Facts**
>
> Philip A. Fisher authored *Common Stocks and Uncommon Profits*. In this treatise, he identified ways the investor can spot excellent businesses that are sure to beat the market if held for long periods of time. Unlike Graham, Fisher was interested in understanding the qualitative side of a business (management talent, corporate image, etc.) as well as the quantitative.

The Least You Need to Know

- Your objectives are determined by both your goal and how fast you need access to the money.

- In most cases, you should invest only in assets that have characteristics that fit the risk profile of your objective.

- If you are investing for capital preservation, never accept a very real potential loss of principal in exchange for a few extra percentage points.

- Speculation should be done in a separate account to preserve the integrity of your long-term investments.

Chapter 5

What Do You Have Right Now—and What Will You Need?

In This Chapter

- ◆ Creating a personal balance sheet
- ◆ Creating a personal income statement
- ◆ Real-life examples of personal financial statement
- ◆ Calculating what it will take to fund your dreams
- ◆ Major life mistakes to avoid

A high net worth is the result of rational, disciplined decisions. There are no arcane formulae that turn lead into gold, nor are extraordinary feats necessary. In order to make intelligent decisions, however, you need to be armed with cold, hard facts. This chapter is designed to help you answer three key questions:

- Where am I now?

    The income statement and balance sheet are the tools we use to answer this question. Collectively, they show you exactly how much you have, how much you owe, how much you make, and how much you spend.

- Where am I going?

    Setting goals and attaching definitive, measurable metrics to them is extremely important. If your objective is to buy a home, live comfortably, and retire with $500,000, your decisions will be necessarily different than someone who aspires to retire with $10 million.

- How am I going to get there?

    Finally, you'll discover how to use a derivation of one of the time value of money (TVM) formulas you learned in Chapter 2 to calculate the amount you will need to invest in order to go from where you are now to where you want to be.

You also learn how to avoid the most common mistakes made by investors and how you can use the 10 percent habit to start saving today.

Where Am I Now?

Before we can begin selecting individual accounts and investments (which you learn about in the remainder of the book), we have to figure out where you are right now—at this very moment. It may not be pleasant. It may even be a little terrifying. But it's important that you face reality; otherwise, you can't begin to craft a plan to achieve your dreams.

To accomplish this task, you are going to prepare two personal financial statements—a balance sheet and an *income statement*.

Your Personal Balance Sheet: A Snapshot of Your Finances

Let's start with the *balance sheet*. A balance sheet shows your *assets*, *liabilities*, and *net worth*. Your net worth is the difference between your assets (what you own) and your liabilities (what you owe). It's a snapshot of your finances at a specific moment in time.

Investor's Idiom

A **balance sheet** is like a photograph of your finances at a given moment in time. It shows what you own (your **assets**) and what you owe (your **liabilities**).

Your **net worth** is the difference between assets and liabilities. Net worth can be positive (if assets are greater than liabilities) or negative (if liabilities are greater than assets). An **income statement,** in contrast, shows the flow of money through your life. It allows you to compare your income with your expenses.

To create a personal balance sheet for you or your family, fill out the following worksheet. Make a habit of doing this once a year so you can compare your progress.

John and Suzie Q. Personal Balance Sheet as of 00/00/00

Assets	Liabilities
Cash _____	Credit Card Debt _____
Checking Account Balance _____	Student Loans _____
Savings Account Balance _____	Other Personal Loans _____
Individual Investments _____	Home Mortgage _____
Profit Sharing (401[k], 403[b], etc.)_____	Car Loan _____
Home (estimated value) _____	Other Debt _____
Car (estimated value) _____	
Collectibles (antiques, stamps, etc.) _____	
Furnishings (estimated value) _____	
Total Assets _____	**Total Liabilities** _____

Fiscal Facts

To estimate what Social Security will pay you during your leisurely retirement, call (800) 772-1213 or visit the Social Security website at www.ssa.gov. You'll need to fill out Form SSA-7004. Social Security will send you your very own Social Security Statement. Check it carefully for bureaucratic boo-boos.

Note that on the asset side, we have left out two potential retirement benefits that some financial advisors would include: Social Security and earned pension benefits. You may add them in if you are close (five years or less) to retirement, but otherwise exclude them because:

- They cannot be converted to cash if necessary.

- They don't technically belong to you right now. In some cases, a former employer may offer to meet your earned pension sum by offering a lump-sum payment, prompting you to transfer the sum to a rollover IRA and include it under the profit-sharing line.

Your first goal is to get your assets to exceed your liabilities. Your ongoing goal is to continually widen that spread so that you maximize your net worth. There are two ways to do this:

- Increase the total return on your assets

  This can be accomplished by either earning more money or cutting expenses. This will result in a higher net income on your income statement, which we discuss later, and, as a result, more assets on your balance sheet.

  The key to true financial independence is in maximizing *income-producing* assets. If you purchase furniture for your new home, for example, you still have the same amount of assets—you just transferred your capital from cash to a loveseat—but the cash has now been taken out of the compounding process. You saw in Chapter 2 the dramatic effect time can have on even the smallest amounts. For that reason, $1 invested in stocks, bonds, mutual funds, and other income-producing assets is more valuable than $1 in hard goods (for you purists out there, we must mention that this ceases to be true in periods of high inflation).

- Decrease the cost of your liabilities

  When you reduce the interest rate you pay on your debt, you not only increase your net worth by the amount of interest expense saved, but also by the profit generated from those funds if invested.

  To illustrate: You have a $100,000 loan that matures in ten years with a current interest rate of 8 percent. You refinance at 5 percent. You invest the $3,000 you save annually. The investment generates returns of 8 percent per annum for the next 10 years. Using the future value of an annuity formula from Chapter 2, you see that you will be $43,460 richer—$30,000 resulting from reduced interest expense and $13,460 from the profit of investing that capital. Following is the equation for figuring this out:

$100,000 \times 8$ percent old interest expense = $8,000

$100,000 \times 5$ percent net interest expense = $5,000

Annual Interest Savings = $3,000

Get a Grip with a Personal Income Statement

A great deal of financial planning is just getting a clear view of your situation. Before you can get a handle on your spending, you'll need to tally up your expenses and compare them to your income. If your expenses are 90 percent or less of your income, great! If they are equal to or are greater than your income, well, now you know there is a problem and can take remedial action.

For most people, getting a truly accurate picture of your expenditures is eye-opening. Consider the following: A 22-year-old recent college graduate stops by Starbucks on the way to work to purchase a drink and a muffin, spending $5 each morning. That works out to around $1,300 per year. If this young professional skipped the morning routine, ate at home, and instead opted to invest that money in the stock market each year, earning a 12 percent long-term rate of return, she would have $1,405,407 when she retired at age 65. She will have given up 11,180 cups of coffee and the same number of muffins, but her retirement will be much fatter.

For some of you, skipping the gourmet coffee isn't an option. That is where individual choice comes into the picture. Armed with this data, you can ask yourself the question, "Is giving up my morning coffee and muffin worth $1.4 million by retirement?" There is no right or wrong answer—that is the art of living.

"But isn't the point of being rich so that I don't *have* to control my consumption?" you ask. Au contraire! In his bestselling book *The Millionaire Mind*, Dr. Thomas Stanley revealed that the average American millionaire, despite having a median net worth of $4.3 million and annual income of $436K, has never spent more than $41,000 for an automobile or $340K for a home; a stark contrast to the popular image most people have of the wealthy.

By tracking your costs through a personal income statement that clearly delineates your income and expenses, you become aware of expenditures—such as gourmet coffee—and the ultimate economic cost to you and your family. Unlike the balance sheet, which is a snapshot of your assets and liabilities at a specific point in time, the income statement covers a range of dates—January 1 to December 31, for example. If you prepare an income statement once a month, you can really get a grip on how much money is coming in and how it's being spent. Before you fill out the following worksheet, you might want to make 20 or so copies of it. Fill out one using yearly figures and use the others to create an income statement each month.

John and Suzie Q. Personal Income Statement Twelve Months Ending 00/00/00

Income	Expenses
Salary _____	FICA, etc. _____
Gifts to You/Yours _____	Federal Taxes _____
Income from Savings[1] _____	State Taxes _____
Alimony Received _____	Life Ins. Premiums _____
	Rental/Mortgage Payments _____
	Real Estate Tax[2] _____
	Food _____
	Clothing _____
	Alimony Paid _____
	Medical/Dental _____
	Entertainment _____
	Gifts Given _____
	Auto Payments _____
Income	**Expenses**
	Student Loan Payments _____
	Credit Card Payments[3] _____
	Other Loan Payments _____
	Auto Related (gas, service, etc.) _____
	Home Repairs _____
	Furnishings _____
	Vacation _____
	Utilities (gas, electric, phone) _____
	Education Related _____
	Other _____
Total Income _____	**Total Expenses** _____

(1) Limited to savings for car, etc.

(2) If not included in mortgage payment

(3) Deduct sums covered elsewhere (e.g., clothing, etc.)

There are a few things you can do immediately to increase the income side without affecting your current lifestyle:

♦ Divert any raises you get at work toward your investments.

♦ Make sure your savings are with the bank that offers the highest interest rate in your area.

♦ Be sure to put any cash gifts into your savings/investing accounts. This is "found" money for you. And you might hint to family members that you would prefer cash to gifts going forward.

A Happy Couple on the Right Track

If you've had a little trouble filling out your personal financial statements, here's an example. Let's call this couple Mark and Tammy. They are both 33 years old, have one 3-year-old child, and own their condo. Mark is a private school teacher and Tammy works part-time at a retail firm. Credit cards are paid off in full each month.

Balance Sheet – Mark and Tammy   July 15, 2005

Assets			Liabilities	
Savings		$20,000	Student Loans	0
Investments			Other Personal Loans	0
Bill (403b)	$12,000			
Pension	$5,600			
Mary (401k)	$600			
Child	$5,000			
Roth IRA	$2,000	$25,200		
Home		$240,000	Mortgage	$99,000
Auto		$5,400	Auto Loans	0
Total		$290,000	**Total**	**$99,000**
Net Worth:	**$191,600**			

Income Statement – Mark and Tammy   July 15, 2005

Income			Expenses	
Salary:	Bill	$37,000	Mortgage	$8,184
	Mary	$11,000 $48,000	Real Estate Tax	$1,416
Investment Income		$800	FICA	$702
Gifts (cash)		$1,000	Medicare	$684
			Federal Tax	$6,004
			State Tax	$2,950
			Medical Plan	$1,344
			Pension	$2,064
			Gifts	$1,000
Income			**Expenses**	
			Auto Repair	$1,000
			Credit Cards	$200
			Home Insurance	$783
			Auto Insurance	$510
			Phone	$672
			Electric & Gas	$1,192
			Food	$5,200
			Clothing	$6,500
			Home Repairs	$2,000
			Entertainment	$2,600
			Vacation	$1,000
			Balance Savings/ Investments	$3,795
Total		**$49,800**	**Total**	**$49,800**

Incidentally, Mark and Tammy are still young enough to be able to keep all their investments in stock, and therefore can take advantage of the high returns available.

Looking good!

Your Typical Young Guy Living Hand to Mouth

Here is another example. Fred is also a teacher, but he's 30 and single. You can see how the unpaid balance on credit cards hinders his opportunities for savings and investment.

Fred's Balance Sheet as of 7/05

Assets		Liabilities	
Checking	0	Car Loan	$1,000
Retirement Plan	$7,088	Student Loans	$17,400
Car	$2,000		
		Credit Cards	$8,325
Total	$9,088		$26,725
Net Worth: –$17,637			

Income Statement as of 7/05 (Monthly)

Income		Expenses	
Salary	$2,517	Federal Tax	$275
Other	$147	State Tax	$170
Gifts	$90	FICA	$165
		Medicare	$39
		Workers Comp	$2
		Union Dues	$51
		Retirement Plan	$160
		Student Loans	$367
		Credit Cards	$350
		Rent	$515
		Auto Insurance	$70
		Auto Club	$5
		Gas	$50
		Telephone	$40
		Electricity	$50

continues

continued

Income		Expenses	
	Cable	$45	
	Water & Sewer	$12	
	Food	$170	
	Entertainment	$120	

Income		Expenses	
	Other	$20	
	Auto Loan	$58	
	To Savings	$0	
$2,754		$2,734	

Fred has a negative net worth and lives hand to mouth on a month-to-month basis. The credit cards are his big handicap not only because he is making such large payments, but because the interest rates are high enough that it will take him decades to pay off the balance at his current pace. Paying off this debt should be Fred's highest priority (you'll learn how to decide whether to invest or pay off your debt in Chapter 7).

The good thing about looking unflinchingly at your finances like this is it forces you to face your problems—and every problem has a solution. In Fred's case, for example, he might consider taking a part-time job for a year to pay off the balance.

His next goal needs to be to develop an emergency cash fund to protect him from life's unexpected (and often unpleasant) surprises.

Super Strategy

When developing an emergency cash fund, your objective should always be capital preservation. This means money should be kept in the most liquid and marketable investments possible—things like money market funds or Treasury bills. Why? It's not likely that you'll be able to postpone surgery to match up with a Treasury note to mature so you can get your principal back!

Fred's situation is typical of recent college graduates. Although his situation will definitely improve if he catches a break such as getting a promotion and/or raise, he will never be financially independent unless he learns to responsibly manage his current resources.

Where Am I Going?

Now that you know where you are, it's time to turn your attention to where you want to go. Perhaps you have your eye on your dream home. Maybe you really do just want to make sure your golden years are comfortable. The key to success in this arena is to identify, specifically, what it is you want in quantitative terms. It isn't enough to say, "I want to save for the down payment on a home." Instead, you need to say, "I want to save $80,000 for the down payment on a home within the next five years." The latter statement contains enough specific information that you can begin to draft a plan based on—you guessed it—cold, hard facts steeped in a cup of rationality and discipline.

How Am I Going to Get There?

The great mathematician Jacobi was famous for saying "invert—always invert." This backward-working approach to problem solving is an excellent way to structure your life—both financial and otherwise. Using this approach, you can ask yourself the question, "What do I have to do *now* in order to meet each of my investment goals?" These step-by-step instructions will help you formulate an answer:

1. Grab a sheet of paper and write down, in financial terms, precisely what you want (such as I want to save $80,000 for a down payment on a house).

2. Decide upon a timeframe for each goal (for example, I want to accomplish this within the next 5 years).

3. Using the timeframe as your guide, assign one of the investment objectives you learned in Chapter 4 to each goal (for example, capital preservation is my goal because I cannot afford to risk the principal).

Fiscal Facts

For a variety of reasons, many financial pundits believe the stock market returns going forward will be significantly lower than they have been over the past two decades. In the interest of conservatism, you may want to limit your estimate for long-term growth to 10 percent (versus a current average of 12 percent). This will build in a margin of safety and protect you from coming up short in the end.

4. Conservatively estimate the after-tax rate of return you can reasonably expect to earn on each goal based upon the investment objective (for example, I expect to earn 6 percent on certificates of deposit at the local bank). Remember, the shorter the timeframe, the lower the rate of return.

5. Use a derivation of the future value of an annuity formula to solve for the amount you will have to save annually to accomplish your goal. Don't panic! Despite the fact that sentence sounds like something out of a math-camp nightmare, you already know everything you need to solve the problem. Like all of the TVM formulas, it is simply a matter of mixing around the variables to answer a different question—in this case, "how much would I have to invest annually in order to end up with $X in Y years at a rate of return of Z?"

No Pain No Gain: Calculating What it Will Take in Actual Dollars

Solving for the Payment of a Future Value of an Annuity

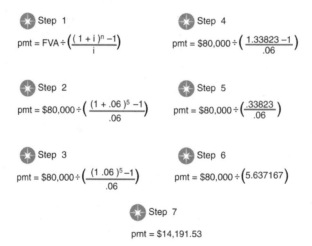

Step 1

$$pmt = FVA \div \left(\frac{(1+i)^n - 1}{i} \right)$$

Step 4

$$pmt = \$80,000 \div \left(\frac{1.33823 - 1}{.06} \right)$$

Step 2

$$pmt = \$80,000 \div \left(\frac{(1 + .06)^5 - 1}{.06} \right)$$

Step 5

$$pmt = \$80,000 \div \left(\frac{.33823}{.06} \right)$$

Step 3

$$pmt = \$80,000 \div \left(\frac{(1 .06)^5 - 1}{.06} \right)$$

Step 6

$$pmt = \$80,000 \div \left(5.637167 \right)$$

Step 7

$$pmt = \$14,191.53$$

In the example—you want to save $80,000 for the down payment on a house within the next five years and you expect to earn 6 percent on your savings—the answer of $14,192 is the amount you would need to invest annually in order to meet your goal. That works out to something like $273 per week.

In the beginning of the chapter, we told you there was nothing magical about building wealth. If you manage to save $273 per week for five years at a 6 percent after-tax rate of return, you *will* end up with your $80,000 down payment on a house. It really is that simple. The most difficult part is deciding which sacrifices you are willing to make in order to meet your goal.

Avoiding Major Mistakes

In this chapter, you've learned the steps necessary to achieve your financial goals. Now, we're going to talk about common mistakes you want to avoid so you don't sabotage your efforts. In fact, it can be argued that the single biggest contributor to building wealth is simply the avoidance a few large-scale, dumb decisions.

- ◆ **Marrying the Wrong Person.** It's no secret that the number one cause of divorce is money. If you have aspirations to build a large net worth yet your spouse is charging thousands of dollars on credit cards, you are headed for emotional and financial disaster. There are enough obstacles in life; you shouldn't have to swim against the tide in your own home. To add insult to injury, you are liable for all debts incurred by your spouse during your marriage—even if your name is not on the account.

- ◆ **Carrying Credit Card Debt.** Credit cards can be a useful tool but they are not a substitute for your own capital. It is impossible to get ahead when you're paying 18+ percent interest. In Chapter 7, we'll discuss how you can decide whether to pay off your debt or invest.

- ◆ **Waiting to Begin.** If you're still not astounded by the power of compounding, take a look at the following chart. It assumes you have a goal of saving $10 million for retirement by 65 (hey—you don't think small!) and earn a 12 percent rate of return.

Starting Age	Years Until Retirement	Annual Savings Required	Monthly Savings Required
18	47	$5,862	$489
25	40	$13,036	$1,086
30	35	$23,166	$1,931
35	30	$41,437	$3,453
40	25	$75,000	$6,250
45	20	$138,788	$11,566
50	15	$268,242	$22,354
55	10	$569,842	$47,487
60	5	$1,574,097	$131,175

Note: The chart was calculated by solving for the payment in the future value of an annuity. You learned the formula earlier in this chapter.

Fiscal Facts

Think 18 is young? Parents or grandparents that want their posterity to have $10 million by retirement would only need to invest $759 per year starting at birth—or $63.25 per month! When the child grew old enough, he could easily fund the investment himself.

If you started investing at 18, you would reach your goal of $10 million by saving $489 per month. If you waited until you were 40, on the other hand, you would have to save $6,250 per month, or nearly 13 times as much! It's true that a vast majority of teenagers aren't thinking about the time value of money, but point is still valid. Every year you wait to invest, your potential future wealth is drastically reduced.

♦ **Taking on excessive leverage.** Utilizing excessive leverage (debt) is foolish. The only reason otherwise rational people choose to do it is because they are eager to get rich too quickly. The thing they don't realize is that, should they fail and suffer a serious capital loss, the compounding cycle has been irreparably damaged. Famed economist and investor John Maynard Keynes once quipped, "markets can stay irrational longer than you can stay solvent." He was right.

♦ **Refusing to live within your means.** You work hard and you don't want to be restrained by meaningless budgets or spending limits. "I don't want to live that way," you say defiantly. That's fine—as long as you are fully aware of the ultimate economic cost. Your life should be one of design, not accident. A flexible budget is merely a tool to achieve your dreams; in the *Richest Man in Babylon*, the reader is told that a budget is merely a tool for protecting your true desires from your casual wants.

King Solomon, the wealthiest man who ever lived, said, "where there is no vision, the people cast off restraint." This is true in any field—if you have a vision, a dream of losing weight, for example, you restrict your calories and make yourself exercise. Likewise, if you have a dream of financial independence, you restrict your casual wants, instead focusing on the bigger goal. This ability to exercise self-control goes back to our central key to success—rational, disciplined decisions.

The Least You Need to Know

- Before you begin investing, you need to answer three questions: "Where am I?", "Where do I want to be?", and "How do I get there?"

- Personal financial statements can be used as a tool to increase your net worth.

- It is important to be specific when identifying financial goals; otherwise, you can't develop a logical plan of action to achieve them.

- Avoiding major mistakes is just as important as making good decisions.

Part 2 Creating a Plan

Um, we have a personal question: what's the interest rate on your maxed-out credit card? Eighteen percent? Youch! So what if your investments are earning 12 percent if you're paying 18 percent to those sharks? Kinda defeats the purpose, wouldn't you say?

Well, you're in luck! This section is about wiping out debt, improving your credit score, purchasing a house, funding your own (or a child's) education, and planning for retirement—all the things you need to establish a firm financial foundation.

Chapter 6

Retirement Plans 101

In This Chapter

- ◆ Defined benefit vs. defined contribution plans
- ◆ 401(k) loans
- ◆ The differences between a traditional and Roth IRA
- ◆ Avoiding the 10 percent early withdrawal fee on nonqualified IRA distributions

In this chapter, you'll learn about the different types of retirement accounts available to you and how to choose the one that is most appropriate. Although we won't focus on selecting individual investments just yet—we're saving that for Part 3—rest assured that the right investment vehicle can mean the difference between a comfortable, and a downright plush, retirement.

How Gold Do You Want Your Golden Years to Be?

If planning for retirement is the furthest thing from your mind, you're not alone. According to the *2005 Retirement Confidence Survey* conducted by The Employee Benefit Research Institute, only 42 percent of all workers have figured out how much they'll need to retire. What's more:

♦ Twenty percent of those who say they are very confident about retirement preparation are not currently saving for retirement, 52 percent do not have an IRA opened with money saved outside of an employer's retirement plan, and 37 percent have not done a retirement needs calculation.

♦ More than half (52 percent) report that the total value of their savings and investments, excluding the value of their primary residence, is less than $25,000.

♦ Fifty-five percent of folks feel like they are a "little" or "a lot" behind schedule in funding their retirement while only 7 percent feel like they are "a little" or "a lot" ahead of schedule.

And for some weird reason, the percentage of smug individuals who say they are "very confident about retirement" has remained flat at 20 to 25 percent for the last eight years. (Who are those people, anyway?) This means that three quarters of us have either blocked the entire disconcerting business out of our minds or toss and turn enough at night to wrinkle our wrinkle-free sheets.

Unless you want to spend your twilight years pushing a shopping cart around town looking for recyclables, you must add retirement into your overall investment-objective picture. What does this mean, exactly? Just this: a comfortable retirement is the manner in which you will maintain your present standard of living without heading off to the salt mines 40-plus hours a week. Presently, you probably don't often have to do without or scrimp; you have the means to eat well and entertain when you wish. When you retire, you'll have roughly the same expenses, with four possible exceptions:

♦ **Car expense.** If you have two cars now and one is primarily used for commuting, you might be able to get by with one after retirement. This will mean significant savings on car payments, insurance, gas, and maintenance.

♦ **Home expense.** If you have a four-bedroom colonial, you might consider moving to a smaller house or condo when the kids leave the nest. This would free up capital and reduce monthly payments and taxes.

♦ **Clothing expense.** Not going to work means not having to wear a different snazzy suit or dress everyday. Bermuda shorts and Converse hi-tops are a lot cheaper.

♦ **Taxes.** Income tax will come down as your income declines; property taxes can be reduced if you sell a large home.

Because these expenses are likely to be reduced once you retire, and because the dollars you're saving now for retirement will become dollars you can consume, a good rule of thumb is to expect that you'll require an annual retirement income of 50 to 70 percent of your present salary. The range accounts for a mortgaged home versus one owned free and clear. So, for example, if you live comfortably now on $60,000 a year and you expect to pay off your home by the time you retire, you need to save a pool of money that will generate 50 percent of $60,000, or $30,000, per year for your retirement.

Now the question is do you spend down that pool of money you have accumulated by age 65, or do you leave it to your heirs? It's probably wiser to assume that you'll spend it to zero by, say, age 90. If you include your savings as part of your retirement support (and face the gruesome fact of your own actuarial mortality!), you'll have to save far less to reach your goal. It's very important when planning your financial security to set realistic, reachable goals. If you establish a goal that requires too much scrimping and saving, you'll eventually shrug your shoulders and say, "Well, whatever happens, happens." Better to set a goal you recognize as doable. Start now, save consistently, get reasonable rates of return, and you'll have that pool of money when you retire.

Defined Benefit Plans

In a defined benefit plan, an employer guarantees a specific annual sum upon retirement (the "benefit") to an employee and is liable for ensuring that sufficient assets are set aside to make good on that promise. The most popular form is a good, old-fashioned pension. Because defined benefit plans are more expensive to run than defined contribution plans—which we'll talk about later in the chapter—companies have moved away from them.

Most defined benefit plans have four characteristics:

♦ A vesting schedule requiring that you work a minimum number of hours per year—a thousand, for example. This eliminates part-timers.

- A minimum number of years must be vested before qualifying for the pension; five years is common. This is to discourage job hoppers. The total of vested years you've accumulated is called "credited service."

- The value of the pension increases as you put more years in at the company.

- The value of the pension is weighted so that the last few years generate a disproportional chunk of the ultimate benefit you will receive. This is to encourage you to stay at this company until you retire. You maximize your pension by staying put.

How the Amount of Your Monthly Pension Is Determined

In the end, the amount of your pension is based on a formula that takes all these factors into consideration. For example, Ralph's Dog Biscuit Company figures out its employees' monthly retirement benefit based on the following convoluted formula:

- Take 2 percent of final average monthly pay.

- Multiply it by number of vested years (credited service) up to a maximum of 35 years.

- Subtract 1⅔ percent of Social Security benefit and then multiply the resulting number by credited service up to a maximum of 30 years.

- Finally, subtract the latter from the former.

- This equals the monthly benefit at age 65.

Fiscal Facts

Just in case some of you have forgotten how to convert a mixed fraction to a decimal, here's the trick: Multiply the denominator (the bottom number of the fraction) by the whole number. Add the resulting number to the numerator (the top number of the fraction). Now, divide the denominator by the new numerator. For example, for the mixed fraction 1⅔:

3 (the denominator) × 1 (the whole number) = 3;

3 + 2 (the numerator) = 5, giving you a new fraction of ⅝;

5 ÷ 3 = 1.66

Whew!

Let's look at an example. Assume loyal Ralph's Dog Biscuit Company employee Lindsay Jackson will be 65 on January 1, 2003, and will have 20 years of fully vested, credited service at that time. Let's say her Social Security benefit in 2005 is $1,007 a month. Let's also assume that her final average pay is $2,500 a month ($30,000 a year). Now we can apply the formula.

Figure out 2 percent of $2,500 (final average monthly pay), and multiply it by 20 (total vested years of slaving away).

> 2 percent = .02
>
> 2,500 × .02 = 50.00
>
> 50.00 × 20 = $1,000

Then, take 1⅔ percent of $1,007 (the S.S. benefit), and multiply that by 20 (those hard-earned years again): 1⅔ percent expressed as a decimal is 1.66. Finally, subtract that number from the number above.

> 1,007 × 1.66 = $16.72
>
> 16.72 × 20 = $334.40
>
> 1,000 − 334.40 = $665.60

Monthly Benefit = $665.60

Ms. Jackson will receive a monthly pension of $665.60, as well as $1,007 per month from Social Security. Her total monthly retirement income, unless she has other investments, will be $1,672.60.

A Whole Lotta Lumps or Just One: The Lump-Sum Option

Pensions are a promise or guarantee from your employer to you to pay a certain sum at a certain age until death. As you learned in Chapter 2, a regular payment over time like this is called an *annuity*. In some cases, you may be given a choice between the monthly pension payment and receiving the entire pension upon retirement as a lump sum.

How can you tell if the lump sum is better than the monthly payment? Well, first it depends on how involved you want to be. Some people are simply intimidated by large sums of money and are grateful to get a monthly check from their former employer. But you could shop the lump sum to several reputable insurers for their annuity rates and then compare. Many insurers "write" annuities and may offer you a better deal (i.e., higher monthly payment) for your lump sum than your employer's plan does. You can also use your broker or friendly banker to help in the process. However, you will not be given all the time in the world to decide which plan is best for you, so be aware that you need to give this some thought before the day of your retirement party.

If Your Employer Drops the Ball

Note that a defined benefit plan like a pension is a promise to pay on the part of the employer. The employer, or plan sponsor, is totally responsible for providing pension payments to retired employees (traditional profit-sharing plans, on the other hand, only tie the employer's contribution to the plan to the level of profitability of the corporation: no profit, no contribution).

Fiscal Facts

Safeguards to prevent pension plans from defaulting on paying retirement benefits to employees were an important reason for the passage of the Employee Retirement Income Security Act of 1974 (ERISA). ERISA also codified 401(k) and 403(b) plans and prohibited employers from conducting certain transactions with retirement plan dollars.

The employer is supposed to be making annual contributions to the company's retirement fund and investing this money wisely. If the company goes broke or anything else happens to its ability to pay the benefits promised to retirees, responsibility for the pension is turned over to a federal agency called the Pension Benefit Guaranty Corp., (PBGC). Probably not who you expected to be handling your future, but at least it's a backup plan.

Defined Contribution Plans

Defined contribution plans, unlike defined benefit plans, limit the employer's role and responsibility. Employees decide ("define") how much they are going to contribute to their retirement account and then choose individual investments from a menu of options provided to them. There are no promises or guarantees; ultimately, your economic well-being depends upon the total amount contributed and the performance of the investments chosen.

401(k) and 403(b) Plans

The most popular defined contribution plans are the 401(k) and the 403(b). These accounts, codified by the Employee Retirement Income Security Act of 1974 (ERISA) provide an attractive way for the average worker to save for their retirement.

- 401(k) plans are for employees of private-sector companies.

- 403(b) plans are for employees of nonprofits, such as public schools, philanthropic foundations, and hospitals.

- Eligible state or local government employees have so-called Section 457 plans ("457s"). Named for Section 457 in the IRS Code, they are set up similar to a 401(k).

Benefits of 401(k) and 403(b) Plans

There are several benefits to defined contribution plans. Chief among these are:

- **Tax-Deferred Growth:** Capital gains, dividends, and interest income generated by the investments held in your 401(k) or 403(b) plan are not subject to income tax until they are withdrawn. Over time, this can result in much more wealth for you! Consider this: $10,000 invested annually each year for 40 years would grow to $3.97 million if the profits were taxed at 20 percent capital gains rates at the end of every year. If the same investment were held in a tax-advantaged account, however, and all of the profits were subject to ordinary income taxes of 35 percent at the end, the portfolio would grow to around $5 million! Why the drastic difference? In a tax-advantaged investment vehicle such as a 401(k), there is more money working for the investor in the form of deferred taxes.

- **Researched Investment Options:** The menu of investment options your employer offers through its defined contribution retirement plans has been carefully chosen and is probably quite solid. Managers of mutual funds and other investments compete intensely to convince corporations to offer their funds as 401(k) plan options.

- **The Employer Match:** Many employers offer to match a percentage of employee contributions in order to encourage saving for retirement. Do the math; if your employer matches you dollar-for-dollar on the first 4 percent of your salary and you contribute $1,000, it will deposit an additional $1,000. You have instantly made a 100 percent return on your investment. There is no other way you can so quickly and safely increase your net worth.

Can I Borrow from My 401(k)?

Can you take or borrow money from your 401(k)? Yes, but only under certain conditions enforced by the employer (and dictated by the federal government). If you borrow, you will have to pay competitive interest rates established by the employer. It is strongly recommended that this option be utilized only for a dire emergency, and that any sum borrowed be repaid ASAP!

You are required, ordinarily, to repay your 401(k) loan within five years. If you are using the money to purchase a home, however, you may be able to extend the repayment period over the length of the mortgage—up to 30 years. Of course, there is one catch (besides the fact that you are taking away money that could be compounding, tax advantaged, for the next several decades): If you cease to work for your employer—either voluntarily or involuntarily—you will only have 2 months to repay the loan. *If you are unable to repay during this window of time, the loan balance will be taxed (and charged a 10 percent penalty fee) as if it were a withdrawal!*

What If I Change Employers?

What happens to your 401(k) if you leave your employer? Following are your options:

Crash Alert

Bear in mind that when you leave a job you have only 60 days to shelter your 401(k) before the IRS swoops down on it. Even though changing jobs is hectic, make sure you either transfer it to your new employer's 401(k) or to a rollover IRA.

- You could leave your 401(k) with your old employer. Some employers allow you to maintain your account in their 401(k).

- If your old employer won't allow you to do that, or you don't want to, you could transfer your 401(k) assets into your new employer's 401(k) plan. No tax will be generated by this transfer.

♦ You could establish a separate IRA account and transfer your assets to this account. You have 60 days to do this before the assets will be taxed and subject to a 10 percent penalty. Because you are *rolling over* your assets into another account, this is called a rollover IRA.

♦ Finally, you could cash out your IRA (after your employer deducts taxes and penalties) and buy a new car. But would we recommend that? Noooooooo!

Once you create a rollover IRA, you can't move those funds to a traditional IRA or a 401(k) plan in the future.

Contribution Limits

Like all good things, Uncle Sam restricts the amount of *pretax dollars* you can contribute to your 401(k) or 403(b) plan. Take a look at the limits that are currently in place.

Annual Deferral Limits for 401(k) and 403(b) Plans

Year	Under age 50	Over Age 50
2005	$14,000	$18,000
2006	$15,000	$20,000

Total contributions (employee and employer contribution combined) are limited to the lesser of 25% of compensation or $42,000 in 2005.

Why would the government put limits on the maximum amount you can save for your retirement? This is to prevent the very highest-salaried employees from being able to shelter a much larger share of their income than lower-salaried employees can. It also encourages companies to offer a higher level of matching funds. If the fat cats at the top of your company could shelter huge chunks of their salaries in retirement accounts and the company had to pay them, say, 50¢ on every dollar they saved in their 401(k) plans, pretty soon the company might decide it can only afford to pay 25¢ on the dollar, thus lowering the retirement benefit for everyone.

Investor's Idiom

The money that is deducted from your pay before taxes are applied is called **pretax dollars.** This enables you to avoid paying taxes on whatever you contribute to your 401(k) or 403(b).

Should You Put All Your Eggs in the Company Basket? Ask the Folks at Enron ...

Often, a company will offer its employees an opportunity to buy its stock as part of the menu for its 401(k) plan. At first glance, this might seem like a pretty good idea. Why not have your company act as a stockbroker for you? You give them all your blood, sweat, and tears, why not let them work for you? Well, because on closer examination this may not be such a great idea. Even if the stock is being offered to you at a discount, you'll be putting all of your eggs in the company basket. Your future is already heavily invested in the success of your company—you work there!

Crash Alert _____

We've seen several instances where employees had money in company stock and the company went bankrupt, leaving them with nothing. We're not trying to scare you, and you may work for one of the biggest and sturdiest companies in the world, but history is littered with fallen giants that were once thought untouchable—the Great Atlantic & Pacific Tea Company, the Pennsylvania Railroad, PanAm, and Kmart, just to name a few.

When Enron, the energy conglomerate, came under investigation by the SEC in 2002, about 62 percent of the funds held in the 401(k) plans of 11,000 employees were invested in Enron stock. That money was wiped out when Enron's stock tanked, and so were the retirement dreams of many employees. Surprisingly, it's not unusual for company employees to hold so much company stock. According to a survey by DC Plan Investing, General Electric employees are 77 percent invested in G.E. paper, and Procter & Gamble's fund is almost 95 percent company stock. Common, yes. Smart, no.

If you do want to own some company stock in your 401(k), you should limit it to what you would invest in if you were creating your own equity portfolio. And don't worry—your employer can't punish you for taking minimal or no participation in the company stock option. There are laws against that. Don't let 'em pressure you (it was widely rumored that Enron execs were pushing their employees to buy more Enron stock while dumping it out of their own retirement accounts). One advantage of share ownership, though, is that it entitles you to receive annual reports and other information that goes to stockholders, so you can keep current on your company and its fiscal healthiness (or lack thereof), if you so desire.

What About Stock Options? Go for It.

If your company offers you *stock options*, as opposed to stock, go for it. These can be very profitable. You'd be amazed how many top executives in corporate America own little or no stock in their companies, but have large stock option grants.

Because there is no risk—you don't exercise your option unless the exercise price is less than the current price and you can make a profit—stock options are really a form of compensation.

If you are eligible for stock options, there are two things you can do with them:

◆ **Buy and sell on the same day.** You immediately exercise your option because the strike price is less than the current price and you can make a profit. You purchase the shares and sell the shares on the same day. This saves you the trouble of having to raise the money to buy the stock. You simply go to your human resources department and say you want to exercise your stock option (this may not be necessary because many companies establish services with brokerage firms that allow employees to manage their options directly over the Internet). Your profit is taxed at ordinary income tax rates. You pay tax on the capital gain resulting from the difference between the exercise price (sometimes called the "strike" price) and the sales price.

Investor's Idiom

A **stock option** is the right, but not the obligation, to buy a stock at a fixed price after a specified period of time (usually 12 months) for a fixed period of time (10 years). Prices and time periods are all specified in the option contract.

◆ **Hold on to the stock now, sell later.** You can buy the stock and hold it, hoping that its price will go up and you can sell at a profit. First, you'll need the money to buy the stock. It can come either from your own savings or by borrowing from your friendly banker. Then you exercise your option, or buy the stock. If you hold the stock for at least one year, you are taxed at capital gains rates (maximum of 20 percent), which is probably lower than your income tax rate.

What would we do? Well, we prefer the bird in the hand rather than trying to search through those darn bushes, so we'd probably choose the same-day transaction and deal with the ugly income tax. But, hey, this is your decision. You know your inclination, you know the company's prospects, and you know your personal financial situation. Take all of these factors into consideration before you make your decision.

Individual Retirement Accounts

What's an IRA? Nope, it's not the Irish Republican Army, although it can pack the same punch. Instead, it's a retirement account that you set up for yourself, as opposed to a 401(k) or 403(b) which would be set up by your employer.

The IRA itself is not an investment; it's a tax-sheltered account into which you put money that you can then invest as you choose. That money can be used to buy stocks, bonds, mutual funds, certificates of deposit, real estate, and other investments. The IRS does not permit you to use your IRA to purchase collectibles (fine art, gems, etc.) or life insurance contracts. An IRA can be set up with a bank, brokerage firm, or a mutual fund company.

There are several different kinds of IRAs, each with its own quirks and purpose. We'll discuss a few of them in-depth, but for now, here's a quick overview:

- ◆ **Traditional IRA:** Developed in 1975 to help people who were not covered by an employer-sponsored retirement plan to save for retirement; contributions to a traditional IRA are tax deductible. Your money grows in the account until you are 59½ years old; at which point you can begin to make regularly scheduled withdrawals without incurring a 10 percent penalty fee. You must begin withdrawing funds by age 70½. As the funds are pulled out, the proceeds are taxed as ordinary income.

- ◆ **Rollover IRA:** Used to shelter retirement savings that have been taken out of a 401(k) or cash pension due to a job change.

- ◆ **Roth IRA:** Created by the Taxpayer Relief Act of 1997 in order to give people more flexibility when saving for retirement, buying a house, or financing a child's education.

- ◆ **SEP-IRA:** A Simplified Employee Pension, or SEP-IRA, is a solution for small business owners. It allows an employer to make deductible contributions for the benefit of participating employees (including the employer him/herself). The contributions are made to individual retirement accounts (IRAs) set up for participants in the plan (again, including the employer). The maximum contribution for 2005 is 25 percent of a participant's compensation with a maximum compensation (for contribution limit calculation purposes) of $210,000. It is more complicated for the employer or a self-employed person, because you have to adjust (reduce) the compensation figure for the self-employment tax deduction. The IRS has a special worksheet you can use to do the calculation.

Incidentally, your employer's SEP-IRA contributions are excluded from your gross income for tax purposes. They will not show up on your W-2!

◆ **Simple IRA:** The Savings Incentive Match Plan for Employees is another option for small employers, including those who are self-employed, that has been growing in popularity because it is very easy to use. An employer can match up to 3 percent of your total compensation or your contribution, whichever is less. (Remember, if you're self-employed, *you* are the employer and the employee!) Contributions are presently limited to $10,000. If you are 50 or older, you are eligible for additional "catch-up" contributions of $2,000 in 2005 and $2,500 in 2006 on top of the $10,000 regular limit.

Old Faithful: The Traditional IRA

There was once a time when the traditional IRA was the only kid on the block. That ship has sailed, but old faithful is still a very good option for individuals that do not qualify for a Roth IRA. Here are the important things you need to know:

◆ **Tax Deduction:** Contributions to your traditional IRA can be deducted from your taxes. According to IRS Publication 590, however, this deduction begins to be phased out if you are covered by a retirement plan at work and your adjusted gross income (AGI) is:

  ◆ Between $65,000 and $75,000 for married couples filing a joint returns or a qualified widow(er)

  ◆ Between $45,000 and $55,000 for a single individual or head of household

  ◆ Less than $10,000 for a married individual filing a separate return.

◆ **Tax Deferral:** All of the dividends, interest, capital gains, and other income generated by your investments while they are parked in a traditional IRA will grow tax-deferred. When you begin to make withdrawals, the proceeds are taxed as ordinary income.

◆ **Withdrawals:** You can begin making withdrawals from your traditional IRA at age 59½ . If you make withdrawals before this age, you will pay taxes as well as a 10 percent penalty. You *must* take withdrawals by the age of 70½—otherwise, you could end up paying a 50 percent excise tax on the undistributed portion of your assets!

The New Kid on the Block: Roth IRA

Less than 10 years old, the Roth IRA offers extraordinary flexibility when compared to its stodgy, more rigid sibling. Here are the important things you need to know:

- **Tax Deduction:** Unlike a traditional IRA, contributions to a Roth IRA are not tax deductible.

- **Tax Free Growth:** All of the dividends, interest, capital gains, and other income generated by your investments while they are parked in a Roth IRA—brace yourself for this—will *never* be taxed as long as you make a qualified distribution ("qualified" meaning either after the age of 59½ or one of the specific exceptions permitted, which we'll discuss in a moment).

- **Passing Along the Wealth:** If you don't need the money you put into your Roth IRA to keep you in golf balls during retirement, the Roth offers an amazing tax break for your heirs. First, you don't have to start taking distributions at 70½, like you do with the traditional IRA. So you can leave your kids quite the tax-sheltered pile.

  If you name a child (or children) as beneficiary, the monthly distributions from a traditional or a Roth IRA will go to that child upon your death. With the traditional IRA, the distributions are taxable. With the Roth, they aren't. And, of course, the money passed onto them continues to grow tax free.

- **Withdrawals:** There is no age at which you must begin to make mandatory withdrawals. In practice, this means you could still be 105 years old and compounding your wealth into the stratosphere. Another huge benefit is that you can withdraw contributions to your Roth IRA without penalty, at any time.

  For example, you have a Roth IRA and you contribute $4,000 to it this year, never touching it again. Five years later, your IRA has grown to $6,500. You face an emergency and want to take cash from your account (not a good idea, but hey …). You could withdraw up to the amount of your contributions (in this case, $4,000) without penalty. The $2,500 in profit, however, is subject to the customary rules, restrictions, and red tape.

- **Income Restrictions:** If you are married and filing jointly and have an adjusted gross income (AGI) of $160,000 or more, or you are a single, head of household, or married and filing separately with an AGI of $110,000 or more, you cannot contribute to a Roth IRA. No exceptions. It's tragic, we know. Attempt to console yourself with your 6-figure income or run for Congress to change the law.

Avoiding the 10 Percent Early Withdrawal Penalty

The members of the United States Congress, being the kind souls that they are, permitted a handful of exceptions to the 10 percent penalty on early withdrawals. Here are a few ways cash taken out of your IRA can escape this dastardly fate (note that withdrawals from your traditional IRA are still subject to ordinary taxes):

◆ Proceeds are used to pay medical expenses that are not reimbursed and exceed more than 7.5 percent of your adjusted gross income.

◆ You become disabled and unable to secure gainful employment due to your injuries.

◆ You die (in which case, you probably don't care abut the 10 percent early penalty, anyway …).

◆ You are receiving distributions in the form of an annuity.

◆ The distributions are used for qualified higher education expenses—such as tuition, fees, books, supplies, and required equipment—for you, your spouse, your children, or other family members.

◆ You buy or build a first home for yourself, your spouse, your or your spouse's child, grandchild, parent, or other ancestor. There is a $10,000 lifetime limit to this exemption.

If you are considering taking an early withdrawal from your IRA, head over to www.irs.gov, read IRS Publication 590 and consult with a tax professional so you don't run afoul of the law and find yourself faced with a hefty penalty.

Which Type of IRA Is Right for Me?

If you qualify, it is better to go with a Roth IRA due to its added flexibility and superior tax treatment. If your income fluctuates, you may want to set up both a Roth and a traditional IRA. That way, you can contribute to the Roth IRA in the years your income is low enough for you to qualify and contribute to the traditional IRA when your income is higher.

Traditional and Roth IRA Contribution Limits

Regardless of which type you ultimately choose, both the traditional and Roth IRA share the same Congressionally-mandated contribution limits.

CAUTION

Crash Alert _____

If you make a contribution to your Traditional or Roth IRA and suddenly realize you have gone over the Congressionally-approved limit for the year, you can generally withdraw the cash with no tax consequences as long as you do it before the date of your tax filing for that year. If you fail to correct the situation on time, however, you will be subject to a 6 percent excise tax on the excess contribution!

Year	49 and Younger	50 and Older
2005	$4,000	$4,500
2006	$4,000	$5,000
2007	$4,000	$5,000
2008	$5,000	$6,000

The Least You Need to Know

◆ If your employer matches your 401(k) contributions, take advantage of this free money—even if you are currently in debt!

◆ If you have a defined benefit plan, ask human resources to help you figure out your monthly pension.

◆ Don't over-invest in your company's stock.

◆ Stock options can be very profitable employment benefits.

◆ For those who qualify, a Roth IRA is superior to a traditional IRA.

Chapter 7

Solving Debt and Credit Problems

In This Chapter

◆ Checking your credit history

◆ Building good credit

◆ The five components of your FICO score

◆ Paying off debt vs. investing

Credit can be either a tremendous boon to your financial life or a dangerous drain, depending upon how wisely you use it. Human beings have struggled with its temptations for centuries.

Credit preceded the coining of money by more than 2,000 years. Coinage is dated from the first millennium B.C.E., but old Sumerian documents, circa 3000 B.C.E., reveal a systematic use of credit based on loans of grain by volume and loans of metal by weight. These loans often carried interest.

About 1800 B.C.E., Hammurabi, a king of the first dynasty of ancient Babylonia, gave his people the earliest known formal code of laws. A number of the chief provisions of this code regulated the relation of debtor to creditor. The maximum rate of interest was set at 33⅓ percent per annum for loans of grain repayable in kind, and at 20 percent per annum for loans of silver by weight. All loans had to be accompanied by written contracts witnessed before officials. Land and other assets could be pledged against a debt. So could the creditor, as well as his wife, concubine, children, or slaves (and you thought you had it bad!). According to Sidney Homer in *A History of Personal Interest Rates*, personal slavery for debt was limited to three years.

Creditors may no longer be able to take your first born, but nothing can screw up your financial goals more than a whopping debt or a bad credit report. In this chapter, we show you how to avoid credit mishaps so you can get into great investing shape.

Fiscal Facts

When you apply for a credit card, a bank loan, or any other form of credit, you typically sign something that gives permission to the creditor to obtain your credit history. The creditor subscribes to credit reporting agencies, which forward your credit report. The information on the credit report is based on what other creditors have reported about you.

What Does Your Credit Report Say About You?

Before a credit card company issues you a card or a bank lends you money, they will check out your credit report. There are credit-reporting agencies (CRAs) that do nothing but gather information about you from bankers and other creditors and sell that information to banks, stores, and other issuers of credit.

If you've ever defaulted on a student loan, failed to pay off a charge account at a department store, or forgotten to pay a bill because you moved, rest assured that these transgressions are on your credit report in black and white. In addition, your report carries your Social Security number, your past and present addresses, and any other details of your financial life the credit-reporting agency has been able to snag. Pretty creepy, huh?

CRA Horror Stories

Nothing can be more upsetting than to discover—the hard way—that you have a bad credit report. Ed was shocked when he was turned down for a credit card recently. He exercised his right to request a free copy of his credit report. (Whenever you are turned down for credit, you can contact the credit agency whose information was used to turn you down and get a copy of the report for free.)

Ed's report was clean as a whistle, except for one little detail: a state tax *lien* of $130, filed on June 10, 1997, for the transfer tax on a home sold back in 1991. The actual tax was a measly $25; the $105 was interest.

Investor's Idiom

A **lien** is a legal right to take someone's property and hold it until the owner pays a debt.

Ed made a slew of phone calls. Finally someone at the state tax department explained that the state had gone after both the buyer and seller of Ed's house, but the buyer never responded and the seller (Ed) did not have a current address in their system. So the state filed the lien. It's a good thing Ed and his wife found this out before they refinanced their mortgage several months later, because it took a month to clear up.

Debra was stunned when a mysterious "unpaid loan" for $2,000 showed up on her credit report. It took six months of persistent phone calls and letters before she determined that her alma mater had mistakenly assigned a single college loan two identification numbers. This made it look like she had actually had two college loans—and had failed to pay off one of them.

What about you? Do you have something like this lurking in your report? Want peace of mind to know you haven't been the victim of identify theft? Do you want to wait until you try to buy a car, a house, or a gym membership to find out?

How to Check Your Credit Reports

We recommend that you look at your credit reports from at least the top three CRAs every year. These are:

- ◆ Trans Union: www.transunion.com
- ◆ Experian: www.experian.com
- ◆ Equifax: www.equifax.com

By law, you are entitled to request a free copy of your credit report from each of these agencies once every 12 months. You can find information and complete the process at www.annualcreditreport.com. If you discover a discrepancy, you can use the contact information we provided in Appendix A to reach the appropriate CRA who can then help you resolve the problem.

If you own a business, you will want to run a credit check on it periodically, too. You might also want to be able to check on your customers' credit. The top credit-reporting agencies in this field are:

♦ Dun & Bradstreet: www.dnb.com

♦ Experian: www.experian.com

How do you get a copy of your report? Each CRA has slightly different policies, but basically you will have to answer several security questions, such as the originator of your outstanding loans, Social Security number, and address. Our information is accurate as of May 2005 but you can always contact the Federal Trade Commission. The FTC website is www.ftc.gov.

No Credit Is Not Good Credit

Don't make the mistake of thinking that because you've never used credit, you have good credit. What you have is no credit, and if you have no credit, you'll have a difficult time getting approved for mortgages or auto loans. Many *credit card* companies won't approve you, either. You need to establish a personal credit history that shows you can make regular payments on a debt over time.

Investor's Idiom

A **charge card** allows you to "charge" an item, or buy it without paying cash at the time of purchase. You are expected to pay the purchase off within 30 days, whereas with a **credit card** you can make monthly minimum payments indefinitely.

Although banks and credit card companies tend not to lend to people with no credit history, department stores are usually willing to let someone with no credit history open a *charge card* account. A charge account lets you buy something without paying cash for it at the time of purchase. You are expected to pay the purchase off by the end of the month. Some charge accounts let you pay off only a minimum balance monthly and charge you interest on the remaining balance.

When you get your first charge account, make a few purchases each month and pay for them by the end of the month. Never miss a payment or pay late.

Finally, make sure your efforts to establish good credit are being reported to the CRAs. Check your reports six months after using a charge account or other credit regularly and if no positive information has been reported, ask the issuer of the credit you're using to send a report to the CRAs. Request a copy for yourself, also.

Debit Cards—A Better Choice?

Debit cards enable you to make purchases with a direct deduction from your checking account rather than a charge to a credit card account. They are often packaged together as a combination cash card (which can be used for deposits and withdrawals at banks or ATMs) and debit card.

Debit cards are very convenient, and you do avoid interest charges by using them instead of credit cards, but they can make it even more of a hassle to balance your checking account. You have to keep track of every little purchase you make with your debit card and enter it into your check register. You can quickly lose control of your balance and run into overdraft and service charges.

Investor's Idiom

A **debit card** can be presented like a credit card when you make a purchase, but the cost is deducted at the time of sale from your checking account.

To avoid the risk of overdraft charges or bounced checks, open a line of credit with your checking account. Typically, there is no charge unless you actually use the line, whereupon the rate is around 11–12 percent. Guess what, though? If you apply for a line of credit, your bank will check your credit report. If there are any problems, you will be turned down for overdraft protection.

Credit card or debit card? The choice is yours. But if you opt for the debit card, keep close tabs on your checking account balance. This includes communication and coordination with your significant other! Also, (and perhaps this is the most important part) your debit card is not going to be reported to your credit agency. This means that it will do absolutely nothing to improve your FICO score.

The Mysteries of Your FICO Score

A good credit score, also known as your FICO score (short for Fair Isaac Credit Organization), can make purchasing a home, financing an education, buying a car, or obtaining capital for your own business easy. Yet many individuals don't have a clue how their FICO score is calculated—or even worse—where they fall in the spectrum.

Range of FICO Scores (Chart)

500 to 559 (Worst)

560 to 619

620 to 674

675 to 699

700 to 719

720 to 850 (Best)

The FICO system is tiered; in practical terms, this means that if you have a 725 score, you are going to get the same deal as someone with an 830. Your score is determined by five variables, each weighted differently. These are discussed in the following sections.

Paying Your Bills on Time (35 Percent)

Whenever you make—or miss—a payment, it is reported to the credit bureaus. This data allows potential creditors to gauge the probability of you making your payments on time. If you haven't paid your bills in the last few months, for example, no one is going to lend you money at a reasonable rate because they can surmise that you are headed for trouble.

Ratio of Debt to Total Credit Limit (30 Percent)

Say you have several credit cards. You don't carry a balance on any of them; none have annual fees. Still, you decide you want to improve your credit so you cancel all but one. Smart move? Wrong! You have single-handedly taken a chainsaw to your credit score and the damage can take years to repair. (We know it doesn't sound logical, but that's how the system works! It's based on the theory that if other people are willing to lend you money, you are a better risk.)

Here's why: the second largest component of your credit score is the ratio between your debt balance and your available credit. If you carried $2,000 on one credit card and had six other cards with credit lines totaling $20,000, your debt-to-credit-limit ratio would be 10 percent ($2,000 balance divided by $20,000 available); very favorable. If, however, you cancelled all of these cards but the one—which had, say, a $3,000 limit—your ratio would skyrocket to 67 percent! Your FICO score is going to get hammered, driving up the interest rate you pay on your existing variable debt and any future borrowings.

An ideal solution is to cut up all but one of your cards. This way, you can't charge to the account, yet your ratio remains unaffected.

Length of Credit History (15 Percent)

The third largest component of your FICO score is the length of credit history. All else being equal, the longer your accounts have been open and in good standing, the higher your score. This is another reason you don't want to cancel your credit cards—doing so could hit you with a double-whammy on both the ratio of debt to total credit limit *and* the length of credit history components.

New Accounts, Credit Inquiries, and Recent Applications (10 Percent)

Each time you request a new credit card or apply for a new loan, this is noted on your credit report. If there is a lot of activity in a short amount of time—say, the most recent six months—this negatively affects your score. Lenders are wary of anyone who attempts to get a lot of credit quickly; they assume you may be in financial trouble. In order to protect this component, only request credit when absolutely necessary and you've done your research.

Mix of Credit Cards and Loans (10 Percent)

Fixed charges are far less attractive from the standpoint of a lender. The reason is simple. If you get into trouble, you can make smaller payments on your revolving accounts, such as credit cards. You don't have this option when writing the check for your car payment, student loans, or mortgage. That's why the type of debt you carry—fixed or revolving—affects your score.

Should I Pay Off My Debt or Invest?

With even small decisions affecting your credit score, how should you determine if you should pay off your debt or invest? As with all financial quandaries, the question can be answered using simple math. The secret? If you can earn a higher after-tax return on your investments than the after-tax interest expense on your debt, you should invest. Otherwise, you should pay off your balance.

Generally speaking, there are two categories of debt: good and bad. "Good" debt is debt which carries a low interest rate and, in many cases such as student loans and mortgages, the interest expense is tax deductible. When put to the test, this type of debt will, more often than not, result in diverting cash to build your portfolio instead of paying off your balances. "Bad" debt, to the contrary, is subject to high, often non-deductible, interest; the archetype being credit cards. Except in extraordinarily rare cases, this kind of debt should be eliminated as soon as possible.

Let's take a look at two examples:

◆ **Example 1:** Ruby has $10,000 in credit card debt. The interest rate on her cards is currently 18 percent; it is not tax deductible. She has twenty years until retirement. Should she pay off her debt or invest?

First, we see that Ruby has a long-term horizon. Thus, she has the luxury of riding out the volatility of the stock market and earning a rate of return in the neighborhood of 10 to 12 percent. None of this money is in a tax advantaged account, such as a 401(k) or an IRA, making her actual, expected after-tax return somewhere between 8 and 9.6 percent.

It is clear that she has no reasonable hope of generating a return on her investments anywhere near that which she is paying on her debt. As a result, she should stop contributing to her investments and, instead, pay off the balance of her credit card entirely.

Super Strategy

Even if you are paying astronomical interest rates on your credit cards, you should contribute to your 401(k) up to the point of your company's match. The reason? By taking the match—which is completely free money—you are instantly earning a 100 percent return.

◆ **Example 2:** Aaron, a recent college graduate, has $20,000 in student loans, currently consolidated at a fixed rate of 2.5 percent. He just landed a new job with a starting salary of $50,000. He is wondering whether he should start building his portfolio or pay off his debt first.

Student loan interest is tax-deductible. Assume Aaron's effective tax rate is 25 percent; lowering his after-tax interest expense to 1.875 percent. Because he has his entire career ahead of him, he expects to earn 10 percent after-tax on his investments through his equity investments in the stock market.

Clearly he should make the absolute minimum payment on his student loan and stretch out the term as long as possible. In this case, the benefit for doing so is even more compelling because his cost of borrowing—in effect, the cost of keeping that $20,000 capital at work in his portfolio—is less than the historical long-term rate of inflation (3 percent). Thus, in actual *economic* terms, he is actually being *paid* 1.125 percent to not pay off the loan! (Here's the math: 1.875 percent after-tax interest expense minus 3 percent inflation = (1.125) percent interest; how can you have negative interest? He is paying off the loan with dollars that are less valuable than they were the previous year. This wouldn't be possible if the interest rate were variable as opposed to fixed).

The Least You Need to Know

◆ Nothing can screw up your financial goals more than a bad credit report.

◆ Check your credit history once a year to catch errors.

◆ No credit is not the same as good credit; you have to use credit to build a credit history.

◆ If you want to use a debit card, get overdraft protection.

Chapter 8

Home Ownership: What You Need to Know

In This Chapter

◆ Down payment do's and don'ts

◆ Timing the real estate market

◆ Owning vs. renting

◆ Choosing between fixed-rate and adjustable-rate mortgages

◆ Interest-only mortgages

Most everyone starts adult life renting rather than owning. The reason is simple: It's cheaper! Initially, you may not even be able to afford to rent on your own, hence your roommates and their socks on the living room floor. But some 5 to 10 years after you enter the work force, with perhaps marriage and children either present or on the way, the subject of purchasing your own home needs to be reviewed. In this chapter, we run you through key questions to ask yourself before you make the big life change from lowly renter to king or queen of your castle.

The Down Payment

Do you have the down payment necessary to buy a home? You will need to put down at least 10 percent, and in some cases up to 20 percent, of the purchase price of the home in order to obtain mortgage approval. There are also some first-time home-buyer programs that don't require such high down payments—for example, VA loans and HUD programs.

Here are the best sources for your down payment, in order of preference:

◆ Savings. You planned ahead by putting aside the savings for 10 percent down, and you're ready to go.

◆ A loan from good old Mom and Dad (or your spouse's mom and dad). "We can pay it back at our convenience? At 0 percent interest?" Or how 'bout: "It's a gift? We couldn't possibly … well, if you insist!"

Super Strategy

Consider moving through a series of steps toward owning your dream home. Most people end up doing this: rental to condo to town house to starter home to the big comfy house in the 'burbs. Skipping any of these steps may leave you financially strapped.

◆ Tapping your retirement plans (Roth IRA, 401(k), etc.). Borrowing from the Roth IRA is preferable. If you borrow from your 401(k), it's considered a loan that you must pay back.

Do not borrow the money for your down payment. The cost of carrying what amounts to a first and second mortgage will most likely overtax you financially. If you approach your mortgage banker already carrying a debt like that, you might be turned down for the mortgage, anyway.

Timing Is Everything

The next question to ask is: what's the real estate market like? Hot, medium, or cold? If it's hot, you run the risk of paying inflated prices, potentially coming in at the top of the market. This translates to a higher down payment and higher monthly payments (principal, interest, and, in many cases, real estate taxes). If you then have to move for any reason, you run the risk of having to sell at a loss.

If possible, follow your local real estate market for several years before even considering home ownership. Most local newspapers carry charts or tables that show you whether home sales in your area are trending up or down, and to what degree. You can also get a feel by going to open houses and requesting sales literature on around a dozen homes that might meet your needs.

Specifically, you'll want to observe two indicators:

♦ Has the asking price been reduced, and, if yes, how much and how many times?

♦ How many days has the house been on the market?

In a "hot" market, homes are gobbled up in a matter of days, and the buyer pays the asking price. In a really hot market, with two or more buyers vying for the same property, the "winner" ends up paying more than the asking price. You definitely do not want to make your first home purchase in this environment.

You should also check out mortgage interest rates, but home prices are a more important indicator of whether or not it's the right time to buy. In inflationary environments, high mortgage rates and high home prices often go hand-in-hand—but not always. Seven years ago the trend was higher mortgage rates and lower home prices. Starting around August 1998, on the other hand, we saw lower mortgage rates and higher home prices. That trend is still in place as of this writing, with 40-year lows in mortgage rates and historically high home prices.

Super Strategy
A good rule of thumb: if you can handle the monthly payments on the home you want and you think it's selling at a good price, don't concern yourself with mortgage rates. Just focus on home prices. Don't forget, you can always re-finance your mortgage if and when rates fall.

Re-Fi Mania

With current mortgage rates so low, refinancing has become an effective way to reduce household expense. But when and how should you refinance? In short, you want to ensure your savings will make up for the additional costs within a year or two or it's not worth doing. Here's how to figure that out:

1. Total all your closing costs (document fees, appraisal, Title, etc.). Exclude the one month interest you'll be charged (interest is paid in arrears), because you'll make that up with a one month "holiday" on the new mortgage.

2. Deduct the new proposed monthly principal and interest payments from the existing P&I.

3. Divide item 2 into item 1. If the number is 12 (one year) or less, go for it. If above 24, forget it (remember, the average person only lives in his/her home for five years).

Evaluate Your Mortgage-Worthiness Before a Banker Does

After you start to keep tabs on the real estate market, make it a point to sit down with a mortgage banker and determine what he or she looks for in a successful applicant so you can compare that profile to your present situation. If you can't find a mortgage banker willing to do this, go to a knowledgeable and experienced real estate broker. Basically, if you present your personal balance sheet and income statement (which you learned how to create in Chapter 5), the expert can tell you if you could qualify for a mortgage and how large a mortgage you could handle. If you don't qualify, you can spend the next few years both following the local real estate market and getting in better financial shape.

Compare Renting to Owning

If you are thinking about buying a home, sit down and calculate the total cost of home ownership vs. renting. When you rent, you pay a monthly rental fee and utilities. You may also pay for parking and laundry. That's about it. Home ownership, on the other hand, is not just about a monthly mortgage payment and taxes. There are many expenses you may not have considered, such as:

◆ Outside maintenance—yard work, painting, and equipment such as a lawn mower and leaf and snow blowers.

◆ Inside maintenance—carpet cleaning, floor sanding and coating, appliance maintenance, plumbing repairs, painting, and papering.

◆ Major repairs and replacements. Retain an inspection service to ascertain the expected life of your hot water heater, roof, siding, deck, etc. People stay in one home an average of five years, so for anything that will probably need to be replaced within five years, determine the cost and divide it by 60. Add this cost to your monthly payments.

On the bright side, your interest and taxes on a home are deductible, and you are gradually building up equity (ownership!) in your home. In addition, you won't be hit with yearly rent increases.

Over Time, Owning Should Save You Money

It's hard to come up with a specific example that is applicable to everyone, so let's make some broad assumptions and compare renting to owning over a 60-month (five-year) time frame:

Per Month	Rent	Purchase
Rent: $2,000 × (4% annual increase ÷ 2) =	$2,217	
Parking	160	
Utilities	100	$200
Laundry	24	12
Principal and Interest*		1,231
Transportation	50	50
Maintenance		250
Homeowners Insurance		50
Repairs		250
Taxes		300
Totals	2,551	2,343

Assumptions: $225,000 purchase price, 10% down, the balance financed at 6¼% over 30 years.

In this example, we have a pretty clear-cut case favoring purchase on cash flow basis alone. Considering you also own an asset that now has the potential to appreciate in value while building equity, and there is no question that owning is a better choice. Your case may be different.

Renting Pluses

Although it's generally considered preferable to buy, continuing to rent is definitely preferable to buying the wrong home at the wrong price at the wrong time in the real estate market. That's why we suggest spending some time watching the market and getting a feel for what constitutes a bargain in your price range and your area.

Owning your own home has always been considered part of the American Dream, but for people who bought when the real estate market peaked in the 1980s and suffered huge losses when they needed to move, the American Dream turned into a nightmare. That may be the case right now.

Remember, you're in charge; you decide when the time is right, and another year or two in a rental is not the end of the world. Be cool.

Fiscal Facts

The Consumer Price Index (CPI) is a group of prices that are followed by economists in order to gauge whether inflation is on the rise or waning. The CPI is probably the most well-known and widely reported inflation number we have. What is not well-known is that housing prices for both rental and owned residences makes up 40 percent of the benchmark.

How Much of Your Income Should You Spend on Housing?

Twenty-five percent of your gross income is a reasonable sum to spend on housing. Some experts use up to 33 percent or even 50 percent, but let's be conservative! Our recommendation means that someone earning $100,000 can afford roughly $2,000 per month for housing. Assuming a 6¼ percent mortgage rate and a 30-year mortgage, principal and interest would equate to roughly $1,539 per month on a $250,000 mortgage, leaving $461 per month for taxes. That feels about right. And with 10 percent down and closing costs, you're looking at a $275,000 purchase. Naturally, taxes vary, as do home prices and what you get for your money. That $275,000 probably buys you a lot in Nebraska or North Dakota, but little (if anything) in San Diego, Boston, Chicago, or New York City.

Fixed Rate vs. Adjustable Rate Mortgage

Your mortgage banker may offer you a choice between the following:

◆ A fixed-rate mortgage that locks you into a given interest rate for the life of the mortgage, which is traditionally 30 years.

◆ An adjustable rate mortgage.

How long you intend to stay in the house is the key to your decision. An adjustable rate mortgage can be a good deal if you plan to stay in your house for no more than five years, and if the rate is sufficiently below the rate for a 30-year fixed-rate mortgage. If the adjustable rate is not at least 200 basis points (2.0 percent) below the 30-year rate, it's not worth the risk of escalating interest rates to commit to it. Right now, for example, short-term and long-term interest rates are all very low and there's not much difference between them, so fewer new homeowners are taking out adjustable rate mortgages.

I.O. for U?

I.O. (interest only) mortgages are the latest product in home financing. As the name implies, the monthly payments are for interest only, with nothing going to pay down the mortgage. In other words, you are going to be paying less each month but you are never going to make progress on paying down the principal. Here is a comparison of an I.O. vs. an *ARM*. In each case, the principal amount being financed is $200,000, the mortgage rate is 5⅛ percent, and the fixed term is five years.

	I.O.	**ARM**	**Difference**
Monthly payment	$854	$1,089	-$235
Five-year totals	$51,240	$65,338	-$14,098
Mortgage reduction	—	$16,019	+$16,019

Even if we assume that the $235 monthly difference is invested at 5 percent per annum, the total of approximately $15,900 is still slightly below the mortgage pay down of the ARM. So are there any circumstances in which the I.O. would be preferable to an ARM? Yes, two:

- The I.O. allows you to qualify for a larger mortgage or a more expensive home. In some cases, it could be the only way you could qualify.

- If you have no other means to fully commit dollars to your 401(k), 403(b), 457 plan, IRA, or emergency fund, etc., then maybe this is a good option. But you risk just spending the difference. Be careful that the I.O. doesn't just become another I.O.U.

The Costs of Closing

Closing costs vary from state to state, depending on whether the state says attorneys are required to handle the closing and on real estate tax rates. Typically, you should be prepared to cover closing costs of around 3 percent of the price of the house before the keys are yours. In some cases, you can gain a concession from a motivated seller and convince them to pick up these expenses.

Following is a summary of a typical closing statement. As you can see, there are columns for the borrower (buyer) and seller. Looking just at the columns pertaining to the buyer, we see that the buyer ends up paying over $6,000 in closing/settlement costs.

Line:			
101	Contract sales price	$252,000.00	The amount you agreed to pay for the home
103	Settlement charges	6,384.81	Detailed below
120	Gross amount due from buyer	258,384.81	Total of lines 101 and 103
Less:			
201	Deposit of earnest money	25,300.00	Down payment
202	Principal amount of new loan	100,000.00	The buyer's new mortgage

220	Total paid by buyer	125,300.00	Total of lines 201 + 202
303	Additional cash from buyer	133,084.81	Sum buyer must come up with at closing Summary of Settlement Charges (Line 103)
802	Loan discount	2,000.00	Buyer paid "points" (two) to get lower mortgage rate
904	Three months real estate taxes	1,548.22	Three months real estate taxes
905		6.94	Property overlaps two municipalities
1107	Attorney's fees	950.00	For the "closing"
1108	Title insurance	1,708.00	Required
1201	Recording fees	70.00	Required
1204	Notice of settlement	16.00	Required
1303	Faxes	45.65	
1304	UPS	40.00	
1400	Total Settlement Charges	6,384.81	Lines 802–1304

Second Mortgages—Pros and Cons

Once you own a home, you will be bombarded with offers for a second mortgage. Second mortgages are tax-deductible, but they place you in a financial straight jacket. With a second mortgage, you sign for a fixed-rate loan for the full amount of equity in your home. You might not need or use all the money, but you sure are paying interest on it.

A home equity loan is a better deal because it is a revolving line of credit—you only pay for what you use (like a charge card), and you can still deduct the interest from your taxes. A second mortgage is either a desperation step for someone who wants to finance a dramatic career shift, or a short-term means of coming up with the down payment on your first (starter) home. Do not enter into it lightly.

Pluses & Pitfalls of Paying Off Your Mortgage

Mortgage (or rent) represents the largest single expenditure for the average tax payer. It's wise, therefore, to try to retire your mortgage before you retire yourself. There are three ways to accomplish this:

◆ Stay in your home for 15–30 years and pay off the mortgage.

◆ Pay off half the mortgage, sell your home and buy a condo/town house at half the price of your former home.

◆ Benefit from escalating home values. If your home rises in value 50 percent in five years, for example, sell your home and buy a condo/town house at half the price. This is beyond your control.

All of that extra cash can improve your standard of living and provide investment capital for you to build your portfolio (and increase the size of the estate you ultimately bequeath to your heirs or charitable causes).

The biggest drawback, however, is that a lack of a mortgage can seriously affect the components of your FICO score, which we discussed back in Chapter 7. This could make it difficult for you to obtain financing for future purchases and possibly even increase the interest rate you are paying on your existing debt.

Should You Shorten Your Mortgage?

Moving from a 30-year to a 15-year mortgage can make a big difference. Here's an example using a 60-month occupancy assumption and a $200,000 mortgage. The figures are very rough and just for purposes of illustration.

30-year mortgage, 6¼ percent*, monthly principal & interest = $1,231

15-year mortgage, 5¾ percent*, monthly principal & interest = $1,660

Difference per month = $429

*You can get a rough approximation by adding or subtracting $15 for each 1/8 percent rates go up or down.

In essence, making a bigger monthly mortgage payment goes a long way toward building equity and reducing the mortgage on your property. In addition, you're going to save a substantial amount of interest expense. For a $200,000 mortgage with a 6.5 percent rate, for example, the total interest paid over 30 years would amount to around $243,319; on the 15 year mortgage, the total cumulative interest would only be $108,672, a savings of $134,647.

The 15-year mortgage just forces you to save. Depending upon the interest rate you are paying, however, it might be more profitable to take the longer mortgage and its smaller mortgage payments and invest the $429 that you save each month into a tax-deferred investment. This way you get the tax break and the benefits of compound interest.

Fiscal Facts

There is a capital gains tax exclusion on your home of $250,000 for an individual and $500,000 for a couple. But to qualify you must have lived in the house for at least two of the past five years. Are there any exceptions? Yes! For job (transfer) or health reasons. Simply divide the number of months you actually lived in the home by 24 months (minimum required). Now multiply that figure by either $250,000 (individual) or $500,000 (joint return) to get your exclusion. Want more info? Request IRS Publication 523.

The Least You Need to Know

- Don't borrow the money for your down payment; you might get turned down for a mortgage.

- Try to follow your local real estate market for several years before buying a home.

- Evaluate your mortgage-worthiness before a banker does.

- Continuing to rent is definitely preferable to buying the wrong home at the wrong price and time.

- Retire your mortgage before you retire yourself.

Chapter 9

Funding Your Own (or Your Child's) Education

In This Chapter

- ◆ Setting up educational funds
- ◆ Withdrawing from a Roth IRA to pay for college
- ◆ Coverdell Education Savings Accounts
- ◆ Evaluating qualified tuition programs

When it comes to educating yourself, your children, or grandchildren, there's both good and bad news. The bad news is that college expenses continue to grow by at least two times the overall inflation rate in this country and the average family income. The good news is that an increasing percentage of college enrollees are getting financial aid. In addition, several options, such as 529 Plans and Coverdell Education Savings Accounts, make saving for college easier than ever.

Expenses for college vary dramatically, depending upon whether your child attends a state school or a private college or university. Gross expenses include tuition and fees, room and board, books and supplies.

Figure on spending roughly $12,000–$15,000 per year in gross expenses for a state school, if you reside in state; add $3,000–$4,000 if you live out of state. Ivy League schools average around $34,000–$36,000. Over the last ten years, tuition costs rose about 6 percent per year so you can use that figure to estimate future tuition costs.

These are just ballpark figures, of course, but they give you an idea of the magnitude of the challenge faced by families trying to put several kids through college.

An Investment That Really Pays

One of the best investments you will ever make in your life is an education. On average, a person that holds a Bachelor's degree will earn $1 million more over the course of their lifetime than someone who graduated from high school only; a very real return on both time and capital employed. More important, an education will provide you with an improved ability to think, analyze, and study—traits that can make it easier for you to spot opportunities.

You already learned the difference between "good" and "bad" debt in Chapter 7. Student loans are certainly one of the most attractive types of debt available thanks to the relatively low cost, the ability to lock in an interest rate through consolidation, the deductibility of interest expense for income tax purposes, and the subsequent increase in earnings that results from a higher education. Still, for those of you who want to start your life off with little or no debt, we're going to give you the low-down on the investing options available to you so you can be prepared to write a check when the bursar calls.

Put Your Financial Security First

Maybe you're a parent who wants to start planning for your child's college education. That's a fine, noble goal. However, it should be the last thing on your list. Contributing to your retirement plan, building an emergency cash fund, purchasing a house, paying down debt—all of these should come first. There are numerous loans, scholarships, grants, work-study programs, and other options to help your child attend school. There are not, however, any special financial programs to help you fund your retirement. In other words, your child has many options at age 18: college first; work, then college; work-study program; no college; the military; and so on. Your retirement only has two options: either you have the money to retire or you don't. And don't forget two other issues:

◆ Where your child goes to college is driven more by his or her academic and extracurricular accomplishments than by your checking account.

◆ Your child is capable of contributing to his or her college education via summer or part-time work, and probably will be a better person for doing so.

Super Strategy
Involve your child in the decision about where to go to college by getting him or her a copy of *The College Handbook*, published by the College Entrance Examination Board. The handbook profiles 3,215 colleges and will definitely get you and your soon-to-be campus star excited and motivated.

Establishing an Education Fund

There are three questions that need to be answered when setting up funds for a college education:

1. What is the most appropriate investing vehicle for your education fund? Your best options include:

   ◆ Traditional or Roth IRAs.

   ◆ Coverdell Education Savings Accounts (ESAs). These used to be called Education IRAs.

   ◆ 529 Plans or QSTPs (Qualified State Tuition Programs).

   ◆ Patriot Bonds (formerly EE Savings Bonds)

2. What scholarships, grants, and loans are available for student expenses or reimbursement? Presently, programs available include:

   ◆ Hope Scholarships

   ◆ Pell Grants

   ◆ Lifetime Learning Credits

   ◆ Student loans

   ◆ Employer-paid educational assistance

3. Finally, should the securities or other assets you intend to save be in your name or the child's name?

Using a Traditional or Roth IRA to Save for College

In Chapter 6, you learned that the 10 percent additional tax on withdrawals from an IRA before age 59½ can be waived for qualified higher education expenses. "Qualified" expenses include tuition, room and board, books, fees, and supplies.

Investor's Idiom

The Education IRA was introduced in 1998. It has since been renamed Coverdell Education Savings Accounts (ESAs). The contribution limit was raised from $500 per year per child to $2,000. You can make contributions annually until your kids hit 18. Withdrawals for qualified educational purposes are tax-free.

Coverdell Education Savings Accounts (ESAs)

Like the Roth IRA, the Education IRA was introduced in the late 1990's. It has since been renamed the Coverdell Education Savings Account (ESA). Contributions are tax-deferred, but not deductible and are limited to $2,000 per year, per beneficiary. You can make contributions annually until your little rascal(s) turn 18. Withdrawals for qualified educational purposes are tax-free. The income eligibility for married contributors was raised by the 2002 tax law changes to $190,000. As a couple's income increases from $190,000 to $220,000, which is double the range for unmarried persons, their contribution limit phases out.

Qualified Tuition Programs (Section 529s)

Public or private schools may now establish tax-exempt prepaid tuition programs, also referred to as Section 529 Plans. Section 529 plans are accounts that may be established by anyone—parents, other relatives, or friends of the family. The investment grows tax-free and distributions are tax-free when used to pay for tuition and other education expenses at any accredited college or university.

This is a smart idea for grandparents, who can contribute up to $11,000 per year ($22,000 for couples) without triggering the federal gift tax. You can even make a one-time contribution of as much as $55,000 ($110,000 from a couple) and spread the gift tax exclusion over the next five years. Not a bad way for grandparents to help out and avoid estate and gift taxes.

Interestingly, unlike ESA and custodial accounts, you don't give up control of the Section 529 plan when the child reaches 18. You still control when withdrawals are taken and for what purposes. A delight for the control freaks among us!

Prior to 1998, these programs had to be state-sponsored. Withdrawals from qualified programs may be made for tuition, fees, room and board, books, and supplies. And, thanks to the Tax Relief Act of 2001, these specific withdrawals are tax-free. You can't contribute to both qualified tuition programs and an ESA in the same year, however.

Here's how a typical plan, the UNIQUE College Investing Plan, sponsored by the State of New Hampshire and managed by Fidelity Investments, works:

- To fund your account, you can sign up for Fidelity Automatic Account Builder (FAAB), with automatic transfers from your checking account of as little as $50 per month. All contributions must be in cash (via check). Families who don't establish automatic contribution plans can start an account with as little as $1,000.

- Your funds are invested in "lifestyle" portfolios consisting of Fidelity Mutual Funds that automatically shift the allocation of your assets between equity and fixed income as the beneficiary (your child) ages. A newborn might be invested 88 percent equity/12 percent bonds, while at college age the ratios might shift to 20 percent equity/40 percent bonds/40 percent short-term bonds and money market instruments—freeing up funds to pay for college. The stock/bond ratio for your child would be dependent upon his or her age upon entering the program. Alternatively, you can invest in fixed asset allocations.

- Fidelity uses no-load mutual funds so the account will be charged only for the operating expenses. In addition, there is a fee of 0.30 percent of your account assets per year and a $30 annual maintenance fee (waived for accounts over $25,000 or if you sign up for FAAB).

- You can increase your monthly contributions with FAAB at any time if you start earning more money or decide that you've underestimated potential education costs.

◆ Earnings grow tax-deferred until they are distributed. If the distributions are for qualified educational expenses, they are exempt from federal income tax; check with your state to determine state tax status.

◆ There are no adjusted gross income (AGI) restrictions or qualifications.

◆ Multiple accounts can be opened for your child by grandparents and other relatives. Joint accounts are not allowed, however. You cannot contribute more than the amount necessary to provide for the qualified education expenses of the beneficiary.

◆ You can change the beneficiary to another child. If you distribute the assets to someone besides the designated beneficiary, however, or if the funds are not used to pay qualified education expenses, you will be socked with state and federal taxes, as well as a 10 percent penalty.

◆ Contributions are considered completed gifts, so the value of an account won't be included in the donor's estate when he or she dies. You can also give up to $55,000 ($110,000 if filing jointly) in one year without gift tax as long as you opt to apply the $11,000 annual exclusion over five years.

◆ You can invest in both a UNIQUE Plan and a Coverdell ESA in the same year. Your child can also benefit from Hope Scholarship and Lifetime Learning Credits, which are discussed below. If you claim these credits, however, you cannot make a tax-free withdrawal to pay for the same expenses. If you do, your 529 withdrawal may be taxable.

◆ You can use the assets to pay for qualified education expenses at any accredited institution of higher learning, not just New Hampshire schools.

◆ Qualified withdrawals may also be tax-free at the state level if you are a resident of that particular state.

◆ Qualified education expenses include tuition, fees, room and board, books, and supplies.

This is just a summary of the UNIQUE Plan. You will want to delve more deeply into the matter before proceeding, but it looks pretty nifty to us.

Because word is still getting out, we expect 529 plans to be the most rapidly growing asset pool of this decade. Fidelity, Vanguard, TIAA-CREF, Merrill Lynch and Salomon Smith Barney are just some of the big names offering new 529 plans.

All the plans seem to use mutual funds exclusively and offer either age-based (meaning that a pre-set stock/bond ratio is used, depending on the tyke's age: for example, heavy on stocks at age 2; heavy in bonds at 16). Finally, each plan has different fees, so shop around. We suggest you start by contacting your State Treasurer's office. You can also mine the State Treasurer's website at www.collegesavings.org. Alternatively, check out www.savingforcollege.com.

Pros and Cons of 529 Plans

Just so we are on the same page, you understand that 529s are for college and university expenses, right? Good (just checking to make sure you're awake)! Now a quick summary of the pros and cons:

Pros

◆ Contributions qualify for annual gift tax exclusion.

◆ Assets enjoy tax-free growth.

◆ You have the option of accelerating the annual gifting provision five fold (e.g., $11,000 \times 5 = \$55,000$).

◆ Distributions can cover tuition, fees, books, equipment, room, and board.

◆ The donor (you) has the power to change the beneficiary.

◆ Payment does not have to be made directly to the school; you can reimburse the beneficiary.

Cons

◆ A penalty is assessed if the funds are used for any purpose other than education.

◆ Contributions must be in cash.

◆ Although you can change the beneficiary, there may be gift tax consequences.

◆ Whatever you give for the 529 must be deducted from your annual max ($11,000) or the five-year max ($55,000).

◆ Be careful if you mix 529s with the Hope or Lifetime Learning Credits we will discuss in the next section.

Tax Breaks for Education Expenses

As we said at the beginning of this chapter, there are all kinds of ways to defray expenses for college—and more are coming on line all the time. Here's a breakdown of the ... breaks!

The Hope Scholarship Credit

Started in 1998, the Hope Scholarship Credit allows parents to take a credit against federal income taxes for tuition and related expenses. The credit is limited to the first two years of undergraduate education and consists of 100 percent of the first $1,000 of qualified expenses, and 50 percent of the second $1,000. Thus, the maximum credit you can take in the first two years is $1,500 per year. Warning: The credit is phased out for married taxpayers filing jointly with a modified AGI between $85,000 and $105,000 ($42,000 and $52,000 for individual filers). These amounts are adjusted for inflation.

Lifetime Learning Credits

Lifetime Learning Credits were also introduced in 1998. These are credits you can take for education expenses that are not eligible for the Hope credit. Included are expenses incurred to acquire or improve job skills. The credit is 20 percent of expenses up to $10,000 per year. The Lifetime has income credit AGI phase-outs identical to the Hope.

Mix and Match Carefully

Assume you are looking at a $3,000 tuition bill (obviously, your kid is going to a state school!), and you take the Hope credit, which reduces your income taxes. But you still have to come up with $3,000. Use the 529? Wrong! You can use the 529 for the first $1,000, but the other $2,000—equal to the Hope credit—must come from some-place else: your pocket, your checking account, Aunt Martha .... If not, you owe taxes and a 10 percent penalty on the amount involved.

The Education-Loan Interest Deduction

Those of you with a modified AGI of less than $65,000 (individual return) or $130,000 (joint return) may be eligible to deduct the interest paid on your student loans. This deduction can decrease your income taxes by up to $2,500. Incidentally, the interest paid is deducted "above the line," meaning you do not have to itemize to claim the deduction. What's the best choice? Be guided strictly by your AGI. If you qualify, go for the Hope/Lifetime credits; otherwise, use the tax deductions.

Patriot Bonds (formerly EE Savings Bonds)

Following the events of September 11, 2001, EE Savings Bonds were renamed The Patriot Bonds. These savings bonds can be either plugged into Coverdell ESAs or Roth IRAs, or used on their own to save for college. There are some disadvantages to using savings bonds, however:

◆ The yield is fixed at 90 percent of a five-year Treasury note, and is recalculated every six months. If Treasury note rates fall, so does the rate on your bond. If the five-year Treasury note is yielding 3.25 percent, the Patriot Bond is yielding 2.925 percent. But if six months later the Treasury note yield drops to 2.75 percent, your bond starts earning only 2.475 percent. Of course, the yields could go up, too!

◆ Although you can redeem (cash in) a Patriot bond after six months, you will pay a three-month interest penalty unless you wait at least five years to redeem it. To avoid the penalty, you have to really plan ahead when using savings bonds for college. You'll need to stop purchasing the bonds five years before the last college bills come due.

◆ You also have to deal with a limit of $15,000 purchase price per purchaser per year.

Patriot savings bonds do have some great advantages:

◆ You can purchase them for as little as $25 ($50 face value).

◆ They make great gifts from relatives.

◆ The interest income on an EE savings bond is free of state and local taxes. The federal taxes on interest income are due only when the EE savings bond is redeemed. In some instances, there is a tax exclusion if the proceeds are being used for postsecondary education.

Cool, but how does this work? First of all, the exclusion is limited to tuition and required fees. In this case, it may not be applied to room, board, or books. Second, the bonds must be registered in the name of the taxpayer, not the child, although the child can be named as beneficiary.

In addition, the qualified tuition and fees paid must be equal to or greater than the amount of money received when the bonds are redeemed. If you pay tuition and fees of $5,000 and the bond proceeds are no more than $5,000, you're qualified for the exclusion. If tuition and fees are $4,000 and the bond proceeds are $5,000, you can deduct only that ratio ($4,000 – $5,000 = 80 percent) of the interest income on the bonds (not the principal). Don't you love how confusing this stuff is?

Finally, to qualify for the tax exclusion, you have to earn less than the modified AGI limits. Currently, benefit is phased out for modified adjusted gross incomes of $89,750–$119,750 for couples filing jointly and $59,850–$74,850 for single filers. In other words, you can get full exclusion if you earn under $89,750, and partial exclusion scaling down to zero once you earn over $119,750. Did you notice that we tucked in the word "modified"?

In this case, modified AGI is AGI plus the interest earned on the redeemed bonds. Ah, the tax code! But wait: there's another neat way to use EE savings bonds for a child's college expense. Buy the bonds in the child's name and file a tax return with the child's Social Security number. Then report the accrued (earned but not received) interest income on the bonds for that year. You won't need to file again and no tax is due unless or until the child's total income exceeds the threshold for taxes owed ($650). If tax is owed, it is at the parent's rate for children under age 14 and at the child's rate at age 14 or older.

It is unfortunate that the regulations on EE savings bonds are so complicated because they have a lot to offer parents saving for college. But that's the Feds for you.

Other Options

We have no intention of exploring every conceivable option for financing an education in this chapter. Our intention was to primarily explore investment options.

But do take a look at two other important prospects:

◆ Student loans or so-called Stafford loans. These are available from the government's "Sallie Mae" program (www.salliemae.com, 1-888-2-SALLIE). Stafford loans are for ten years and the interest rate is set annually on July 1, based on the last 91-day T-bill auction in May. Also, you can take one opportunity to consolidate any outstanding Stafford loans.

◆ Scholarships. First, check with the college your child wants to attend to find out whether he or she is eligible to apply for any scholarships. Definitely call local organizations such as the Rotary Club or Kiwanis, which often sponsor scholarships for deserving students. Remember that grants or scholarships do not have to be repaid, loans do. Your college can also help you determine whether your child qualifies for financial assistance in the form of Pell grants or other government-sponsored grants. Financial aid is defined in terms of demonstrated need; total college expense less family contribution equals demonstrated need.

Sorting Out All the Options

Now, how do you sort out all these complicated alternatives? It seems that the best tax-incentive alternatives are available to low-income parents, who may also be most likely to obtain scholarship dollars for their child.

On the other hand, these parents face a level of complexity that would challenge an accountant. Parents over the AGI limits, meanwhile, can feel very frustrated. Let's list the alternatives we've discussed on a best-to-worst basis, both for those with a qualifying AGI and those above it.

If you earn at or below the AGI minimum:

◆ Coverdell Education Savings Account—Benefit specific (education) and ideal for larger families.

◆ Roth IRA—Not education specific, but same qualifications and benefits.

◆ EE savings bonds—Register in your name; also request gifts in child's name. Not all education expenses covered.

◆ Scholarships—Must pursue and apply shortly before matriculation.

◆ Hope/Lifetime Credits—If you have to borrow, use these tax deductions.

◆ Student Loans—Last resort.

If your earnings are over the AGI minimum:

◆ 529 Plans (qualified tuition programs)—Choose the variable option over the fixed one; this gives you a better shot over time at making more money.

◆ Traditional IRA—Use the education expense option.

◆ EE savings bonds—Keep in child's name; ditto for gifts; don't bother with annual tax filing.

◆ Taxable portfolio—Invest in index equity funds or passive equities; mix with EE bonds.

◆ Hope/Lifetime Credits—See if you qualify.

◆ Student Loans—See Sallie as a last resort.

In Whose Name?

Parents ask us all the time whether they should keep education funds in their name or in the kid's name. This issue revolves around taxes vs. trust. If the assets are put in the child's name, the tax bite is going to be less. But if the assets are in the child's name, the child can choose to cash them in and move to Bali to study puppetry, rather than attend your alma mater. The very thought sends some parents into a spin. Then again, the young woman who designed the award-winning sets for Disney's Broadway production of *The Lion King* went to Bali to study puppetry, to the probable mortification of her parents, and she's doing awfully well! On the other hand, if the assets are in the child's name, it can reduce a child's financial aid eligibility.

We come down on the side of holding taxable education assets in the child's name for the lower tax hit. If you are concerned that your child might abuse these assets, your problems are far greater than financing a college education.

The Least You Need to Know

◆ We've said it before, we'll say it again; don't jeopardize your retirement to pay for your kids' education.

◆ Put your education savings in traditional and Roth IRAs, and Coverdell ESAs and EE savings bonds.

◆ 529 College Savings Plans (QTPs) are tax-exempt, prepaid tuition programs; one of the most interesting is the UNIQUE College Investing Plan.

◆ Several income tax credits are now allowed by the IRS for education expenses.

◆ Hold taxable education dollars in your child's name for a smaller tax bite.

Part 3 — Investing 101

You've made it this far, and now you're ready for the meat and potatoes! In addition to learning about the role of institutions such as the Federal Reserve and the Securities and Exchange Commission, Part 4 will endow you with a thorough understanding of the investments that are likely to make up a majority of your portfolio—common and preferred stock, fixed income securities, mutual funds, and real estate investment trusts. We'll even tell you what you should look for in a broker.

Sit back, relax, grab a big cup of coffee and a highlighter … we're about to demystify that venerable place called Wall Street.

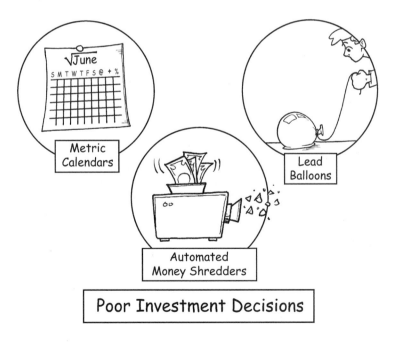

Metric Calendars

Lead Balloons

Automated Money Shredders

Poor Investment Decisions

What Are They Up to On Wall Street, Anyway?

In This Chapter

◆ The purpose of Wall Street

◆ The difference between a bull and a bear

◆ An introduction to the Federal Reserve

◆ Buy side vs. sell side

◆ Choosing a broker

Fifty-odd years ago, the then-head of General Motors Corporation, "Choo Choo Charlie" Wilson, reportedly harrumphed: "What's good for General Motors is good for America."

At the time, his statement may have seemed rather arrogant and self-serving, but to those with shares in the company, his words hit home. In financial terms, the translation goes something like this. Corporate America is not only a key employer of many of the citizens of this country, but it is owned by them. The stock market represents this ownership, and, as we were reminded by the market's reaction to the wave of corporate scandals in 2002, when corporations go bad, that's bad for America.

Investors watched billions of dollars in stock market holdings collapse as Enron imploded, WorldCom filed for bankruptcy, and Global Crossing, Adelphia Communications, and Tyco scandals came to light, followed by SEC inquiries into stalwarts like Johnson & Johnson.

Congress promptly passed a corporate-oversight bill designed to discourage "creative" bookkeeping, diminish conflicts of interest, and crack down on financial abuses. Some folks called it watershed legislation—the most important since the 1930s laws enacted after the Great Depression that brought much-needed regulation to the stock market. Others questioned whether it would really have much impact.

The nerves of investors were understandably frayed by the wild swings in the stock market. The losses were certainly painful. Nonetheless, we live (and hope to prosper) in a capitalist society, and the capital is largely provided by the stock market. Historically, the market has recovered from worse times and has gone on to make investors wealthy. If you learn how it works, you'll learn how to protect yourself from its volatility and still earn great returns on your investments.

The Purpose of Wall Street

Wall Street is a financial district in lower Manhattan where a number of important institutions are headquartered, such as the New York Stock Exchange, American Stock Exchange, and several major commercial banks and brokerage firms. In the vernacular, however, Wall Street is used to refer to the investment community at large. "The Street," as it is known, has two components, each with its own purpose: the primary market and the secondary market.

The Primary Market

Imagine you own a chocolate company. After years of building the business, you've increased sales to $100 million and net income to $25 million. You continue to reinvest the profits and occasionally utilize bank loans to expand, yet you find it difficult to get enough capital to go to the next level. Frustrated, you don't know where to turn.

You're in luck, my friend! Wall Street may have the answer. You can call an investment banking firm, such as Goldman Sachs, and begin a process known as "going public." Here's a grossly over-simplified version of what is going to happen. Your investment banker is going to value your business; in your case, they may tell you the chocolate company is worth $300 million. After some discussion, they decide they want the opening stock price to be $25 per share, so they cut the company up into 12 million shares ($300 million divided by $25 = 12 million shares).

At this point, you will decide how much of your business you want to sell and how much you want to keep. You may, for example, decide to sell 45 percent of the company, or 5.4 million shares worth a collective $135 million, to the public. The investment banker you worked with throughout the process (known as the "managing house" or "lead underwriter") is going to call several other investment bankers on Wall Street and form a syndicate. This syndicate will then purchase those shares from the company. During this time, the underwriting syndicate holds the bag—that is, if the market collapses, it doesn't matter to the company because the underwriter is the one that owns the securities, albeit temporarily. In exchange for this holding risk and other services rendered, the investment banker will be paid a fee; normally around 7 percent of the gross proceeds raised during the initial public offering ("IPO"). In exchange, the business is going to receive a $100-million-plus check for the proceeds of the offering. These funds can be used to open new stores, build new factories, hire additional employees, acquire other companies, or any other activity that management believes will generate attractive returns.

The underwriter is going to sell the shares it has purchased of your chocolate business to the general public through any number of methods; best-effort basis, competitive bid, negotiated purchase, privileged subscription, or direct sale, to name a few. This placement—investors purchasing directly from the underwriter—is known as the "primary market."

The Secondary Market

Whether it is for college expenses, to purchase a home, or because they found a more attractive security, the investors that acquire shares of your chocolate company through the primary market are probably going to sell them one day. On the flip side of the coin, there are going to be investors that did not purchase your shares during the IPO that now want to become partners with you in business. These folks need an orderly market to facilitate trade by matching buyers and sellers. This—investors buying and selling shares of existing businesses from each other—is known as the secondary market. It is what you see on the nightly news.

The Players

There are numerous players on Wall Street. We're going to look at the major ones, particularly the stock exchanges, the Federal Reserve, the Securities and Exchange Commission, the buy side, and the sell side. By understanding the roles of these institutions and how they interact with one another, you can begin to understand the dynamics that help drive security prices.

The Stock Exchanges

The stock market in this country consists of a number of exchanges, plus the NASDAQ over-the-counter market. The exchanges include:

- Philadelphia Stock Exchange

- New York Stock Exchange

- American Stock Exchange (owned by the National Association of Securities Dealers, or NASD for short)

- Pacific Stock Exchange

- Boston Stock Exchange

- Cincinnati Stock Exchange

- Chicago Board Options Exchange

Investor's Idiom

The **ask price** is the lowest price a seller is willing to accept for a stock. The **bid** is the highest price a buyer is willing to pay for the stock. The **spread** is the difference between the ask price and the bid price. If a NASDAQ trader has a seller who is willing to sell a stock for 30 and the trader can get a buyer to bid 30¼, the trader can keep the ¼ as his profit. That quarter point is the spread.

Organized in 1790, Philadelphia is the oldest exchange. The New York Stock Exchange, also known as "the Big Board," is by far the largest and the most well-known. The organization that became the NYSE began trading stocks under a buttonwood tree at what is now 68 Wall Street on May 17, 1792. On March 8, 1817, the traders wrote a constitution and the name "New York Stock Exchange Board" was adopted. The name was changed to "New York Stock Exchange" on January 29, 1863.

Some years later, a rival exchange, the New York Curb Exchange, was founded. While NYSE members had moved indoors, "the Curb" literally traded outdoors until 1921. In 1953, the New York Curb Exchange changed its name to the American

Stock Exchange. Although the short name is "the Amex," old-timers still refer to it as "the Curb."

The NASDAQ is an automated information network that provides quotes (prices) on stocks for brokers registered with the National Association of Securities Dealers (NASD). Trades are done by phone or computer with traders (members of the NASD) profiting from the *spread* between a stock's *bid* and *ask prices*, rather than adding a commission, as they do with exchange-listed stocks.

In rough numbers, there are around 2,768 stocks listed on the New York Stock Exchange, compared to 798 on the Amex. The number for the NASDAQ is huge, probably approaching 40,000.

Fiscal Facts

How the broker who handles a securities trade is compensated can vary. On the New York Stock Exchange, for example, the system is "plus commission," whereas on the NASDAQ over-the-counter market, it's "ex-commission." If you buy 100 shares of ABC stock via NYSE for $90 each, you will pay $9,000 for the shares plus a commission of $25. Your total transaction price is $9,025. If that stock were traded on the NASDAQ, the stock would be priced at $90.25, with the commission built in. You'd still pay a total transaction price of $9,025, but you wouldn't be aware that the extra $25 is commission.

What's With All the Animal References?

There's an old saying on Wall Street: "Bulls make money, bears make money, but pigs get slaughtered." But what's a "bull" and what's a "bear"? Bulls are people who believe a stock or the stock market is going to increase. Bears believe the price of a stock and/or the stock market is going to decrease.

Of course, the question that remains is where did these particular names originate, anyway? There are two explanations that are usually bandied about. The first is based on how each animal attacks: the bear by raking down with his large sharp claws, the bull by tossing up his large sharp horns. The second explanation comes from *The Wall Street Journal Guide to Understanding Money and Markets* (by Kenneth M. Morris, Fireside, 1999) and is a little fancier. According to the *Journal*, the term "bear" comes from sellers of bearskin who had a penchant for selling the bearskins before the bears were caught. Later, the term morphed to represent speculators who, on a hunch that the price would drop, agreed to sell shares they didn't own. Their next move would be to quickly buy the now lower-priced stock and sell it for the previously agreed higher price.

Fiscal Facts _____

New York Stock Exchange volume:

December 15, 1886: First million share day (1.2 million shares)

October 29, 1929: 16.4 million shares traded as the stock market crashed

August 18, 1982: First 100 million share day (132,681,120 shares)

October 28, 1997: First billion share day (1,202,550,000 shares)

January 4, 2001: First 2 billion share day (2,129,445,637 shares)

Because bull and bear baiting were once popular sports, bulls came to mean the opposite of bears. Bulls were those who bought heavily, expecting a stock price to increase.

Whatever explanation floats your boat, the words have carried down through the years, and people to this day describe themselves as bullish or bearish, depending upon their outlook.

The Securities and Exchange Commission (SEC)

According to the SEC itself, "The primary mission of the U.S. Securities and Exchange Commission (SEC) is to protect investors and maintain the integrity of the securities markets. As more and more first-time investors turn to the markets to help secure their futures, pay for homes, and send children to college, these goals are more compelling than ever." Appointed by President Roosevelt in 1934, the first Chairman of the SEC was Joseph Kennedy; father of future President John F. Kennedy.

The SEC accomplishes its mission by requiring companies to provide certain disclosures and information to all investors—whether a multi-billion-dollar pension fund or an elderly retiree with only a few hundred dollars. It has authority over nearly every institution involved in the securities markets: stock exchanges, mutual funds, investment advisors, brokers, dealers, and public utility holding companies.

The key to enforcement success is simple—the SEC carries a very, very large stick. It has the ability to bring action against individuals and entities that engage in insider trading, securities fraud, or a host of other verboten activities. It can even seek lifetime bans from serving as officers of publicly traded companies on individuals that have engaged in these activities!

The Fed's Balancing Act: Dampening Inflation Without Dumping on Us

Probably the most fundamental relationship you'll need to learn is the one between interest rates and the markets. Maybe at times you've wondered how interest rates are determined.

You've probably heard of the Federal Reserve. That's our country's central bank, and it monitors the activity of all banks in the nation. The Fed is charged with only one task, but it's a doozy. The Full Employment Act of 1946 and the Humphrey-Hawkins Act demand that the Fed keep the economy stoked so people can find jobs, yet also control inflation. This is an extremely delicate balancing act—like squeezing a balloon at one end without the other end blowing up with air.

Inflation, as you probably know, is an overall increase in prices. Inflation tends to occur when, as economists love to say, "too much money is chasing too few goods." If everyone in the country has a job and plenty of money to spend, a situation may arise where companies are not able to make enough products to satisfy the demand for them.

If you own a factory that makes stereos and your stereos are flying off the shelves, you will want to make more to satisfy the demand. Only problem is, with full employment, you can't find any workers to hire. So you can't make more stereos. "Well," you think, "all those flush consumers really want to buy my stereos, so I could definitely make some money here. I can't find anyone to help me make more stereos, but I'll bet if I raise the price, people will pay it." This is how full employment can fan the fires of inflation.

The Problem with Inflation

The problem with inflation is that once it takes off, it can outpace wages and lower the standard of living. If you can buy a bag of groceries in August for $60 and by December the same groceries cost you $75 but your salary hasn't budged, well, you're going to have to start eating less or going to fewer movies or playing fewer rounds of miniature golf on the weekend. Now that's no fun!

When the Fed sees evidence of inflation, it takes the one action it can, which is to raise interest rates. If you're one of those folks rushing out to throw a new stereo on your credit card and your credit card company informs you that your rate has gone up from 12.5 percent to 14.5 percent, you may give that purchase a second thought. When the Fed raises interest rates, spending is reduced and inflation dampened.

How does the Fed raise rates? Thanks to the Monetary Control Act of 1980, the Federal Reserve has the authority to require every commercial bank to hold a certain percentage of its deposits as cash reserves, allowing the central bank to control the money supply. Most of these reserves are held as deposits at one of the Federal Reserve banks. From time to time, a bank may run short of the reserve requirement at the end of the day and need to borrow money from another bank. The rate that banks charge each other for these short-term loans is called the *federal funds rate*.

Investor's Idiom

The Fed manipulates the interest rates we pay for auto loans, mortgages, and the like in two main ways. It raises or lowers the **discount rate,** which banks must pay when they borrow from the Fed. If the banks have to pay more, they'll turn around and charge you more. The Fed can also indirectly affect the **funds rate** that banks charge each other by adjusting the ratio of required reserves to total deposits.

Okay, stay with us now. The Fed doesn't set the funds rate directly but can affect it by increasing or decreasing the required ratio of reserves to deposits. In the same way that too much money chasing too few goods causes inflation, if the Fed increases reserve requirement, banks have fewer dollars on hand to lend each other overnight. Since they have less to lend, there will be pressure on the funds rate to rise.

The Fed can also directly control interest rates by increasing or decreasing the *discount rate*. This is the rate paid when banks borrow directly from the Fed.

Now, the one thing you can count on is that when it costs a bank more money to borrow money, it'll turn around and charge you more money to borrow. Consequently, when the funds rate or the discount rate rises, every other interest rate in the country begins to rise as well. Suddenly, it costs you more to buy that stereo or a new house. You slow down your spending; factories slow down their hiring; the economy begins to contract.

Conversely, when interest rates fall, it encourages borrowing, expansion, spending, and hiring. When the Fed thinks inflation is under control but jobs are scarce, it reduces the required ratio of reserves to deposits, therefore increasing system-wide liquidity. This increases the cash available to banks to lend to each other, and the funds rate falls. Interest rates begin to decline—people start buying again; companies begin hiring; the economy expands.

Interest Rates and the Market

What do interest rates have to do with stocks and bonds? Glad you asked! The longest-term U.S. Treasury obligation is considered by the financial community to be the "risk-free" interest rate. That is, the investor is always going to get his money back because the United States can tax and/or turn on the printing presses to ensure that the principal is repaid.

All investments are compared and valued against this risk-free rate. An insurance company may decide it wants a 3 percent risk premium for a corporate bond; therefore, it would only buy the bond if it yielded as much as the long-term treasury rate plus 3 percent. If the Feds increase the risk-free rate by 1 percent, for example, the corporate bond now only offers a 2 percent risk premium. Investors aren't interested so they will sell the bond until the price falls far enough the yield increases to provide a 3 percent-over-risk-free premium once again. This relationship between risk-premium and the risk-free interest rate is the key to understanding why the markets react so strongly when the Federal Reserve takes action. By influencing the direction of rates, the Fed can literally change the value of every asset in the country.

Buy Side vs. Sell Side

What do mutual funds, insurance companies, pension funds, and hedge funds have in common? They are all on what is known as the "buy-side" This group consists of institutions that professionally manage money; purchasing investments on behalf of themselves, their clients, and fund holders. The analysts and portfolio managers of these entities scour financial records, examine industries, and evaluate competing uses of capital all with one goal in mind—to make money for those individuals and organizations for whom they act as a fiduciary.

Those on the buy side have the ability, indeed the desire, to reject investments. They look for what is wrong with a potential opportunity and are free to disregard any companies they don't understand. In some cases, buy-side analysts are compensated based upon how well their recommendations perform. They have a very real interest in selecting only winners.

The "sell side," in contrast, is concerned with promoting and placing the offerings of an investment banking house; a process known as underwriting. For this reason, you should always take their research with a grain of salt as they will paint the rosiest, most optimistic picture imaginable. (If you're feeling depressed, read some sell-side literature. Your disposition will instantly improve!)

Choosing a Broker

Before you can begin investing, you are going to have to open a brokerage account. This account will allow you to buy and sell equities, options, bonds, mutual funds, treasuries, exchange-traded funds, real estate investment trusts, and more. Each time you execute a trade, you will pay your broker a commission. Depending upon the type of brokerage firm with which you have an account, your commissions can be very low (as little as $8.95 per trade or less) or very high (hundreds of dollars depending upon the size of your transaction).

Traditional vs. Discount

A traditional or *full-service broker* is one that offers clients a complete array of services—individual attention through personal contact with a broker that is familiar with your portfolio, research products, and asset allocation advice. All of this comes at a price, of course. Commissions and fees for traditional brokerage accounts can be many times as much as you would pay at a discount broker.

Investor's Idiom

A **broker** will act as an intermediary between you and the stock market. He or she will seek out buyers for stock you want to sell and find sellers of stock you want to buy. **Full-service brokers** also provide research and make recommendations. **Discount brokers** simply execute trades.

A *discount broker*, on the other hand, performs a single task: it executes your order, be it market, limit, or whatever (we'll cover those later in the chapter). In some cases, you don't even talk to a person! The advantage of a discount broker is a lower commission rate. Period. No free toasters, hand-holding, or "hot tips."

How do you know which one is right for you? It depends upon your personality, your investing experience, and the complexities of your trades. If you are capable of making individual investment decisions on your own and don't want input from an outside party, go the discount route. If, on the other hand, you need someone to explain the difference between market capitalization and enterprise value, you may want to go with a traditional broker.

Check Out Your Broker's Background

In most cases, snooping isn't considered polite. When choosing a broker, however, you want to do the intellectual equivalent of dumpster-diving. On Wall Street, the dumpster is the Central Registration Depository. The CRD database, as it is known, contains information about individual brokers and brokerage firms. Through this system, you can quickly discover complaints that have been filed against your broker, regulatory compliance issues, educational and employment histories, and—more important—verify that he is properly licensed. Why is this important? If you open an account with an unlicensed brokerage firm and it later goes under, you may not be able to recover your assets; not the kind of surprise you want.

To tap into the CRD, contact your state securities regulator or the National Association of Securities Dealers (NASD) Broker Check service at 1-800-289-999 or http://pdpi.nasdr.com/PDPI. It's completely free!

SIPC Protection (or What If My Broker Goes Bust?)

There's one last thing you must do before opening an account: Check to make sure that your brokerage firm is part of the Securities Investor Protection Corporation (SIPC) by clicking over to www.sipc.org/who/database.cfm. This ensures that if your broker goes out of business, you will recover up to $500,000 in assets, $100,000 of which may be in the form of cash. SIPC participation does *not* protect you against declines in the market value of your investments. Many firms will purchase additional insurance to give their clients added peace of mind.

If you are still not appeased by the idea that your account could go up in smoke should your broker fail, you can enter into a custodial agreement with your local bank. When you execute a trade, your broker will contact your bank which will transmit the funds necessary to complete the transaction. The broker will then deliver the securities purchased to your bank for safekeeping. In many cases, the custodian will also perform other functions such as collecting dividend and interest income on your behalf and monitoring corporate actions (e.g., stock splits). Despite the added expense, this is a good option if your assets are considerable.

Placing a Trade with Your Broker

Regardless of which type of broker you choose, most of the trades you place with it are going to fall into one of three categories:

◆ **The Market Order:** This instructs the broker to buy or sell at whatever the current market price is, no matter where it goes before your order is filled. You can expect that your broker will complete trades of 1,000 shares or less at or very close to the last trading price recorded. Such orders are typically executed electronically. You can usually get your price confirmed before you hang up after placing the order. Larger orders of 25,000+ shares may have to be "worked." For example, if ABC stock is moving up and you place an order to buy 50,000 shares of that stock, which was trading at 45, you may receive a report from your broker that you purchased:

  10,000 shares at 45⅛

  15,000 shares at 45¼

  10,000 shares at 45⅛

At this point, your broker may say: "I can fill the balance at 45¾." Now it's your decision: do you want to fill at that price or step aside and see if the price declines? If you go ahead, your broker would most likely report the balance of the trade as:

  100 shares at 45½

  100 shares at 45⅝

  14,800 shares at 45¾

Your average stock price (before commissions) would be $45.40.

◆ **The Limit Order:** Using the previous example, you might conclude that ABC stock will settle down in price and instruct your broker to "buy 50,000 shares of ABC with a 45 limit." Next, you must tell the broker if this is a day order (i.e., either filled that day or canceled) or "good 'til canceled" (referred to as GTC). That means the order will stay open until the broker fills it or you cancel it.

The problem with GTCs is you can forget you placed them. Maybe a few weeks later you'll buy alternative stock XYZ only to receive a follow-up call from your broker stating "we just filled your GTC on ABC." Whoops, a little short on money? It's easier to stay on top of things if you cancel and reenter your order each day, although your broker won't appreciate the extra work.

- ◆ **The Stop or Stop Loss Order:** Let's say you bought ABC stock at 30, saw it shoot up to 45¾, and it has now backed down to 42. At this point, you may be more willing to lock in a gain rather than roll the dice to see if it crests the 45¾ high again. So you instruct your broker to place a stop loss order to sell at $40. If the stock goes up, great; if it goes down, you're "out" at 40.

Unless you are a professional investor dealing with large orders, our advice would be to use market orders. Of the three, there isn't the margin of error that exists in the latter two choices. You're still getting in on the action, but you're letting a professional do most of the work.

Asset Management Accounts

In response to the stock market crash of 1929, Congress passed the Glass-Steagall Act. This legislation required a separation between brokerage services and commercial banks. For nearly seven decades, this restriction remained in place until, in 1999, then-President William Jefferson Clinton signed the Gramm-Leach-Bliley Act, which permits the creation of "financial services" firms. Endowed with the powers to engage in various banking, brokerage, and insurance activities, these firms created *asset management accounts* in order to attract customers.

> **Super Strategy**
>
> If you want to deal with a single financial institution only for all of your banking and brokerage needs, an asset management account may be the ideal solution.

Here's how they work. When you make a deposit, the proceeds are automatically swept into an interest-earning money market fund. You can write a check or use your debit card to automatically access the cash, just like a regular bank account. You can also go online or call your bank and purchase stocks, bonds, mutual funds, real estate investment trusts, and most other investments. At the end of the month, you will receive a single, consolidated statement detailing all of your transactions, both banking and brokerage.

There are a few downsides. Most asset management accounts have higher minimum opening balance requirements (e.g., $15,000 vs. $1,000 for a regular brokerage account). Also, the fees and commissions tend to reside somewhere between those charged by traditional and discount brokers; not bad at all if you value the services and convenience it affords.

The Least You Need to Know

- Although Wall Street is a literal place in Manhattan, the term is used as a reference to the investment community at large.

- A bull is someone who believes prices are going to increase; a bear, someone who believes prices are going to decrease.

- The Federal Reserve manipulates interest rates in two ways: by increasing or decreasing the *discount rate*, which is the rate banks pay when they borrow directly from the Fed, and by indirectly affecting the *funds rate* which is the rate that banks charge each other by adjusting the required ratio between reserves and deposits.

- The buy-side consists of those engaged in money management; the sell-side, underwriting.

- The primary responsibility of the SEC is to preserve the integrity of the financial markets.

- Before you open a brokerage account, you should check and see if the broker and brokerage firm, respectively, are licensed and part of the Securities Investor Protection Corporation.

Chapter 11

Common Stock

In This Chapter

- ◆ Investing from a business prospective
- ◆ Researching individual common stocks
- ◆ Calculating dividend yield and payout ratios
- ◆ Spotting an excellent business
- ◆ Building a position in a company through low-cost DRIPs

As you learned in the previous chapter, common stock represents ownership in a company. When you purchase shares in a corporation, you become, in effect, a silent partner (unless, of course, you have the funds to acquire a meaningful percentage of the equity, in which case you can elect yourself to the Board of Directors and enact changes). As such, the value of your investment is directly tied to the operating results of the business over the long-run, just as if you had opened a coffee shop with your best friend, or bought a miniature golf course with your family.

This distinction—seeing common stock as ownership in a business rather than a meaningless symbol on the electronic *ticker*—is one that can give you a very real competitive advantage over other investors. It gives you the freedom to ignore the noise of the market and focus on what really matters. This will help prevent unintelligent actions during the many financial crises you will encounter in your career.

Investor's Idiom _____

In the late nineteenth century, stock quotes were transmitted over telegraph lines to ticker machines. As the information was received, the machine would print it on a small strip of paper known as ticker tape.

Although computers came to replace ticker machines, stocks are stilled tracked by short combinations of letters known as **ticker symbols**. Coca-Cola, for example, has a ticker of KO; the Washington Post, WPO; General Electric, GE; Wal-Mart, WMT; Microsoft, MSFT; Hershey, HSY; and so on. If you wanted to purchase shares Hershey, you would call your broker and say, "Buy 100 shares of HSY."

Own Your Own Business: Investing in Common Stocks

Imagine, for a moment, that you own an extremely profitable soda business. You have a strong balance sheet, a franchise that cannot be replicated by any competitor, a wonderful distribution system that lets you reach the far corners of the world, and pricing power that allows you to pass on increases in manufacturing costs to the consumer without hurting sales. As the owner of this dream company, you would never be foolish enough to sell it. In fact, if someone offered to buy your stake for half of what you believed it was worth, you'd probably laugh in their face.

Yet if this soda company was publicly traded and the share price dropped by half, many investors (i.e., business owners) would panic and sell their fractional ownership out of fear. Don't believe it? It actually happened! The story is frequently told by legendary investor Warren Buffett to illustrate the importance of focusing on the competitive advantages and economics of an enterprise over the short-term movements in the stock price:

> In 1919, Coca-Cola went public at $40 per share. Due to conflicts with the company's bottlers and a dramatic surge in sugar prices, the shares had fallen to $19.50 by the end of 1920. Had you sold your position at that time, you would have experienced a substantial loss.

> Despite these short-term problems, a single share of Coca-Cola purchased in 1919 would have now grown into 4,608 shares through stock splits. That is, if you had purchased one share of Coke in 1919 at $40 and *not* reinvested the dividends, you would now own 4,608 shares with a market value of approximately $230,400. You would also receive around $5,160 in dividends annually.

Had you reinvested those seemingly paltry dividends each year into more Coca-Cola common stock, however, that one share would have grown into more than 100,000 shares; at today's stock price, a market value of more than $5 million. You would also receive nearly $112,000 in dividends per annum. (We talk more about the power of reinvested dividends later in this chapter.) Despite wars, depressions, recessions, stock market crashes, nuclear proliferation, a Presidential assassination, the invention of television, satellites, and the Internet, Coke's products remain relevant to today's consumer. That success translated into dramatic wealth for the owners of the business.

Fiscal Facts

When Coke went public in 1919, it had two underwriters, each of whom earned a $100K fee for services rendered. One firm took payment in cash. The other firm, the predecessor to SunTrust Bank, took its entire fee in Coca-Cola stock. According to the company's most recent 10Q, SunTrust now owns 48,266,496 shares of Coke worth more than $2 billion! In addition, the investment provides SunTrust's shareholders with more than $43 million in dividend income each year.

Also in SunTrust's Atlanta, Georgia, vault is the original copy of the Coca-Cola formula. It is said that only two executives from Coke have access to the priceless document.

But How Am I Going to Make Money?

When you own stock, there are two potential sources of profit:

1. Appreciation in the price of the security (e.g., you buy shares of a company for $10 and the stock prices increases to $25; you've made a $15 profit).

2. Dividends received; this is when the company mails you a check for your portion of the profits paid out to shareholders. Over the last century, around 40 percent of returns have arisen from dividends. Stocks that pay large and increasing dividends over time can be an excellent choice for investors that require current income upon which to live.

Investor's Idiom _____

Market capitalization is the value of all of a company's outstanding common stock. A corporation with 2 million shares outstanding and a current stock price of $50 per share would have a market capitalization of $100 million.

An example may help. The Avalon Candle Company, a fictional enterprise, is a manufacturer of premium candles and scented products. The company has a *market capitalization* of $250 million (10 million shares of stock outstanding, each trading for $25). Last year, the business had a net income of $15.6 million.

Each share of common stock is entitled to a proportional interest in the profit. If you divide the company's net income ($15,600,000) by the number of shares outstanding (10,000,000), you discover that each share is entitled to $1.56 of the profits. This figure is known as earnings per share, or EPS; we'll talk more about it when we explore the income statement in Chapter 16.

Once a year, the shareholders of The Avalon Candle Company vote to elect a Board of Directors. Among other things, this Board is responsible for ensuring the business is run well so that shareholders make as much money as prudently possible. One of the most important decisions it must make is how to pay you—the owner of Avalon's shares—your $1.56 profit.

Generally speaking, the Board has two choices: It can either reinvest the funds in the business to expand future earnings per share by building new factories, creating new products, acquiring other companies, repurchasing existing shares, and paying down debt, or it can send you a check in the mail. Profits that reinvested in the business are known as *retained earnings*. Profits that are paid out to shareholders in cash are known as *dividends*. For the sake of our illustration, assume Avalon's Board decides to reinvest $0.50 of the profits, and pay the remainder, or $1.06, out in the form of a dividend.

If you purchased 500 shares of the company's stock, you are going to receive a check in the mail (in the event you hold these shares through your broker, the funds will be

Fiscal Facts _____

Profits reinvested in the business are known as **retained earnings**.

deposited into your account) for $530 ($1.06 per-share dividend × 500 shares). Your portion of the retained earnings would equal $250 (500 shares × $0.50 retained earnings for the year). In theory, these retained earnings will cause the share price to increase over time.

Dividend Payout Ratio

The ratio between cash paid out to share-holders in the form of dividends and total earnings is known as the *dividend payout ratio*. A company that had net income of $10 million and paid $6 million out as *cash dividends* would have a payout ratio of 60 percent ($6 million dividends paid divided by $10 million net income).

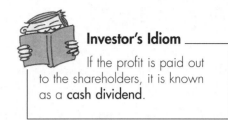

Investor's Idiom

If the profit is paid out to the shareholders, it is known as a **cash dividend**.

The inverse is known as the *retention ratio*, and can be calculated by taking 100 percent subtracted by the dividend payout ratio. Using the same example, the retention ratio would be 40 percent (100 percent – 60 percent dividend payout ratio = 40 percent retention ratio). As you'll see when we discuss return on equity in Chapter 17, these concepts are extremely important because they are used to calculate a company's maximum sustainable growth rate.

Dividend Yield

Another important metric is dividend yield. It tells you how much a common stock is yielding based upon its current market price. It is calculated by dividing the annual cash dividend by the per share market value of a stock.

Take a look at U.S. Bancorp (symbol: USB). At the time of this writing, the shares were trading at $29.53. The indicated annual cash dividend equaled $1.20. By dividing the dividend by the current market price, we find that the U.S. Bank's common stock is currently yielding 4.06 percent. That is, the purchaser of $10,000 worth of the stock today would expect to earn 4.06 percent, or $406, in dividend income over the next year.

Fiscal Facts

Most companies pay dividends quarterly. If you open *The Wall Street Journal* and see that a corporation pays a $1 dividend, it is likely that you are going to receive $0.25 per share, four times a year (Jan. 1, Apr.1, July 1, and Oct. 1, for example). Some businesses, on the other hand, pay dividends annually or semi-annually.

On rare occasions, a Board of Directors may declare a *special* dividend. These are one-time distributions normally arising from excess funds that have accumulated or unusual, non-recurring sources, such as the sale of a business or an award from litigation.

We're Not Talking About Leaky Faucets: Investing Through DRIPs

Most corporations offer a handy service known as a Dividend Reinvestment Program, or DRIP for short. DRIPs are the best way for you to build a position in a company at a very low cost over a long period of time. Advantages of these programs include:

 ◆ In most cases, there is little or no fee for shares purchased through a DRIP. This lowers your cost basis and can increase your returns substantially over long periods of time.

 ◆ You can purchase additional shares of stock directly by sending in a check or having funds withdrawn from your checking/savings account. Most of the time, additional investments can be as small as $10 or $25.

 ◆ You can establish automatic, regular withdrawals from your bank account to purchase shares. This is an easy way to establish a dollar cost averaging program, which you will learn about in Chapter 20.

 ◆ Fractional shares can be purchased. Say you receive $15 in dividends yet the current stock price is $50. Through a DRIP program, you will actually be able to purchase 0.3 shares. This isn't possible through a broker.

Want to know how to get started? First, check and see if the stock you fancy offers a DRIP. You can either find the phone number for the investor relations department on the company's web site or head over to www.equiserve.com.

Next, buy a single share through your broker and then request that he send you a stock certificate; you can also order a single certificate through a special gift service such as OneShare.com. This makes you eligible for participation.

Finally, fill out and mail in the paperwork provided to you by the investor relations department or Equiserve.

Violà! You've done it! Sit back and relax. Without any additional work, the amount of shares you own will increase as your dividends are reinvested.

The Truth About Stock Splits

Notice that we haven't mentioned stock splits as a way to make money? A lot of novice investors make the mistake of thinking that when a stock splits, it's good for their portfolio. Really, it has no effect whatsoever! It's the financial equivalent of getting two $10 bills in exchange for the $20 you have in your pocket. Don't believe us? An example may help.

The Missouri Tea Company has 100,000 shares outstanding, each trading at $30; giving the business a market capitalization of $3.0 million. Last year, MTC had a net income of $250,000, or $2.50 per share.

The Board of Directors declares a 2-1 stock split because it thinks that $30 per share is too expensive for the average investor. It turns on the printing presses and prints an extra 100,000 shares. It then distributes them pro-rata to the existing shareholders (for example, if you owned 100 shares, you would receive 100 shares of the newly created stock).

The result is that the shareholders now hold twice as many shares. But notice that the entire company is still the same size! The $250,000 profit is being split by 200,000 shares instead of the 100,000 that existed previously, cutting the EPS in half to $1.25. The result is that the stock price—which was $30 per share—gets cut in half to $15 per share.

So which would you rather have … 100 shares at $30 each generating $2.50 per share in profit, or 200 shares at $15 each generating $1.25 per share in profit? At the end of the day, you are still in the exact same economic position.

Spotting an Excellent Business

Although a rare breed, excellent businesses share certain characteristics that distinguish them from run-of-the-mill enterprises. We're going to talk about each of these so you can acquaint yourself with the desirable traits that make for a great investment.

Durable Competitive Advantages

An excellent business has numerous durable competitive advantages. Sometimes these come in the form of high barriers to entry. Boeing and Airbus, for example, are not likely to experience as much competition as Saks Fifth Avenue and American Eagle Outfitters. Other manifestations include brand recognition, a strong distribution system, a government-sponsored monopoly (e.g., Fannie Mae and Freddie Mac), patented or copyrighted products or ideas, superior product quality, or being the low-cost producer in a commodity-like industry.

Raise Those Prices!

The ability to increase prices without a significant decrease in sales is perhaps the single most important indicator of a business's inherent economics. A gourmet chocolatier is going to be able to charge a premium for its product because people are willing to pay for brand name and quality, whereas a steel maker competes solely on the basis of price. If you don't believe it, imagine the reaction you'd get if you sent your true love a box of the generic chocolate sold at the dollar-store; not nearly as pleasant as if you had sent Godiva or See's.

> ### Super Strategy
>
> One way to spot excellent businesses is to look for those with pricing power. Unless it is the low-cost producer, a company that cannot raise prices substantially without causing a corresponding reduction in sales is always going to be vulnerable to market forces.

Complimentary Cultural and Demographic Drivers

The dual forces of cultural norms and demographic drivers (age, gender, education, and so on) are very powerful. Before you commit capital to an enterprise, it is important that you look up from the financial statements and examine the world around you. An American investor would probably be quite foolish to assume that a fast-growing kid's-themed sushi restaurant is going to successfully replace the Hamburger Happy Meal at McDonald's any time in the near future, for example. Likewise, if you are examining a chain of baby supply stores in a particular geographic area yet the average child per household is decreasing rapidly, you must recognize the growth potential of the enterprise is, to some degree, limited.

Product Relevance

One of the biggest competitive advantages a company can possess is the sustainability of its franchise. In other words, will the product be relevant to consumers 100 years from now despite changes in tastes and technology? For companies such as William Wrigley, Hershey Chocolate, and Coca-Cola, the answer is an unequivocal "yes." For other businesses, such as software manufacturers, movie studios, and auto makers, the answer is not so clear. There was once a time when horse carriage manufacturers, whip makers, and railroads populated the list of Wall Street's favorite blue chip companies, yet the first two no longer exist in any meaningful way and the latter, thanks to the capital-intensive nature of the transportation industry and cutthroat competition, struggles to maintain profitability.

History of Share Repurchases

Did you know that it is possible for shareholders to get wealthier without actually having a business grow? Many people forget that the overall size of the company is second only to the growth per share. Consider the following example based on a fictional company, Donna's Quilt Shop.

DQS has 5 million shares outstanding and generated $10 million in net income last year. Each of those shares is entitled to $2 of the profit. The stock is trading for $20 per share. Management wants to make the shareholders money but it realizes that the growth market for quilts is not exactly on fire. The company has no debt to pay down, leaving it with two possibilities: distribute all of the profits as cash dividends or repurchase its own stock on the open market.

You already understand dividends; if the first option was chosen, you would receive a check amounting to $2 for each share you owned (e.g., if you owned 10,000 shares, a check for $20,000 would show up in the mail).

Say, on the other hand, management took the $10 million to the open market and repurchased 500,000 shares ($10 million profit divided by $20 cost per share = 500,000 shares purchased). It then destroyed them; they no longer exist.

Now, there are only 4.5 million shares outstanding. Even if the company doesn't grow at all, the $10 million in profit is going to be split among 4.5 million shares—not 5 million, like before. That means that each share is now entitled to $2.22. The per-share earnings grew 10 percent despite the fact that the company's bottom line remained flat!

Fiscal Facts

Over time, share repurchases can make a tremendous difference in your wealth level. Going back to the Coca-Cola example we've used throughout the chapter, you can see in the company's most recent annual report that KO has repurchased over 1 billion shares since it began buying back its own stock in 1984. That amounts to over 34.5 percent of the then-outstanding shares!

Historically, share repurchases have been a more tax-efficient way to return capital to shareholders. Prior to the Bush administration, dividends were taxed at personal income rates. Recently, dividends are taxed at a maximum rate of 15 percent.

Sensible Management with Reasonable Compensation

One of the most frustrating things you will encounter as an investor is finding an excellent business with many of the characteristics on this list and then discovering that the success of the enterprise is being pocketed by management; none is actually flowing through to the shareholders.

Sometimes this happens by means of excessive stock option awards. Every time new stock is issued without old stock being repurchased, the owners of the business (that's you!) are forced to share the net income with more "pieces"; the proverbial pie has been cut into more slices. Other times, management is paid unjustifiably large salaries in cash; a transgression compounded by the fact that the government does not permit companies to write off base salaries in excess of $1 million.

You Want Them Holding the Bag

One of the ways to ensure that management, the Board of Directors, and shareholders all have aligned interests is for the company to establish stock ownership guidelines. An excellent example is Berkshire Hathaway. According to the Chairman's 2004 shareholder letter, every director of Berkshire comes from a family owning no less than $4 million in the company's stock and none of these shares were acquired through options or grants. Likewise, at U.S. Bank, guidelines have been established for upper management regarding the amount of company stock they should own. According to USB's proxy statement, executives are generally given 3 years to comply. The requirements for the CEO are 5 times base salary; other executive officers, 4 times base salary. The best part? Vested in-the-money options don't count toward this ownership requirement.

Open and Honest Communication

A company's annual reports should not resemble a promotional flyer released by the public relations department but, rather, contain direct, open, and honest communication from the stewards of your capital, admissions of challenges and mistakes, and a clear plan for the future. Be wary of a CEO who tells you his priority is paying down debt and shortly thereafter announces an acquisition.

History of Increasing Dividends

Historically, about 40 percent of total stock market returns have been generated by dividends. A shareholder-friendly management is one that consistently raises the dividend over time if the cash cannot be reinvested at a higher rate of return than the shareholders could earn themselves. Take a look at the chart below. You can see that the owner of any one of these businesses would have received ever-increasing checks in the mail.

Example of Rising Per Share Dividends

Year	Coca-Cola	Citigroup	Sara Lee
1997	$0.56	$0.20	$0.42
1998	$0.60	$0.2775	$0.46
1999	$0.64	$0.405	$0.50
2000	$0.68	$0.52	$0.54
2001	$0.72	$0.60	$0.58
2002	$0.80	$0.68	$0.60
2003	$0.88	$1.10	$0.6525[1]
2004	$1.00	$1.60	$0.75

(1)Includes supplemental dividend of $0.325

Dividends, Interest, and Fixed Charges "Earned"

Common sense tells you that if a company has earnings per share of $2, yet it is paying a dividend of $3, this unfortunate state of affairs cannot endure forever. As an investor, you are going to want to make sure that the company can continue to service its dividend to shareholders, interest to bondholders, and fixed charges (leases, etc.) so you are going to insist upon a margin of safety. This can be done only by purchasing companies that have "earned" the dividend several times over. That is, if Jemima's Diner Company is paying a $1 dividend, you want to make sure that it had EPS of $1.50, or $2.00, or more.

There may be some years where a company reports a restructuring charge or a loss. If this is an isolated incident and not part of an on-going trend, you probably don't need to be concerned about the safety of the dividend. Most management teams understand that investors depend upon the dividend, and are unlikely to do away with it unless absolutely necessary.

Little or No Debt

A small amount of leverage can be good for the shareholders of an excellent business. If your company can generate returns of 22 percent on capital, yet its borrowing costs are only 8 percent, the spread is effectively dropping to the bottom line. Too much debt, however, can put the entire ship in danger of capsizing under the burden of high interest payments. An excellent business does not need large amounts of debt because it, by definition, generates tons of cash.

Tons of Free Cash Flow

Some companies require massive amounts of capital to generate $1 of profit while others require very little (imagine if you wanted to start your own business ... a steel mill is going to require millions in startup funding whereas an advertising firm would require a desk, a pencil, and some brainpower).

The best businesses are those that require little investment and generate tons and tons of cash. *Free cash flow*, which we examine in Chapter 18, is the actual money that is left after a company has taken care of its reinvestment needs. It is the amount available to pay down debt, repurchase shares, pay dividends, or expand operations.

A Controlling Shareholder (Well, Sometimes ...)

A controlling shareholder is someone who owns enough of a company's voting power to effectively make all of the decisions. Sometimes, control comes by simply buying a majority of the common stock outstanding. This is simple to understand—someone strolls in with deep pockets, acquires 51 percent of the company, and names himself CEO.

Other times, a founding family will create a special class of stock that outvotes all other shares. Consider the Washington Post Company, which has 1,722,250 shares of Class A and 7,866,357 shares of Class B stock, respectively. The Class A shares, held by the Graham family, are not publicly traded. Those shares have "unlimited voting rights, including the right to elect a majority of the Board of Directors." The Class B shares are traded on the New York Stock Exchange and have the right to elect 30 percent of the Board. For that reason, it is impossible for an outsider to takeover the business. An investor in the Washington Post is, in effect, a silent partner with the Graham family. In the Post's case, this has been a tremendous advantage. The paper is free to focus on the long-term success of the business and ignore Wall Street. This philosophy has led to a stellar track record of intelligent share repurchases and acquisitions.

Were you a partner with Jay Gould in any of his business over a century ago, however, you would have found yourself playing the proverbial patsy. Unlike the Graham family, Gould had no respect for minority shareholders and would routinely manipulate, abuse, and cheat them out of their rightful bounty.

The bottom line: a controlling shareholder can be a huge asset, or a substantial liability. It depends entirely upon the quality, character, and intelligence of the individual or entity. Your pocketbook will thank you if you engage in some due diligence and research the past investments and actions of those in control before committing your hard-earned money.

Market Leadership

There are numerous advantages to holding the leading position in any given industry. In addition to name recognition, economies of scale, and greater financial resources, a leading business has an easier time attracting and retaining talented executives.

Price

The single most important determinant of your investment returns is the price you pay. This concept is so important that we've dedicated an entire portion of the book (Chapter 20) to it! If you are filled with anticipation, skip ahead … we'll be right here, waiting, when you return.

Researching Individual Stocks

Now that you know what you are searching for, let's get into how to actually find these businesses! There are good research resources available to the individual investor, many at your local library. In addition, if you hire a full-service broker, you can indirectly avail yourself of his or her research department.

In our opinion, the two most basic, cost-effective, and objective research tools are the *Value Line Investment Survey* and *Standard & Poor's Stock Guides*. Both may be available at your local library, but if not, or if you wish to have your own personal copies, we have provided subscription information.

The Invaluable Value Line

The basic Value Line service covers approximately 1,700 stocks. For each stock, Value Line provides two rankings: timeliness and safety. Of the two, pay particular attention to safety. Stocks are ranked on a 1–5 basis, with 1 being the safest. Don't consider any stock with less than a 2 rating.

Value Line also provides scores for four other key indicators:

- ◆ Financial strength

- ◆ Stock price stability

- ◆ Stock price growth persistence

- ◆ Earnings predictability

In addition to the rankings and key indicators cited here, Value Line includes a great deal of relevant statistical and narrative information. Value Line reports are updated regularly. The individual company write-ups will take some getting used to, but after a while, you will find that you can easily determine a company's earnings growth rate and the consistency of that growth rate.

Use Value Line to help you select at least 25 stocks that:

- ◆ Are safe or very safe (remember, that means a ranking of 1 or 2)

- ◆ Are growing at an above-average rate

- ◆ Are growing consistently and steadily

What does "above average" mean? We suggest you look for a minimum of 8 percent and, ideally, 10 percent growth. And keep an eye on consistency. For a 10 percent grower, 10 percent a year is perfect but rarely achieved. A range of 8–12 percent is consistent. From 6–14 percent is acceptable. But if the company's earnings swing between 0 percent and 30 percent, for example, it's too volatile to be in your portfolio unless you know exactly what you're doing.

To subscribe to Value Line, call 1-800-634-3583. A one-year subscription costs $598, but you can get a 3-month trial subscription for $75!

S&P Stock Guides: Another Great Tool

Standard & Poor's Stock Guides (Bond Guides are also available) are an excellent research tool. The guides come out monthly and cover over 6,000 stocks, 700 mutual funds, 600 closed-end funds, and 800 preferred stock issues. Annual subscription prices are $220 for the Stock Guide and $370 for the Bond Guide. Special year-end editions are $24.64 (Stock) and $33.00 (Bond). You can order by calling 1-800-221-5277 or visiting the S&P website at www.standardpoors.com.

The Best Newspapers for Stock Info

Finally, two newspapers, *Investors Business Daily* and *The Wall Street Journal*, do an excellent job of tracking the stock market and individual stocks. Either may be available at your local library. To order a subscription to the *Journal* visit http://services.wsj.com. To subscribe to IBD, visit www.investors.com.

If you simply must follow the market during the day, both CNBC and Bloomberg Information TV do a good job of keeping you current. For a nightly wrap-up, check out PBS's Nightly Business Report.

Investor's Idiom

A corporation is expected to issue an annual report once a year that includes an income statement, balance sheet, cash flow statement, and certain disclosures. The company is also required to file a 10-K report with the Securities and Exchange Commission (SEC). The 10K is a more detailed version of the annual report, minus pictures and narrative. A company must also file an 8K report with the SEC within 30 days regarding any event that could affect operating performance.

All the News That's Fit to Print: Annual Reports

The most valuable research you can get your hands on is provided by the companies themselves. After you purchase individual equities, the company (or your brokerage firm) will begin stuffing your mailbox with quarterly and annual reports.

We spend all of Part 4 discussing how to analyze and interpret these documents so if you want those reports before we get there, check the stock tables in *The Wall Street Journal's* Section C. You will find a three-leaf, clover—type symbol next to those companies that provide a free annual and free current quarterly report. To obtain these reports, call the Annual Reports Club at 1-800-654-2582, fax your request to 1-800-965-5679, or order via the Internet at www.wsj.ar.wilink.com.

Annual and quarterly financial statements are like report cards. Avoid the glossy charts and the pretty pictures, and you'll be able to tease out trends. The 10K is the annual report equivalent filed with the SEC. It's sometimes more revealing than the corporate reports to shareholders and comes without the rosy verbiage.

You'll also want to get your hands on a copy of the most recent proxy statement. This document details the proposals put before shareholders at the annual meeting, such as executive compensation programs and the election of directors.

Finally, the 8K form is a report that a corporation's managers must file with the SEC within 30 days of any event that might affect the financial status or share price of the company.

If You Own It, You Better Love It (or the Evils of Market Timing)

Many investors are naïve enough to think that they can consistently beat the market by timing their entry into and out of stocks. In their excellent publication *10 Ways to Beat an Index*, Tweedy Browne managing directors Christopher Browne, William Browne, and John Spears tell us that, "empirical research has shown that 80%–90% of investment returns have occurred in spurts that amount to 2%–7% of the total length of time of the holding period. The rest of the time, stocks' returns have been small." In other words, had you been out of the market on just a handful of the best performing days, your returns would significantly below average.

There's also another very powerful reason to avoid short-term plays: taxes. Whenever you sell an investment you've owned for less than one year, the profit is going to be taxed at your personal gains rate, which can be as high as 35 percent (2005). Long-term capital gains, on the other hand, are not taxed at a rate higher than 20 percent. The longer you defer your tax bill to Uncle Sam, the more capital you have working to compound your net worth. Over an investing lifetime, the difference can be millions of dollars.

Super Strategy

Obviously, there are good reasons sometimes to sell a stock. Maybe you made a mistake in the first place, or the company has fallen apart. But your best bet is to buy the stocks of stable, high-quality companies that you'll feel comfortable owning for a long time. If they pay a growing cash dividend, so much the better.

A Word on IPO's, Penny Stocks, and Hot Tips

Avoid speculative securities. Initial public offerings (IPOs), *penny stocks*, and "hot tips" aren't worth the risk. Even the best traders don't buy all their stocks at what turn out to be lowest prices; mistakes are part of the business. But good quality stocks recover and eventually go on to new highs; losers just curl up and die. IPOs are simple to deal with. The "hot" ones go to large institutional customers; the little person might get a few shares if he/she is lucky. If you are offered a good chunk of an IPO, odds are the broker was unable to unload all the shares to institutional customers and is calling with a "hot tip" because he's got to get rid of them somehow. Penny stocks are a specu-lator's dream. A $40 stock that goes up an eighth equals a yawn, but a $1 stock up ⅛ equals a 12.5 percent gain! There's also the ego boost of saying "I just put away 10,000 shares of X." But "up ⅛" can quickly become "down ⅛." And wait until you see the commis-sion on 10,000 shares! Temptation, get thee hence!

Investor's Idiom

Penny stocks are stocks that are selling for a very low price—typically one, two, or three dollars.

Regarding hot tips in general, please face facts: You're a small player, and when the hot tip gets all the way down the chain to you, it'll be lukewarm at best. If an invest-ment seems too good to be true, it is too good to be true.

The Least You Need to Know

- Investment returns arise from two sources: appreciation in the price of the secu-rity and dividends.

- The payout ratio is the percentage of a company's profit that is distributed to the shareholders as cash dividends.

- DRIPs offer an easy, low-cost way to build a position in a company.

- Excellent businesses possess certain characteristics such as the ability to pass on cost increases to consumers, sensible management with reasonable compensa-tion, a Board of Directors with significant personal holdings, open and honest communication, little or no debt, tons of free cash flow, a history of share repur-chases market leadership, and an attractive price.

◆ You always want to read a company's annual report, 10K, and proxy statement before investing.

◆ The frictional expenses, tax considerations, and unpredictable nature of Wall Street make market timing extremely difficult.

Chapter 12

Slow and Steady Wins the Race: Fixed-Income Securities

In This Chapter

- ◆ Determining if bonds are right for your portfolio
- ◆ How to read a bond table
- ◆ The danger of inflation
- ◆ Calculating taxable-equivalent yield on municipal bonds
- ◆ Earning higher yields through agencies without extra risk

Maybe you're not the type that likes to take big chances. You like to know what's coming around the corner, and, if you can't, you at least like to have a back-up plan to deal with life's little boomerangs. If this is you, there are two words you need to remember: fixed income. A fixed-income security entitles you to regular, fixed payments of interest income on your investments. In this chapter, we're going to give you the lowdown on these securities and how they can benefit you.

The Importance of the Debt Markets

Bonds and *notes* are fixed-income securities that corporations, municipalities, and governments issue to borrow money. When you buy a bond or note, you are agreeing to lend the entity that issued it a certain amount of money. In return, the company gives you a fixed-income security and promises to make specified interest payments to you and return the full amount borrowed when the security matures. The interest that is to be paid to you, the timing of those payments, and the *maturity date* are all spelled out in a document known as the *indenture*.

When corporations raise money using fixed-income securities, it's called *debt financing*. When they issue stock to raise money, it's called *equity financing*. It may surprise you to learn that, although the stock market receives more coverage on the nightly news, the bond market is far, far larger!

 Investor's Idiom _____

Bonds, **notes**, and **bills** are all IOUs that corporations and governments issue when they want to borrow money. The borrower promises to pay you interest as well as return the principal amount you lent it at a specific date in the future (this is known as the **maturity date**). In the case of the United States government, these IOUs are called bonds when the specified date is longer than 10 years from the date the bond is issued. When the maturity date is between 1 and 10 years from issuance, the IOU is a known as a note. When it's 1 year or less from issuance, the IOU is called a bill.

Bonds and other fixed-income securities balance out the risk of carrying stocks in your portfolio. Unless you lend money to a borrower with lousy credit, you can count on getting your money back when the fixed-income security matures. Plus, you earn all that interest income in the meantime.

When the stock market is tanking, it can be a great relief to know that you have some of your money in nice, safe bonds. Even better, when the stock market is performing miserably, the bond market tends to do really well, and vice versa. This seesaw effect keeps your portfolio on an even keel when you own both stocks and bonds. The events of 2001 and 2002 are good examples.

When Do You Get That Groovy Interest Income?

In the United States, most, but not all, fixed-income securities pay interest twice a year; on the annual anniversary of the original issue date, and again six months later (in Europe, most bonds pay interest annually). For example, five-year U.S. Treasury notes yielding 6.625 percent and due May 2007, pay interest in May and November each year. Plus, the Treasury will pay you back the amount you lent it (your principal) on the maturity date, May 2007.

Beware the Call Feature

Some fixed-income investments include a "call" feature. What is this? Well, let's say you have a home mortgage. This is essentially a fixed-income security you sold to your bank. You, as the borrower, agreed to make fixed monthly payments and to pay off the principal by a final maturity date.

You have, however, the right to pay off your mortgage in advance and to refinance your mortgage to take advantage of declining interest rates. This right is the "call" feature. You can "call" your mortgage anytime and pay it off. Some U.S. Government bond issues and the vast majority of corporate and municipal issues also have call features. These give the issuer/borrower the right to pay off ("redeem") the bonds issued.

Crash Alert

Call features benefit only the original issuer; they never benefit the purchaser or owner. Therefore, either don't buy any issues with a call feature, or be very careful about incorporating them into your bond portfolio.

Why would the borrower want this right? Well, let's go back to our example of Treasury notes paying 6.625 percent interest and maturing in 2007, and pretend the issue is callable. What if interest rates declined to 3 percent? The Treasury would love to be able to pay off the note at 6.625 percent and issue a new note. It would save billions of dollars in interest expense!

This would be a drag for you, though, because now you no longer have a 6.625 percent note. Sure you got your principal back, but now if you want to reinvest it, the best you'll do is a new Treasury note at 3 percent. Your interest income has been drastically reduced by this swift move and there's not one thing you can do about it!

Now, let's assume that rates increase to 8 percent. You would be very pleased if the Treasury would call your note so you can reinvest at the higher rate, but the Treasury sure doesn't want to pay 8 percent when it's got you locked in at 6.625 percent.

In this case, the Treasury would not exercise the call right.

Sinkers

Traditionally, if a bond issue has a "sinking fund" it means that the company periodically sets aside resources to purchase the securities either on the open market or through the exercise of its right to call and retire them prior to maturity. The debt level of the enterprise decreased, increasing the safety of the bonds as a result.

As an investor, you could make a tremendous amount of money if you were lucky enough to receive a call during a period of rising interest rates. As the new, higher rates cause the market value of your bond to fall, you would receive the full par value upon cancellation of your bond and be able to immediately reinvest it at the prevailing higher rates.

The opposite is also true, however. If you were unfortunate enough to receive a call on a bond that was trading at a premium due to a decrease in the general level of interest rates, you would only receive a fraction of the quoted market value of your security. You would then have to reinvest the proceeds at the prevailing lower rates.

The bottom line: sinking funds make a bond issue both *more* attractive due to the decreased risk of default and *less* attractive as a result of the call feature that is likely to be embedded in the security. Exercise caution and do your research so you don't encounter any unexpected surprises.

Super Strategy

To paraphrase Will Rogers, "It's not the return *on* your principal, it's the return *of* your principal ...." When buying fixed-income securities, don't just look for notes and bonds with the highest yields. If a borrower is willing to pay high interest rates, its credit must not be very good. Junk bonds, for example, are high-yielding bonds from corporations with lousy credit ratings. They may pay a lot of interest but the risk that you will never be paid back part or all of your principal is also very high—too high to risk. The highest yield, per se, cannot be your objective; it must be the highest yield on the highest quality bonds.

The Wonderful World of Bond (No, Not James)

The bond is a popular fixed-income security. But in the world of finance, you've probably heard the term tossed around with stocks as if they're one and the same: "Stocksnbonds, stocksnbonds." Well, obviously, they're not.

For one, when you buy a stock you are buying equity—ownership in the company that issued the stock. You are now an owner, entitled to share in the profits and to suffer the losses of the company. The company may or may not pay you dividends, depending on whether or not profits rise. The price of the stock you own may or may not rise. If it does, you could sell it and get your investment back many times over. But when you buy a bond, you are buying debt. You are not an owner; you are lending money to the company (or government) and it has agreed to pay you interest and to pay you back at a certain date. You are promised a specific return (the interest) on your investment, as well as the eventual return of your investment. Because you are not an owner, you are not entitled to a share of the company's profits, nor are you expected to suffer its losses. No matter how bad things get, the company is expected to honor its promise to pay you interest and return your principal at maturity.

Unlike bondholders, stockholders are not guaranteed a specific rate of return and they might not even get their investment back. On the other hand, a stockholder might make a huge return on investment if the company in which he or she is invested skyrockets. A bondholder does not share in that possibility. Stocks are riskier investments than bonds, but offer the possibility of higher returns.

When Do You Want Bonds in Your Portfolio?

There are three reasons to own bonds:

◆ To meet current income needs. Bonds provide high current income. This is why, as you approach and eventually reach retirement, bonds will play an increasingly important role in your portfolio. You should be able to live off the income they generate when you no longer earn a salary.

◆ To reduce the volatility or risk in your portfolio.

Fiscal Facts

Each of the two world wars occurred just before a major turning point in the history of bond yields. World War I was accompanied by high and rising yields, and so was every earlier great war of modern times. World War II, in contrast, was accompanied by low and declining bond yields. World War II ended one year before bond yields reached their lowest point this century. In 1946, one issue of the long government bond sold yielding only 1.93 percent. (Source: *A History of Interest Rates*, pg. 335)

◆ In the unlikely event of another depression like the one that decimated stock prices between 1929 and 1932, having bonds in your portfolio can cushion the blow when your stocks take a hit.

Let's look an example. Say there are two portfolios: one is invested 100 percent in equities, and the other has 20 percent in bonds that pay 6 percent annual interest and 80 percent in stocks.

Portfolio One (100% Equities)				Portfolio Two (20% Bonds/80% Equities)			
Bond Return	Equity Return	Total Return	Index Nos.	Bond Return	Equity Return	Total Return	Index Nos.
-	+10	+10	+1.010	+6	+10	+9.2	+1.092
-	0	0	+1.10	+6	0	+1.2	+1.105
-	+20	+20	+1.32	+6	+20	+17.2	+1.295
-	–10	–10	+1.188	+6	–10	–6.8	+1.207
-	+30	+30	+1.544	+6	+30	+25.2	+1.511
Total Return		+50				+46	
Average		+10.0%				+9.2%	
Compound Annual		+9.1%				+8.6%	

The portfolio with bonds returns 8.6 percent. The portfolio invested exclusively in stock earns 0.5 percent more (9.1 percent) but it is much more volatile. Is it worth forgoing that small 0.5 percent difference to invest in bonds and have a more stable portfolio—especially as you get closer to retirement age? For many people, the answer is "absolutely!"

How Inflation Erodes Bonds

Bonds are definitely safer than stocks … unless you are in a period of high inflation, that is. When the cost of living is going up rapidly, an all-bond portfolio carries a wipeout risk that makes the gyrations of the stock market look mild.

In 1971, for example, the year-end yield on long-term government bonds was just below 6 percent. Say you invested your entire net worth—$100,000—in these fixed-income securities at that time in order to generate current income. That year, inflation was running at 3.36 percent making your real return 2.64 percent. Now take a look at what happened throughout the remainder of the decade:

Year	Rate of Inflation	Real, Inflation-Adjusted Value of Your Principal Investment	Nominal Interest Income	Inflation-Adjusted Income (Cumulative from 1971)
		$100,000		
1972	3.41	$ 96,590	$6,000	$5,795
1973	8.80	$ 88,090	$6,000	$5,285
1974	12.20	$ 77,343	$6,000	$4,640
1975	7.01	$ 71,921	$6,000	$4,315
1976	4.81	$ 68,461	$6,000	$4,107
1977	6.77	$ 63,826	$6,000	$3,829
1978	9.03	$ 58,063	$6,000	$3,483
1979	13.31	$ 50,335	$6,000	$3,019
1980	12.40	$ 44,093	$6,000	$2,645
1981	8.94	$ 40,151	$6,000	$2,409

(*Source:* Ibbotson Associates, Inc. Stocks, Bonds, Bills and Inflation® 2004 Yearbook. *All right reserved. Used with permission.*)

By the end of the decade, nearly 60 percent of the real purchasing power of your initial investment had been obliterated! To add insult to injury, the $6,000 you received in interest income each year now only buys you the equivalent of $2,409 worth of goods and services. Although your portfolio still has $100,000 worth of bonds paying you $6,000 per annum, the true economic net worth would be less than it was when you began investing; a terrific tragedy.

Instead you'd much rather own shares of outstanding corporations. Why? Think back to the list of traits exhibited by an excellent business that we discussed in the previous chapter. A good enterprise is capable of passing on cost increases to the customer in the form of a higher selling price without affecting sales. Likewise, because it is not capital intensive, it doesn't have to worry about replacing huge factories that now cost more. The net result is that inflation inflicts far less damage. The moral: an all-bond portfolio can actually be riskier than an all-stock portfolio in real, honest-to-goodness economic terms during periods of high inflation.

Bond Ratings

Bonds are rated by *rating agencies* such as Moody's and Standard and Poor's. Fixed income analysts pour over financial data provided by the issuers of bonds and assign grades to help investors determine the level of risk a bond issue posses. The higher the credit quality, and thus rating, the lower the yield. The reason is simple: Companies that are high-risk have to offer higher interest payments to compensate for the greater probability of default.

Investment Grade	Moody's	Standard and Poor's
Highest Quality	Aaa	AAA
High Quality	Aa	AA
Tier-1 Medium	A-1, A	A
Tier-2 Medium	Baa-1, Baa	BBB
Noninvestment Grade or Junk		
Speculative	Ba	BB
Extremely Speculative	B, Caa	B, CCC, CC
In Default	Ca, C	D

As an individual investor, you should relegate your purchases to the upper levels of investment grade securities. Otherwise, you might find yourself in the unhappy of position of losing your entire investment.

How to Read a Bond Table

Like stocks, bonds are also listed in tables in the financial section of newspapers. Bond tables are useful for two reasons:

- If you own a bond and want to sell it, chances are the price is going to be different than what you paid for it. You need to know how different.

- Most bonds are purchased from the secondary market. The table allows you to research and compare current yields for various issues.

A bond table is a handy way to adjust to changes in bond yields and/or prices. When bonds are first issued, they are priced to sell at *par*, or 100. As they trade, their price moves above or below 100, depending on the demand for the bonds. If a bond's price falls below 100, it is considered to be selling at a *discount*. If it rises above 100, it is selling at a premium. Bonds trade in "32nds"; $\frac{1}{32}$, $\frac{2}{32}$ price movements. For example, in May of 2002, the Treasury sold five-year notes that mature in May, 2007 and pay 4.375 percent interest. By August 1, 2002, the notes were trading at a *premium* price of 104 $\frac{12}{32}$ with a yield of 3.37 percent.

If the yield fell 30 basis points (.30 percent), what would the price of the bond be? Looking in a bond yield book (your broker or banker will have one), you would look down the yield scale to 3.07 percent and then over to 4 years 10 months to maturity to read a price of 105.87. Alternatively, if the yield increased 30 basis points, you would look up to find the price of 103.12. Know the price but want to find the yield? Just reverse the process!

Investor's Idiom _____

Par is the original price of a bond, note or bill. It is also the amount that the security will pay back at maturity and is referred to as "100" (e.g., a $1,000 par value bond that increased in price to $1,100 due to a fall in interest rates would be quoted as "110" in the bond tables). Between issuance and maturity, a fixed-income security may be bought and sold, with its price rising or falling depending on interest rates and other factors. If a bond's price is over 100, the bond is said to be trading at a **premium**. If the price falls below 100, the bond is trading at a **discount**.

Corporate Debt—An Unwise Choice for Small Investors

Corporations issue bonds and notes—both *mortgage* (*secured* debt) and *debentures* (*unsecured* debt)—but these are not wise investments for individual investors. Why not? Well, since you asked so nicely …

- ◆ Corporate debt typically includes call features—a must to avoid. Some corporations also issue a hybrid security called a convertible *debenture*. A convertible claims to give you participation in both the bond market and the stock market. Unfortunately, you just get two watered-down products: (1) a coupon that pays less interest income than a plain old bond and (2) a chance to buy the company's stock that doesn't kick in unless the stock price increases at least 20–25 percent. Avoid convertibles and leave the field to the experts who specialize in these securities.

♦ Most corporations have fluctuating credit ratings. You might buy bonds from a company with a triple AAA rating, only to find that a few years later the company has made some bad business decisions and has had its credit rating downgraded to A or even BBB. Yikes, now you have to worry about whether the company will be able to honor its promise to give you back your principal at maturity.

♦ Outstanding corporate debt typically sells in individual units of 100 bonds ($100,000). Do you want to sink that kind of money into one company's bonds? Not unless you have millions to invest, in which case you don't need this book, you need your own private financial advisor.

Investor's Idiom

A **mortgage bond** is a bond backed by actual collateral, either in the form of real estate or property that can be liquidated in the event of default. Mortgage bonds are also known as **secured bonds**. On the other hand, **debentures** are bonds backed only by the promise of the company to repay; also known as **unsecured bonds**.

♦ Corporate debt is primarily traded over the counter instead of on the New York Stock Exchange or American Stock Exchange, which are more accessible to individual investors. The NYSE might trade around $10 million in bonds on any given day. Amex only does around $750,000. Meanwhile, roughly $100 million a day in corporate bonds is traded in the over-the-counter market. That's a market that small investors don't really have access to, and those bonds aren't quoted in the newspaper bond tables, either.

For all these reasons, corporate bonds are not a good choice for individual investors—meaning you. The higher yields are not worth the added risk and aggravation. Stick with Treasuries and agencies.

Searching for Treasure

Don't feel too bad about staying away from the tantalizing array of corporate debt out there. The U.S. Government issues plenty of options that are much healthier for your portfolio. The best part? Uncle Sam's obligations are considered risk-free. That is, you are always going to get your interest and principal because the debt is backed by the full faith and credit of the United States Government. In practical terms, if the Treasury runs short, the Feds can either turn on the printing presses and print more money or simply raise taxes to increase revenue.

U.S. Government debt is issued by:

- The Treasury Department
- Government and Quasi-Government Agencies

U.S. Treasury debt takes one of three forms:

- Treasury bills (out to one-year maturity)
- Treasury notes (2- to 10-year maturities)
- Treasury bonds (maturities beyond 10 years)

There are also two other forms of Treasury debt:

- Treasury STRIPs are Treasury notes and bonds "stripped" down to their individual coupons and maturity. These are sold at a discount like Treasury bills, and are very useful if you know you will need a sum of money by a certain date (college tuition, for example).

- Treasury debt also appears as inflation-indexed notes and bonds. These include an inflation adjustment, which you get when the bond matures. So if you buy a $10,000 inflation-indexed bond and inflation has risen by 10 percent by the time the bond matures, you'll get your $10,000 principal back plus a $1000 inflation adjustment.

How to Buy Treasuries

Treasury securities are easy to purchase at regular Treasury auctions. You can participate online via Treasury Direct (www.publicdebt.treas.gov/sec/sectrdir.htm). There are weekly T-bill auctions, monthly one-year T-bill auctions, and quarterly Treasury note and bond auctions. Check your local newspaper or *The Wall Street Journal* for advance notices, which usually appear five to seven days before an auction. You can also deal directly with your nearest Federal Reserve Bank or ask your banker or broker to make purchases for you for a small service fee of around $25. The minimum purchase is $1,000 and all bids must be made in $1,000 lots.

Buying Outstanding Treasuries

Besides buying Treasuries at auction, you can also buy outstanding Treasuries on the market. They will be trading either at a discount or a premium (although you will receive your principal back in full at maturity, the par value of a bond will fluctuate in the interim due to changes in interest rates; as rates decrease, bond prices increase and vice versa).

What does this mean to you? Well, a bond or note is selling at a premium because it pays a higher interest rate than current new notes or bonds. So if you buy an outstanding Treasury at a premium, you will get higher interest income than you would from the new Treasuries being auctioned. On the other hand, you don't get all of your principal back when you buy a Treasury that is trading at a premium. Remember, the principal is the amount that the borrower originally borrowed. If you buy a $10,000 Treasury note at a premium, it'll cost more than $10,000, but $10,000 is all you get paid back at maturity.

A discount bond works in just the opposite manner. Let's say you purchase a Treasury bond trading at 96, or $9,600. You'll receive $10,000 at maturity, for a gain of $400. However, you'll get interest income from this note for around $400–$600 less than the current rate. Is it worth it to receive less income in return for greater principal return? That depends on what's more important to you—some people want income, some want a greater return in the long run. If the answer to either question is no, just buy at the auctions.

An Old Favorite: Savings Bonds

Savings bonds—the kind you received from your grandparents when you were a kid—can actually be a great option for the average investor. Like treasuries, savings bonds are backed by the full faith and credit of the United States government.

Patriot Bonds (Formerly EE Savings Bonds)

Following the events of September 11, 2001, EE Savings Bonds were renamed Patriot Bonds. They are purchased for half of their face value (e.g., a $10,000 savings bond will cost you $5,000) and come in denominations of $50, $75, $100, $200, $500, $1,000, $5,000, and $10,000. Patriot Bonds, a type of *zero-coupon bond*, are simple, straight-forward, and absolutely safe. There are some disadvantages, however:

◆ The yield is fixed at 90 percent of a five-year Treasury note, with the yield recalculated every six months. If Treasury note rates fall, so does the rate on your bond. If the five-year Treasury note is yielding 3.25 percent, the Patriot

Bond is yielding 2.925 percent. But if six months later, the Treasury note yield drops to 2¾ percent, your bond starts earning only 2.475 percent. Of course, the yields could go up, too!

- Although you can redeem (cash in) a Patriot Bond after six months, you will pay a three-month interest penalty unless you wait at least five years to redeem it. To avoid the penalty, you have to really plan ahead when using savings bonds for major expenditures such as a college education. In other words, you'll need to stop purchasing the bonds five years before the last college bills come due.

- You also have to deal with a limit of $30,000 face value ($15,000 purchase price) per purchaser, per year.

Patriot savings bonds do have some great advantages:

- You can purchase them with as little as $25.

- They make great gifts from relatives.

- The interest income on an EE savings bond is free of state and local taxes. (Remember, we promised way back in Chapter 9 to get to this!) The federal taxes on interest income are due only when the EE savings bond is redeemed. And, in some instances, there is a tax exclusion if the proceeds are being used for postsecondary education.

Fiscal Facts _____

Patriot Bonds are a type of zero-coupon bond. Instead of sending you your interest payments periodically, the investment is issued at a discount to par. As a result, you received your interest in the form of an appreciation in the price of the bond, rather than interest checks in the mail.

Here's how the exclusion works: first of all, it is limited to tuition and required fees. In this case, it may not be applied to room, board, or books. Second, the bonds must be registered in the name of the taxpayer, not the child, although the child can be named as beneficiary.

In addition, the qualified tuition and fees paid must be equal to or greater than the amount of money received when the bonds are cashed in. If you pay tuition and fees of $5,000 and the bond proceeds are no more than $5,000, you're qualified for the exclusion. If tuition and fees are $4,000 and the bond proceeds are $5,000, you can deduct only that ratio ($4,000 ÷ $5,000 = 80 percent) of the interest income on the bonds (not the principal). Don't you love how confusing the IRS can make things?

Finally, to qualify for the tax exclusion, you have to earn less than the modified AGI limits. Currently, the range of modified adjusted gross income is $89,750–$119,750 for couples filing jointly and $59,850–$74,850 for single filers. In other words, you can get full exclusion if you earn under $89,750, and partial exclusion scaling down to zero once you earn over $119,750. Did you notice that we tucked in the word "modified"?

In this case, modified AGI is AGI plus the interest earned on the redeemed bonds. Ah, the tax code! But wait: there's another neat way to use EE savings bonds for a child's college expense. Buy the bonds in the child's name and file a tax return with the child's Social Security number. Then report the accrued (earned but not received) interest income on the bonds for that year. You won't need to file again and no tax is due unless or until the child's total income exceeds the threshold for taxes owed. If tax is owed, it is at the parent's rate for children under age 14 and at the child's rate at age 14 or older.

It is unfortunate that the regulations on EE savings bonds are so complicated because they have a lot to offer parents saving for college. But that's the Feds for you.

HH Bonds

HH bonds cannot be purchased; they can only be acquired by exchanging your matured EE savings bonds. As of September 1, 2004, you cannot exchange your EE savings bonds for HH bonds. Still, for those of you with these stuffed under your mattress, here's the low-down: series HH bonds are issued at face value in four denominations, $500, $1,000, $5,000 and $10,000 (in other words, if the bond is for $10,000, you pay the full $10,000 for it) and earn interest by a pre-stated formula. They are current-income securities, meaning that the value of the bonds remains constant, never increasing or decreasing. Instead, interest is paid out every six months via direct deposit to your checking or savings account. The rate is locked in for ten years on the day of purchase; currently a measly 1.50 percent. Interest rates are reset on the tenth anniversary of the date of issuance. HH bonds reach final maturity 20 years after they are issued.

I Bonds

Series I bonds are new bonds first issued by the Treasury in September of 1998 that provide built-in inflation protection (remember our discussion about how inflation can erode a bond's value?). The earnings rate of an I bond is a combination of two separate rates: a fixed rate of return and a variable semiannual inflation rate. The fixed rate remains the same throughout the life of the I bond, whereas the semiannual inflation rate is adjusted every six months based on changes in the *Consumer Price Index*. The semiannual inflation rate is combined with the fixed rate to determine the I bond's earnings rate for the next six months.

You must hold I bonds for at least six months to get your original investment and earnings; however, if you cash out before five years, you'll lose three months of interest. With 6-month CDs offering their lowest rates in almost 20 years, I bonds are not a bad parking spot for your savings.

Agency-O-Rama

The Treasury is not the only government agency that issues debt. There are a host of government agency and quasi-agencies (agencies created by an act of Congress, like FNMA) out there borrowing money. Following are some of them:

♦ The Federal National Mortgage Association (known as "Fannie Mae"). FNMA is a quasi-agency. Its debt is an implied (but not a guaranteed) obligation of the federal government. The agency's stock trades publicly on the New York Stock Exchange under the ticker symbol FNM.

Investor's Idiom

Published monthly, the **Consumer Price Index** (CPI) tracks the cost of a basket of goods that includes housing, food, transportation, and more, in an attempt to measure inflation.

♦ Federal Home Loan Mortgage Corp. ("Freddie Mac"). Like Fannie Mae, Freddie Mac is a quasi-agency/private corporation with stock listed on the New York Stock Exchange under the ticker symbol FRE.

♦ Student Loan Marketing Association ("Sallie Mae"). Officially known as SLM Corporation, Sallie Mae is the third and last of the three public/private corporations. Its ticker symbol is SLM.

♦ Government National Mortgage Association ("Ginnie Mae") issues bonds that return both principal and interest, just as you pay your monthly mortgage in a single sum to cover both principal and interest. GNMAs are federally guaranteed. This is the only quasi-agency that enjoys this privilege. "Ginnie Mae" bonds are an example of a class of bonds called mortgage-backed securities (MBS). The MBS is a debt instrument with a pool of real estate loans (perhaps your mortgage included) representing the underlying collateral. As principal and interest payments are paid into the pool, they, in turn, are paid out to GNMA bondholders. Mortgage-backed certificates are issued by banks and insured by private mortgage insurance companies.

♦ Resolution Funding Corporation (RFC). These bonds are guaranteed as to principal, but not interest, and were issued to help resolve the Savings & Loan crisis of the late 1980s/early 1990s.

CDs: A Viable Alternative to Government Debt

If you want the guarantee of the federal government but aren't willing to venture into buying Treasuries, consider your old pal the certificate of deposit. After all, CDs can be purchased in maturities up to 10 years, and for specific sums once you clear the minimum (usually $1,000). The first $100,000 is completely guaranteed by the federal government.

As we mentioned earlier, though, CD rates are currently quite low, so this might be a good time to gather up your courage and visit the Treasury online and learn how to purchase Treasury notes. It's really not that tough, we promise!

Nevertheless, CDs offer an interesting alternative to shorter-maturing government securities. And, if you buy at your local bank, you have the added convenience factor. CD rates tend to be competitive with government paper, especially Treasury bills, but you may need to shop around to determine which bank offers the best deal. The only problem with CDs is the penalty you incur (usually three to six months of interest, depending upon maturity) if you sell prior to maturity. Unlike the new I bonds, they don't offer any protection against inflation.

Municipal Bonds

Municipal bonds are issued by city, county, and state governments. The proceeds of the issue are often used for projects such as building a hospital, facilities for public schools, or improving infrastructure. Unlike corporate bonds, the interest income investors receive from "munis" are free from federal taxes; sometimes, even the state taxes are waived if the investor resides in the state that issued the bonds!

There are two broad categories into which municipal bonds fall—*general obligation* (GO) and *revenue*. The difference arises from the source of repayment. GO munis are backed by the power of an entity to tax whereas revenue bonds rely on the operations of an underlying business such as a hospital or utility.

It is much more difficult to secure information on municipal issues than it is, say, the bonds of General Electric. As a result, you need to do two things:

◆ Examine the credit rating assigned to a municipal bond. Don't even think about buying something that is outside of investment-grade range.

◆ Some municipalities will lower their cost of borrowing by paying for bond insurance. The result is that you—the investor—can buy munis that are guaranteed by a third party; meaning that if the bond issuer defaults, the insurer steps in and foots the bill to ensure that you get your money.

Fiscal Facts

The difference between general obligation and revenue municipal bonds is the source of repayment. GOs rely on the taxing power of the issuer, whereas revenue munis are operations of an enterprise such as a hospital.

Calculating Taxable-Equivalent Yield

There's a quick and easy way to compare the tax-free yields on municipal bonds to those offered by less advantaged issues. Here's the formula:

$$\frac{\text{Tax-Exempt Yield}}{1 - \text{Tax Bracket}}$$

Assume an investor in the 35 percent tax bracket is interested in acquiring a muni that is currently yielding 4.0 percent. Plug this data into the equation.

Step 1. $\dfrac{.04}{1-0.35}$

Step 2. $\dfrac{.04}{0.65}$

Answer = 0.0615, or 6.15 percent

The result tells us that the investor could either acquire a municipal bond yielding 4 percent or a fully-taxable bond yielding 6.15 percent and come out in the exact same financial position once the bill to the IRS had been paid.

In almost all cases, investors that reside in high income tax brackets are going to find munis more attractive than other fixed income securities. Likewise, municipal bonds make absolutely no sense for tax-advantaged institutions such as churches, universities, and other nonprofits.

Money Market Funds

Okay, for you purists out there, we realize that money market funds aren't fixed income investments themselves. Still, because they are invested entirely in fixed-income securities, it makes sense to discuss the topic while we're here.

A money market fund attempts to keep its share price at exactly $1. The funds it receives from investors are placed into short-term, fixed-income securities such as *commercial paper*, Treasury bills with maturities of 30 days or less, and certificates of deposit. The income from these investments is paid out to the fund owners and may or may not be taxable depending upon the type of money market fund chosen.

Investor's Idiom

Commercial paper is an unsecured obligation issued by companies with stellar credit ratings to help meet short-term funding needs. The typical maturity runs from 2 to 270 days. There is a very limited secondary market for commercial paper due to the extremely short maturities.

Although not insured by the FDIC, there is very little risk of loss because the SEC requires the average maturity of the investments held by the fund to be 90 days or less. If you are in-between investments or simply looking for a safe place to park your cash, a money market is an excellent way to get a little extra yield without a substantial increase in risk.

The Least You Need to Know

- ◆ The owner of a bond lends money to a corporation, government, or municipality.

- ◆ In exchange for knowing when (and how much) return you are going to receive, you forgo the chance of extraordinary profits.

- ◆ In high-inflation economic environments, bonds are terrible investments.

- ◆ You can also get a little extra yield without much extra risk by purchasing the bonds of U.S. agencies.

- ◆ For most high-income households, municipal bonds make more sense than their taxable counterparts.

Chapter 13

Preferred Stock: The Hybrid of Wall Street

In This Chapter

◆ Why preferred stock doesn't make sense for individual investors

◆ Cumulative vs. non-cumulative provisions

◆ Participating preferred issues

◆ Convertible preferred stock

Somewhere between common stocks and bonds lies a hybrid known as preferred stock. Although technically equity, preferred issues have many of the characteristics of debt. In this chapter, you learn why these commitments rarely make sense for the individual investor and—for those of you who choose to take the path less traveled—the terms to look for if you do decide to add them to your portfolio.

What Do You Get When You Mix Stocks with Bonds?

First, let's examine three basic characteristics of preferred stock:

- ◆ **Higher Dividends:** The main attraction to preferred stock is that it offers dividends that are substantially higher than those available on the common stock (which may or may not receive any cash distributions). Unlike common dividends, which are declared in nominal per share amounts, preferred dividends are spelled out in a prospectus and normally stated as a percentage of *par value*.

Fiscal Facts

The dividend for a preferred stock is usually stated as a percentage of par value. Put another way, when you are researching preferred stocks, you will notice in the title something like "ABC Company Cumulative 9% Preferred"; this means that the dividend is going to be 9 percent of the stated par value. If, for example, those shares had a $100 par, the dividend would equal $9 annually; a par value $25 would result in a dividend of $2.25.

- ◆ **Liquidation Preference:** In the event of bankruptcy, preferred stockholders rank beneath the bondholders and above the common stockholders. (For example, if there is anything left of the company after the bondholders' claims are satisfied, it will be distributed to the holders of the preferred stock. The common stockholders come last.)

- ◆ **No Residual Right:** In exchange for the higher dividend and liquidation preference, preferred stockholders forgo any residual right to excess profits. After they've received their juicy dividend, they have no further expectation of profit from the success of the enterprise—all of that bounty goes directly to the holders of the common stock.

It Just Doesn't Make Sense

As you can see, the preferred stockholder has all of the drawbacks of bond ownership (no residual right to profits) as well as all of the drawbacks of common stock ownership (subordinate rank in the event of bankruptcy). Why, then, would anyone purchase preferred stock? Believe it or not, it can be a great investment for corporations. To understand why, we must voyage into that Oz-like land of tax law. Here's all you need to know:

- When a corporation *issues* bonds, the interest it pays out to the bondholders is tax-deductible. When it issues shares of stock—whether common or preferred—the dividends are not.

- When a corporation *invests in* the bonds of another corporation, the interest income received is fully taxable. On the other hand, 70 percent of dividends received on equity investments—whether common or preferred—are excluded from the calculation of tax (unless the investor is an insurance company, in which case it can exclude only 59½ percent).

The result is that a corporation would generate higher after-tax rates of return by receiving dividend, rather than interest, income. Therefore, a corporation choosing between a bond and preferred stock issue, each yielding 5 percent respectively, would almost always opt for the latter despite the fact that it was subordinate to the bonds.

Prior to the Bush tax cuts, individual investors paid personal income tax rates on both interest income and dividends received. Now, dividends are taxed at a maximum rate of 15 percent. Absent this recent incentive to invest in equities, it makes more sense to purchase fixed income securities; in addition to being at the top of the list in the event of bankruptcy proceedings, you have a greater chance of receiving your money on time. Believe us—although corporations loathe either scenario, missing a bond payment is a much more serious transgression than passing on a preferred dividend.

Bolstering Capital

The fact that preferred stock is more popular among corporate investors leads to many custom-tailored *private placement* issues created with specific goals and objectives in mind. Say you owned a chain of hotels and were low on cash due to rapid growth-driven expansion. Through a series of events, one of your competitors falls upon hard times and is interested in selling out to a larger concern: a once-in-a-lifetime opportunity. You'd love to jump at the offer but you have some hesitations. First, you don't want to issue bonds and increase your level of outstanding debt. Second, you don't want to issue additional common stock, diluting the ownership of your existing shareholders.

Investor's Idiom

Private placements are investments sold directly to institutional investors such as corporations, insurance groups, pension funds, mutual funds, and investment partnerships. Private placements are not publicly traded and, in many cases, are nontransferable. Unlike public placements, registration with the SEC is not required.

You don't necessarily have to pass on the opportunity. You could approach a cash-rich corporation and offer to create a special class of preferred stock, tailored to the needs of both parties. You receive the proceeds of the sale, providing the capital necessary to complete the acquisition, and the other corporation gets the promise of earning higher rates of return than it would otherwise be possible on its idle cash balances. As you'll see throughout the remainder of the chapter, the myriad of options available for customizing the issue are limited only by the imagination of the participants; cumulative vs. noncumulative, participating vs. nonparticipating, voting vs. nonvoting, convertible vs. nonconvertible, higher penalty-rates in the event of nonpayment of dividends, and mandatory redemption provisions, just to name a few.

It's a Family Affair

Sometimes a company's founding family wants to go public to raise capital and expand the business, but doesn't want to pay out all of the earnings as dividends, slowing growth.

Throughout history, creating a special class of preferred stock has often been a solution to this problem. The new class of preferred shares could have a mandatory annual dividend (such as 5 percent of par) that is payable under all but the most dire circumstances. It could have voting power to elect a set percentage of the Board of Directors. In some cases, it may even be participating.

If you have any stake in a company—common stock, preferred stock, or bonds—you need to be aware of the existence of a capitalization structure, such as the one just described, that may cause the controlling family to have interest divergent with your own. This information isn't likely to be in the annual report. Instead, you'll have to turn to the 10K.

What to Look For in a Preferred Stock

The odds are fairly good that you are neither a corporation, nor a member of a controlling family about to take a company public. That being the case, for those of you who are still interested in acquiring preferred stock for your portfolio, the least we can do is offer you a checklist of things to look for and/or avoid when searching through the minefields. All of these details can be found in the prospectus for the preferred stock issue you are considering. You can get a copy of the prospectus by contacting the Securities and Exchange Commission.

Cumulative vs. Noncumulative

As an investor, you expect to receive your dividends. On rare occasions (for example, a company facing the possibility of missing an interest payment to its bondholders) a Board of Directors may decide to withhold the dividend that would otherwise be paid to the preferred stockholders.

What happens when and if prosperous times return? If your preferred stock is cumulative, the dividend that you did not receive is known as *in arrears.* This means that before dividends can be paid on the common stock, the company must make up all of the past skipped payments to the preferred stockholders. If your shares were noncumulative, you would simply be out of luck; when the Board of Directors passed on the dividend, it was lost to you forever. Tough break!

Investor's Idiom

When a dividend is **in arrears**, it means that it is owed, but not paid, to the preferred stockholders. In order to protect the preferred shares, companies are often prohibited from paying dividends on their common stock until the balance has been paid in full.

It shouldn't be hard to see that the single most important consideration for a preferred stockholder is whether an issue is cumulative or noncumulative. Repeat after us: "I will purchase only cumulative issues." Now, say it again.

Voting Rights

Most of the time, preferred stock has no voting rights. Sometimes, however, the prospectus may contain a provision granting voting rights to the preferred stockholders if dividends are not paid for a specific length of time.

Take Avalon Bay Communities, one of the largest apartment rental real estate investment trusts in the United States. The company has an 8.70% Series H Cumulative Redeemable Preferred Stock. Diving into the prospectus, you find just such a provision:

> "As a holder of Series H Preferred Stock, you will generally have no voting rights except as required by law. However, if we fail to pay dividends on any shares of Series H Preferred Stock for six or more quarterly periods, our Board of Directors will increase the number of directors of Avalon Bay by two. As a holder of Series H Preferred Stock, you will be entitled to vote, separately as

a class with the holders of all other series of preferred stock upon which like voting rights have been conferred and are exercisable, for the election of such two additional directors until we have fully paid all dividends accrued on the shares of Series H Preferred Stock (or until we have declared such full dividends and set aside a sum sufficient for the payment thereof)."

The presence of conditional voting power seems fair and desirable. It can provide you with reasonable assurance that management isn't going to pass on the preferred dividend simply to enlarge the empire.

Redemption Rights

Remember the call provision we discussed back in Chapter 12? When a stock is redeemable at the option of a company, it is never good for the preferred stockholder. In effect, it means that the Board of Directors could decide to cancel your certificates and send you a check in the mail at a predetermined price—even if you didn't want to sell the investment.

Some issues are redeemable at the option of the stockholder. This means that you could force the corporation to repurchase your shares at a previously agreed-upon price, most often during a small window of time every few years. These are almost always good for you. In effect, it can establish a floor to the stock.

Participating Provisions

Remember when we told you that preferred stock has no residual right to excess profits generated above its fixed dividends? That was true ... unless, of course, the issue contains a participating provision!

Participating provisions allow the preferred stockholders to receive extra dividends, based upon a formula spelled out in the prospectus, when and if the dividend on the common stock exceeds a certain level. This potential for additional income is going to cause the preferred stock price to fluctuate far more than it would otherwise. Don't worry, though. As long as the fixed dividend is paid, it tends to act as a stabilizing force (unlike common stock, it's not probable your preferred stock would lose 70 percent of its value if the dividend is still being, and expected to remain, paid).

Adjustable Rate Provisions

Some preferred stock issues have adjustable rate provisions. Instead of a fixed dividend expressed as a percentage of par, the payout is determined by the movement in an established benchmark, such as U.S. Treasuries.

Unlike traditional preferred stock, the dynamic nature of the dividend payout on adjustable rate issues generally results in a relatively narrow range of market prices. Although this is good for you, it doesn't overcome one big shortcoming—you don't know how much you are going to receive in dividends each year! When investing for current income, you need to know how much cash you can expect to have in hand.

Riding with the Top Down: Convertible Preferred Stock

An entirely different beast altogether, convertible preferred stock offers the owner the option to convert their preferred stake into shares of common stock. The terms of conversion are determined at the time of issuance and are carefully spelled out in the prospectus. Consider the following hypothetical scenario:

> To raise capital, my company issued shares of $100 par value, 5 percent convertible preferred stock with the right to convert the security into 4 shares of common stock at $25 per share; at the time, my common stock was trading at $15 per share. By offering you the conversion privilege, I was able to get away with paying you a dividend that most investors would have otherwise rejected as insufficient.

> Upon issuance, the conversion privilege has little or no value (why would you convert a $100 preferred stock into 4 shares of common stock, effectively paying $25, when the current market price is only $15?). Instead, you hold your position because you are interested in the $5 annual per share dividend. The potential to profit from a move in the common stock without the associated risk is simply icing on the proverbial cake.

> A few years pass and the price of my common stock has increased to $40. Now, the conversion right offers some real gravy! An *arbitrager* could purchase shares of the preferred stock on the open market, convert them, and instantly experience a profit of $15 per share ($40 per share selling price – $25 per share cost = $15 per share profit). Due to the basic law of supply and demand, the resulting buying frenzy will cause the market price of the preferred stock to rise, say, to $160 per share. Here you are, sitting on your original shares, with a $5 annual dividend arriving in the mail every year and a $60 unrealized capital gain due to the conversion feature. Life is sweet.

There's only one problem. You originally purchased your shares strictly for investment purposes—that is, you wanted current income in the most old-fashion of ways. Your shares, which originally yielded 5 percent ($5 annual dividend divided by $100 per-share market value) now only yield 3.125 percent ($5 dividend divided by $160 market price) thanks to the conversion-driven increase in the market value!

Had you purchased your position before the conversion boom, you would be fine in the event of a collapse in the underlying common stock. Your investment would return to its former price and you would continue to receive your dividend check in the mail. Had you purchased the shares after the price contained some sort of reflection of the conversion privilege, however, you would have effectively been speculating in the common stock! The only redeeming factor is that the presence of the preferred dividend, in most cases, establishes a practical floor that protects you from losing everything.

There are portfolio managers who spend their entire lives specializing in nothing but convertible arbitrage. This is a field dominated by specialists. For those of you who insist on playing in this sandbox, remember that arrogance can be financially ruinous; seek the advice of professionals.

The Least You Need to Know

- Preferred stocks often make more sense for corporate investors than for individuals.

- Preferred dividends are usually expressed as a percentage of par value.

- Never invest in a noncumulative preferred stock.

- Check for the existence of capitalization structures that may cause the interests of a founding family or other entity to diverge with your own.

- Leave convertible issues to the pros.

Chapter 14

Navigating the Mutual Fund Universe

In This Chapter

- The difference between open-end and closed-end funds
- Avoiding unnecessary fees and expenses
- How to pick a winning fund
- The benefits of index funds
- Why you shouldn't invest in bond funds

If you were to make a list of growth businesses for the 1990s, you'd have to place the mutual funds business at or close to the top. Although the first mutual funds were created before the 1929 stock market crash, funds have truly exploded in popularity in the last 15 years.

Why did they become so popular? There are a few reasons:

- Mutual funds have become the product of choice for 401(k) plans.
- Some mutual fund firms have developed enough critical mass to justify advertising on—gasp!—television during prime time, reaching all those folks who probably have a little extra cash to burn.

◆ Some mutual fund managers have become cult figures who are frequently quoted and interviewed in major publications nationwide.

◆ With the downturn in the stock market in the late 1990s and the more recent turmoil, individual investors who got burned by holding only a few stocks are realizing that mutual funds offer much wider diversification than they could achieve on their own. Such diversification reduces the risk of investing in just one or several stocks.

What Exactly Are Mutual Funds?

A mutual fund is a company that invests on behalf of customers. The "customers" may be individual investors like you, or even big companies. Either way, the mutual fund pools the money it collects and manages it with investment objectives that are carefully spelled out in a document called the *prospectus*.

Investor's Idiom

A **prospectus** is a legal document sent out to potential investors. It describes a fund's objectives, strategies, risks, and other pertinent data designed to help an individual determine if the fund is right for his or her personal needs.

For example, one fund might invest only in technology stocks. Another might invest in small, emerging companies; another in government securities, or in corporate bonds. There are funds that mimic the S&P 500 index or other indices; these are passively, not actively, managed—meaning that the fund's managers do very little. When you buy "shares" in a mutual fund, you own a piece of its investments proportional to the amount you've invested. Because the mutual fund is investing millions of dollars, it can develop a diversified portfolio far beyond anything you could likely afford to create by yourself.

Open-End and Closed-End Funds

All mutual funds are registered with the Securities and Exchange Commission (SEC) under the Investment Advisers Act of 1940. Most mutual funds are open-ended. This means that they are always open to accepting more deposits from more customers and can continue to grow in size with no limit to asset size. Some funds are closed, meaning they accept no more deposits after their initial offering. Closed-end funds only sell a fixed number of shares—similar to a corporation. And, like many corporations' shares, closed-end funds are primarily listed and traded on the New York Stock Exchange or the American Stock Exchange. Closed-end funds only hold around 2 to 3 percent of the total assets invested in mutual funds.

One important distinction is between a fund that is "closed" and a closed-end fund. Sometimes, a fund becomes so successful that the portfolio manager will choose to "close" the fund to new investors. This means that, unless you already had shares before a predetermined cut-off date, you cannot invest in the fund. Why is this done? Performance. In money management, the more capital you have under your control, the harder it is to beat the market (imagine trying to allocate $30 billion! Suddenly, that brilliant little company with a market capitalization of $250 million simply isn't an option—even if stock doubled, it would barely affect your bottom line by a fraction of a percent). Other times, portfolio managers will close a fund if they don't see any attractive opportunities, only to open it back up again later.

Investor's Idiom

Net asset value (NAV) is the dollar value of all the marketable securities owned by a mutual fund, less expenses, and divided by the number of the fund's shares outstanding. When you want to buy shares in an open-end mutual fund, the price you will pay is based on the net asset value. Because the shares of a closed-end fund trade on the market, however, its share price may differ from its NAV.

You can buy shares in a mutual fund by contacting its distributor. The price you'll pay for shares is based on the net asset value that day, provided your order is received and accepted before the close of business (currently 4 P.M.). Orders received after 4 P.M. are priced at the next day's *net asset value (NAV)* figure.

With a closed-end fund, though, differences can develop between a share's net asset value and its market price because shareholders are competing to buy a fixed number of shares. If the shares are selling above the net asset value, they are selling at a "premium." In contrast, shares trading below NAV are said to be selling at a "discount." Some closed-end funds sell at a discount of 20 percent or greater.

If you buy shares in a fund that's selling at a hefty discount and later the fund's share price bounces back, you could make a tidy profit. So if you are interested in closed-end funds:

- ◆ Stick with discounts.
- ◆ Study the historical discount range to determine whether the current price is at the top, middle, or low end.

Why would a fund choose to be closed rather than open? Fund managers are concerned with sell-offs that could be triggered by bad news or other events. For this reason, emerging market equity funds, specialized equity funds, and municipal bond (especially state-specific) funds tend to be set up as closed-end funds because holders of the shares who wish to sell don't turn to the fund, but to the market. This protects managers from having to raise the money to buy back shares in the event of a sell-off.

Crash Alert _____

Sometimes closed-end funds become open-end funds, thereby eliminating the discount that may have made them an attractive buy in the first place. You can check the current premium or discount by looking in the Monday *Wall Street Journal* (Section C near the end), and also in the Sunday *New York Times* "Money & Business" section (again, near the end).

Avoid Load Funds

Do you simply pay the NAV times the number of shares you want to purchase when you buy shares in an open-end mutual fund? Not always. Some funds deduct a sales charge from your principal; this is referred to as a "front-end load." Funds that charge this fee are called "load" funds. Loads currently make up 5.0 to 5.5 percent of your investment and go to whomever sold you the fund (your broker, for example); they do not go to the fund itself. Funds that do not charge this fee are called "no load" funds—and they are a much better deal. Here is a simple example of how front-end load can hurt your investment. Let's say you purchase $10,000 of a fund with a NAV of $10.00 and a 5 percent load:

	Load Fund	No Load Fund
Principal Amount	$10,000	$10,000
Less Sales Commission	$500	$0
Net Available	$9,500	$10,000
Net Asset Value	$10	$10
Number of Shares	950	1,000

If you buy the load fund, you lose $500, or 5 percent, of your principal before it even has a chance to work for you! Over time, the result can be millions of dollars in forgone wealth.

Back-End Loads and 12b-1 Fees

Some funds also charge you when you redeem (sell) your shares. This charge is referred to as back-end or back-door load. It is also called a deferred sales charge. The intent here is to penalize investors who make frequent fund purchases and sales.

Back-end loads may run as high as 6 to 7 percent of the amount you sell in the first year, scaling down to zero by, say, the seventh year. This charge, if applicable, is deducted from your gross proceeds when you make the sale. Finally, many funds charge a shareholding servicing fee, often referred to as a 12b-1 fee. This fee, limited to .25 percent, is used as an inducement to brokers who have helped or may help sell fund shares. It is vital that you learn before purchasing shares in a fund whether it charges front- or back-end load, and/or a 12b-1 fee. It's your money, after all! Simply ask your broker, call the fund company, or request a prospectus.

Index and Tax-Advantaged Funds

If you can shelter all the dollars you want to invest in IRAs and 401(k)s, great. But if you put some of your money directly into equity mutual funds without the shelter of an IRA, you will have to pay taxes on any gains the fund makes, even if you immediately reinvest them back into the fund. To avoid this situation, you can limit your mutual fund holdings to one of two types of stock funds—index funds and tax-advantaged funds:

♦ Index funds mimic the behavior of stocks in a particular *index* (such as the S&P 500). Because there are few trades, few capital gains are generated, meaning a lower tax bill for you. The irony is that most actively managed mutual funds (the "smart money") fail to beat low-cost index funds (the "dumb money") over long periods of time! The oldest, largest, and least expensive fund is the Vanguard Index 500, which mimics the S&P 500 Index. You can contact Vanguard at 1-800-662-7447.

Investor's Idiom

An **index** is merely a list of assets used as a barometer. The Dow Jones Industrial Average, for example, is the most widely recognized index. It is a list of 30 blue-chip stocks selected by the editors of *The Wall Street Journal* (a publication of the Dow Jones Company) price-weighted (that is, a stock that is $50 per-share would have a greater effect on the Dow than a stock that was $30). Other famous indices include the S&P 500, the Wilshire 5000, the Russell 2000, and the NASDAQ composite.

◆ Tax-advantaged funds make a conscious effort to minimize taxes by minimizing trading. The fund managers don't completely ignore opportunities to improve the portfolio by buying and selling, but they do it as little as possible to avoid generating taxable capital gains. The fund managers will also attempt to offset gains with losses whenever possible—again, to reduce taxes.

Exchange-Traded Funds

In addition to index mutual funds, you can now purchase and hold index funds that trade on an exchange (like closed-end funds). ETFs have grown like crazy since their introduction several years ago. Fund expenses are low, if not lower, than those for index mutual funds, and you can buy or sell at any time during normal trading hours. In contrast, regular mutual fund shares can only be traded after closing prices are reported. They work best, however, in a buy-and-hold mode because you do incur commission costs every time you make a trade. If you can minimize commissions and are not a compulsive trader, ETFs are an excellent choice.

SPDRs

Think healthcare stocks are poised to outperform the broad market? Maybe you like retail, instead. Now, thanks to an ETF known as SPDRs, you can instantly purchase a particular *sector* of the S&P 500. As of this writing, there were nine Select Sector SPDRs available:

SPDR	Symbol
Consumer Discretionary	XLY
Consumer Staples	XLP
Energy	XLE
Financial	XLF
Health Care	XLV
Industrial	XLI
Materials	XLB
Technology	XLK
Utilities	XLU

If you were to purchase the consumer staples SPDR, for example, you would acquire ownership in over 30 separate companies; a lot of diversification with only one commission! As of June 2, 2005, your top ten holdings would consist of:

Investor's Idiom

A **sector** is a subset of the broad market. The financial sector, for example, consists of banks, underwriters, and insurance companies.

Company	Ticker	Percentage
Wal-Mart Stores	WMT	14.33%
Procter & Gamble	PG	12.39%
Altria Group	MO	12.27%
Coca-Cola	KO	8.90%
Pepsi	PEP	4.89%
Gillette	G	4.72%
Walgreen	WAG	4.25%
Anheuser-Busch	BUD	3.35%
Kimberly-Clark	KMB	2.82%
Colgate-Palmolive	CL	2.39%

For more information, visit www.spdrindex.com

iShares

With tiny expense ratios, iShares can be an excellent, low-cost way to achieve instant diversification across numerous asset categories. These ETFs allow you to invest by security (equities, fixed income, or real estate), style (value or growth), individual areas of the market (sector or industry), internationally (by country), or even in precious metals such as gold! Head over to www.ishares.com to check out your options.

HOLDRs: An Alternative to ETFs

Invented by Merrill Lynch, HOLDRs are trust-issued receipts that represent owner-ship of a basket of stocks. There are currently 17 different varieties; biotech, broadband, B2B Internet, Europe 2001, Internet, Internet architecture, Internet infrastructure, market 2000+, oil services, pharmaceuticals, regional banks, retail, semiconductor, software, telecom, utilities, and wireless. There are no management expenses, unlike a mutual fund. Instead, the investor pays an annual custodial fee—currently 8 cents per share—that is waived if dividends are not paid on the underlying stocks.

Here's how it works: you call your broker and purchase a round lot (100 shares) of the Regional Bank Holder (symbol: RKH). The most recent trading price was $135.41 per HOLDR, so your entire investment equals $13,541. According to the most recent 8K form filed with the SEC, here's what you would own:

Name of Company	Ticker	Share Amounts
AmSouth Bancorporation	ASO	12
BB&T Corporation	BBT	10
Bank of America	BAC	27.765
Comerica Incorporated	CMA	5
Fifth Third Bancorp	FITB	13.5
KeyCorp	KEY	13
Marshall & Ilsley Corporation	MI	6
Mellon Financial Corporation	MEL	14
National City Corporation	NCC	18
Northern Trust Corporation	NTRS	7
Piper Jaffray Companies	PJC	0.5683
State Street Corporation	STT	10
SunTrust Banks, Inc.	STI	9
Synovus Financial Corp.	SNV	8
The PNC Financial Services Group, Inc.	PNC	9
US Bancorp	USB	56.83
Wachovia Corporation	WB	41
Wells Fargo & Co.	WFC	24

Had you bought these stocks individually, you would have paid 18 separate commissions!

Another great advantage of HOLDRS is that, unlike an ETF, you can actually take possession of the underlying securities. In exchange for a cancellation fee of $10 per round lot, the HOLDR trustee (the Bank of New York) will un-bundle the stocks. Why would you want to do that? Maybe you need to sell off some assets to pay a tax bill or raise cash for a down payment on a home. You could dispose of the stocks you cared for the least, while retaining those you thought had above-average prospects.

For more information, check out www.holdrs.com.

What's Out There in the Fund Universe?

With nearly 17,000 mutual funds in existence, how can you determine which ones fit your investment needs and objectives? As in most situations, the best thing you can do is turn to the experts. In the world of mutual funds, no one holds a candle to Morningstar.

Founded well over one hundred years ago in a Chicago apartment by a man named Joe Mansueto, Morningstar now reigns supreme in the business of mutual fundranking and analysis. Premium subscribers can use the firm's website (www.morningstar.com) to research individual funds, expense ratios, top holdings, annual turnover statistics, analyst recommendations, minimum investment requirements, and more.

Additionally, our good friends, *The Wall Street Journal*, *Barron's*, Yahoo! Finance, and MarketWatch, participate in the Fund Info Service. Whenever you see a mutual fund listing at one of these sources with a "club" symbol next to it, you can contact a web site or toll-free number to quickly obtain a prospectus, information kit, and an application. The financial information can be downloaded instantly or hardcopy versions can be mailed within 24 hours.

Why Funds Are a Great Investment Option

There are several key reasons why you should consider mutual funds:

- ◆ **Professional Management:** The manager of a given mutual fund may not be more intelligent or luckier than you, but he or she can devote full-time attention to what you can, at best, only give a portion of your time. Also professional investment management has access to research and to market information that would either not be available to you at all or only after a time delay.

In addition, corporate "road shows" stop off at various professional management offices to bring them up to date, but don't expect them to come knocking on your door. Finally, influential Wall Street professionals share their opinions first with large, commission-generating customers—like mutual fund managers.

◆ **Instant Diversification:** We're going to tackle the issue of diversification when we talk about asset allocation in Chapter 21. For now, realize that to achieve even bare-bones diversification on your own at a reasonable cost, you would need several hundred thousand dollars to invest.

Investor's Idiom

There are 100 **basis points** in one percentage point. So 100 basis points = 1 percent.

◆ **Low Costs:** We've pointed out layered fund expenses such as front- and back-end loads and 12b-1 fees. Funds also charge management expense fees that approximate 50 to 75 *basis points* (.50 to .75 percent), and go as high as 75 to 150 basis points for some equity funds. If you stick to no-load funds that keep expenses low, however, you'll find that investing in mutual funds is a great deal cheaper than investing in stocks on your own and paying commissions and transaction costs. Some index mutual funds have expenses as low as 12 basis points (.12 percent). Try topping that!

◆ **Terrific Variety:** Whatever you want, the fund industry offers. Want to invest in Japanese companies? Health care? New Jersey municipal bonds? Indonesian utilities? There's a fund somewhere doing just that.

◆ **Ease and Convenience:** Usually, you can complete your transaction with one phone call and a bit of paperwork. And if you stay within a particular fund family, you can switch funds with no—or at the very least, minimal—expense, over the phone.

These are some of the more significant reasons why mutual funds have reached unparalleled popularity in this country (other than those primetime TV ads). You just have to use your head in making your selections. Start by requesting annual and quarterly reports and prospectuses from funds that interest you. And actually read them before you buy!

How to Pick a Winning Fund

How do you pick a fund? Well, for starters, don't read those glossy financial magazines with the eye-catching headlines screaming from the newsstand about can't-lose mutual funds. Okay, read them if you must, but take a look at who's buying the ads that keep these mags afloat. That's right: mutual funds.

We have a better suggestion. Simply apply the following criteria, and you'll make excellent choices.

- **Performance:** Is the fund rate of return above average for its category for the latest one, three, and five years? Notice that we are not recommending that you buy the funds with the highest return or even the ones in the top 10 percent. We prefer to sacrifice some historical returns for consistency. Don't run out and buy a fund that just hit a home run; it might strike out the year after you buy it. Better to seek funds that consistently hit singles and doubles. If you get consistent above-average returns, you'll get superior results over the long haul.

- **Management:** Make sure that the same team has been managing the fund for at least the last five years. When a fund changes managers, you simply don't know whether the new management will do better or worse. You also may not be able to find out the track record of the new manager.

- **Size:** With index funds, go for the largest size fund because it would (or should) have the lowest expenses. But with actively managed funds, avoid unproven funds of small size, as well as very large, ponderous funds that may lack the flexibility to move from stock to stock or industry to industry as conditions warrant. Just for you, we've arbitrarily selected a range of $250 million to $5 billion. Minimum asset size per category is over $2 billion for the large-cap stock funds, $2 billion for most bond funds, and $500 million for small-cap stock funds.

- **No Load:** You know our feelings on this. We want to start with $1 working for us, not 95¢.

- **Expense Ratios:** We expect the administrator and the investment adviser for the fund to make a profit. But we don't want that green monster called greed to rear its ugly head. Stick with funds that keep expenses under 1.25 percent for equity funds, 0.75 percent for fixed-income funds, and 0.50 percent for lower-yielding fixed-income funds (municipal bond funds and intermediate-term taxable bonds).

The Problem with Bond Funds

Mutual funds are great … for equities, that is. When you buy individual government securities (or municipals) for the bond portion of your portfolio, you should do so directly because, as we see it, there are two problems with bond funds:

◆ Much of the yield is eaten up by management fees.

◆ When you buy into a bond fund, you can't stagger interest income to meet your personal needs the way you can when you buy individual bonds and know their maturity dates. We really like the idea of buying bonds of different maturities so that after you retire, you have interest income coming in every month that matches up with your monthly expenses, as well as annual bond maturities to reinvest as you see fit.

Lifestyle and Tax-Efficient Funds

Two other new types of funds deserve mention. One is the so-called lifestyle fund. This fund allows you to set a target retirement date, and, as you approach that date, the asset allocation automatically shifts to less equity exposure. Be aware that a generic stock/bond ratio might not be appropriate for most investors because the ratio makes assumptions that might not apply to your age or risk tolerance. Nevertheless, the automatic asset allocation rebalancing concept is appealing. Vanguard seems to be the leader at this point.

We are wholeheartedly enthusiastic about a new concept that we discussed earlier for individual investing: so-called tax-efficient (or tax-managed, tax-preferred, and so on) funds. The concept is only several years old, with no more than 40 funds available at present. Once again, Vanguard appears to be the leader.

The Least You Need to Know

◆ Low-cost index funds can be an excellent choice for building a diversified portfolio.

◆ Look for open-end funds that keep expenses low and don't charge load or 12b-1 fees.

- Mutual funds are great for the equity portion of your portfolio, but for the fixed-income component, skip bond funds and buy individual securities.

- Keep an eye out for developments in lifestyle and tax-efficient funds; these could be good buys.

Chapter 15

Real Estate Investment Trusts (REITs)

In This Chapter

- ◆ Advantages of hands-off real estate ownership
- ◆ Why you should avoid mortgage REITs
- ◆ Economic characteristics of different equity REITs
- ◆ Calculating funds from operations

Everyone needs a place to live, and in Chapter 8, we talked about how to put a roof over your head and finance it, too. In this chapter, we take a look at real estate as an investment, not just shelter.

The REIT Stuff

When you own shares in an ordinary corporation, you are taxed twice; once, when the company pays its tax bill, and then again when the after-tax profits are paid out to you in the form of a cash dividend. In 1960, Congress created real estate investment trusts, or REITs; a special type of corporation not subject to this double-taxation.

Why would the folks on Capitol Hill take such action? It was done to encourage individual investors to pool their assets together for property investment, providing the economies of scale that were previously available only to the wealthy.

Crash Alert _____

For years, there was one excellent reason to own real estate—any losses on your properties could be used to offset income and reduce your taxes.

Unfortunately, the 1986 Tax Reform Act took away what was one of the greatest appeals of a real estate investment for a taxable portfolio. The Act rules that real estate losses may be used only to offset other real estate income—not your income from salary or other investments. The Feds strike again.

Although the law governing REITs was tweaked in both 1986 and 1999, there remain four tests that every enterprise must pass in order to qualify for this special tax treatment. According to Ralph Block in *Investing in REITs: Real Estate Investment Trusts*, these are:

◆ The REIT must distribute at least 90 percent of its annual taxable income, excluding capital gains, as dividends to shareholders.

◆ The REIT must have at least 75 percent of its assets invested in real estate, mortgage loans, shares in other REITs, cash, or government securities.

◆ The REIT must derive at least 75 percent of its gross income from rents, mortgage interest, or gains from the sale of real property. And at least 95 percent must come from these sources, together with dividends, interest, and gains from securities sales.

◆ The REIT must have at least 100 shareholders and must have less than 50 percent of the outstanding shares concentrated in the hands of five or fewer shareholders.

Advantages of Investing Through REITS

In addition to the rather attractive tax break afforded to these entities, there are numerous advantages to acquiring property through REITs when compared to direct ownership. These include:

◆ **Professional Management:** Very few people can devote their every waking hour to studying real estate markets and searching for attractive opportunities. A large REIT, however, has the resources necessary to put together a team of dedicated, talented, and seasoned professionals. By purchasing a few shares, you are able to profit from their experience.

Super Strategy

Perhaps the single most important determinant of a REIT's success is the quality of management. Always evaluate the past track record of a management team before committing your capital. Your portfolio will thank you.

◆ **Less Hassle:** Unless you can afford to hire a building or property manager, you're going to have to deal with middle-of-the-night phone calls to fix flooding pipes. For young, passionate, entrepreneurial go-getters with no need for sleep, this isn't a problem. It's not so appealing for the other 99 percent of us! As the owner of a REIT, you can rest assured you will never receive a call from one of your tenants.

◆ **Access to Capital:** Whereas the individual investor is predominately limited to funds secured through personal equity and bank debt, well-managed REITs are able to raise capital from multiple markets at rates and terms far more attractive than would otherwise be possible.

◆ **Ability to Acquire Attractive Properties:** Due to the human and financial capital available to them, REITs are able to undertake substantially larger and potentially more lucrative projects than are available to the average investor.

◆ **Diversified Property Base:** An investor with $100,000 could either acquire a handful of properties on his own or a fraction of thousands of properties in numerous geographic regions through a REIT. This can reduce overall risk insomuch as you are not dependent upon rental income from a few tenants or vulnerable to a housing bubble in a specific market.

◆ **No Need to Use Leverage:** REITs, which are traded just like stock, can be purchased with the cash in your brokerage account; no need to tap your equity or employ *leverage* by taking out huge mortgages. For those of you who are extremely risk adverse or uncomfortable carrying large debt loads, this is a major plus.

Investor's Idiom _____

To buy something on **leverage** means to finance its purchase with debt. When you take a mortgage on a real estate property, you are borrowing money from a bank to buy the property. Leverage is measured by the debt-to-equity ratio:

Debt ÷ Equity = debt-to-equity ratio

As you pay off the mortgage, your debt-to-equity ratio changes because the debt gets smaller and equity (ownership) gets bigger.

- **Quick Liquidation:** Think the real estate market is going to turn? Unlike direct property ownership, REITs can be liquidated in a matter of seconds. All it takes is a quick call to your broker.

- **Higher Yields:** As a result of the Congressionally-mandated payout requirements for special tax status, REITs tend to offer relatively high yields compared to other asset classes. For investors seeking current income, this can be particularly attractive.

- **Lower Correlation to Stocks:** REITs respond to two different stimuli: interest rates and the real estate market. They are considered conservative investments and tend to mimic the bond market (which is driven by interest rates). On the other hand, they are sensitive to trends in their particular real estate market (Atlanta, Georgia vs. San Francisco, California, for example). They are especially sensitive to trends in property values and rental rates. As a result, prices of REITs often run counter to the general stock market. This can help stabilize your portfolio.

- **DRIPs:** Many REITs offer dividend reinvestment programs, just like stocks. As you learned in Chapter 11, this method of investing can help you build a large portfolio at a very low cost.

Types of REITs

There are three categories of REITs:

- **Equity REITs:** These enterprises acquire, manage, renovate, build, and sell real estate. Equity REITs are often focused in a specific type of operation such as retail, apartment complexes, industrial, hotel and resort, and self-storage.

- **Mortgage REITs:** These entities invest primarily in real estate mortgages. We recommend that you exclude mortgage REITs and concentrate on equity and hybrid REITs because the former, for all intents and purposes, serves as a fixed income security. You'd be better off investing in Treasuries.

- **Hybrid REITs:** A blend between equity and mortgage REITs, the hybrid can be an attractive option for your portfolio.

Not All REITs Are Alike

To increase performance, REITs tend to focus on one or two areas of core competence. Some specialize in building residential real estate; some in corporate parks.

Regardless of the specialty in which you invest, there are a few standard questions you should ask yourself when acquiring a REIT.

- What type of property does the REIT own—low, middle, or high income?
- In which geographic markets does the company operate?
  - Are there high barriers to entry that could make it more difficult for competitors to open new units and compete effectively?
  - Are any of those markets currently experiencing a pricing bubble or depression?
  - Will expected changes in interest rates materially affect the results of the business?

Now, let's get into some of the individual specialty REITs you are likely to come across in your research.

Residential

Probably the most familiar and easily understood REITs are those that focus on residential properties such as apartment communities. The most potent danger for companies operating in this market is the potential for overcapacity. Often, during cyclical booms, the number of available units in a given geographic area will increase. As long as economic conditions permit, all players profit. At some point, however, the excess supply will necessitate a lowering of average rental rates in order to maintain high occupancy rates.

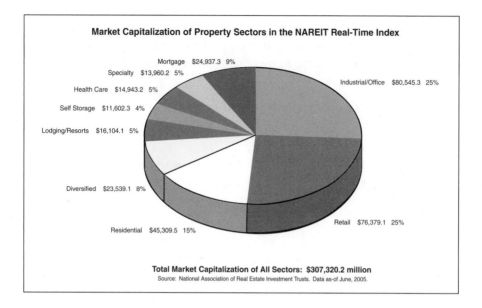

Market Capitalization of Property Sectors in the NAREIT Real-Time Index

Mortgage $24,937.3   9%

Specialty $13,960.2   5%

Health Care $14,943.2   5%

Self Storage $11,602.3   4%

Lodging/Resorts $16,104.1   5%

Diversified $23,539.1   8%

Residential $45,309.5   15%

Industrial/Office $80,545.3   25%

Retail $76,379.1   25%

Total Market Capitalization of All Sectors: $307,320.2 million
Source: National Association of Real Estate Investment Trusts. Data as-of June, 2005.

Retail

A popular endeavor for REITs engaged in retail properties to undertake is the development of shopping malls and centers. One of the attractive characteristics of this specialty is the high barrier to entry caused by the large amounts of capital necessary to fund a project. There also tends to be a first-to-market advantage in that if a town or city with a stable population already has a major mall, it is unlikely a competitor will risk its time and capital competing head-to-head.

Office and Industrial

The office and industrial sector of the real estate market is long-tail in nature, meaning that leases are often locked in for multiple years. During periods of declining rents, this can cost the property owner substantial sums of money as it takes much longer to unwind less-profitable leases than in the residential sector. Office properties tend to be more volatile due to the cyclical nature of the economy. Industrial properties, surprisingly, are far more consistent thanks to higher lease renewal rates.

Self-Storage

The biggest drawback to self-storage REITs is the low barriers to entry; an entrepreneur with a decent amount of capital can afford to build a self-service storage facility, increasing competition and lowering rents. This part of the REIT market tends to be more recession-proof than many of the others.

Hotel and Resort

These REITs are the most vulnerable to economic and geographic risk. When times are bad, people vacation less, business travel falls, and there is little the owner of a hotel or resort can do to increase occupancy under such conditions.

Health Care

The biggest risk to the owners of hospitals, assisted-living facilities, and nursing homes is not so much geographic or economic (in the middle of a heart attack, a victim is not going to insist upon the hospital the next county over because he finds the accommodations more pleasing), but rather, political. This is because the property owner depends upon the health of the underlying business which is dependent upon Medicare reimbursements.

Funds from Operations

In almost every business, *depreciation* is a very real expense (we'll talk about that concept in-depth throughout Part 4). When purchasing a building, the underlying property is likely to appreciate over extended periods of time and, assuming reasonable maintenance, rents will increase as well, making depreciation less of an economic cost. For that reason, the reported net income figure on the income statement of all REITs is considered by many pros as an insufficient metric of profitability.

Fiscal Facts _____

In real estate, **depreciation** is defined in terms of the minimum useful life of the property. For residential property, the useful life is defined as 27.5 years (or 3.64 percent per year); for all other real estate, the useful life is 39 years (2.56 percent per year). How do we get these numbers? One hundred percent divided by 27.5 = 3.64 percent. And remember, you cannot depreciate the land upon which your residence is built.

How do we deal with the depreciation of the land portion of your real estate investment? Your tax bill should be broken down into an appraised value of the land and an appraised value for "improvements" (or your "structure" or "building"). Take the land dollar sum and divide it into total appraised value to get a percent (e.g., $20,000 ÷ $100,000 = .20, or 20 percent). Multiply your current professionally appraised market value by this percent and deduct it. This is your depreciable value (e.g., $150,000 × .20 = $30,000; less from $150,000 = $120,000 depreciable base).

Instead, you should calculate *funds from operations* by taking net income, adding back in depreciation expense, and backing out the gain on the sale of any properties during the period. Then, you should back out the capital expenditures necessary to maintain the business as-is and the amortization of improvements that do not increase the long-term value of the property.

Super Strategy

When purchasing REITs, you shouldn't focus exclusively on reported net income. Rather, calculate **funds from operations** by taking net income, adding depreciation expense, and backing out the profit from any property sales during the periods, if applicable. After that, subtract the capital expenditures required to maintain the property as well as any amortizations of leasehold improvements that do not increase the value of the asset.

I'll Pass on the Accounting

Those of you who don't want to get into the complexities of accounting should get your hands on Standard and Poor's research. For starters, check out the REITs that are included in the S&P 500 and S&P 400 MidCap indices. Combined with the advice of a trusted financial advisor, it should be a snap to build a real estate portfolio in short order.

REITs Included in the S&P 500

Name	Ticker Symbol
Apartment Investment & Management Co	AIV
Archstone-Smith	ASN
Equity Office Properties Trust	EOP
Equity Residential	EQR
Plum Creek Timber	PCL
ProLogic	PLD
Simon Property Group	SPG

REITs Included in the S&P MidCap 400

Name	Ticker Symbol
AMB Property	AMB
Developers Diversified Realty Corp.	DDR
Highwood Properties	HIW
Hospitality Properties	HPT
Liberty Property Trust	LRY
Mack-Cali Realty	CLI
New Plan	NXL
Rayonier	RYN
Regency Centers	REG
United Dominion Realty Trust	UDR
Weingarten Realty Investors	WRI

Two REITs on the list, Equity Office Properties and Equity Residential, are quite famous because they are run by multibillionaire Sam Zell. Known for buying properties based solely on valuation—not prestige—Zell was a pioneer in the industry. In 1988, he helped Merrill Lynch open the first real estate fund, personally committing 10 percent of the initial $400 million in capital.

Some Additional Resources

To help you further your REIT education, here are some additional resources that can provide valuable insights into accounting, tax, and other considerations.

◆ Green Street Advisors (www.greenstreetadvisors.com): This institutional research firm is the preeminent authority on REITs and other publicly traded real estate securities. Check out the sample reports on the company's site.

◆ Invest in REITs (www.investinreits.com): Free guide to REIT investing, glossary of terms, charts, tables, and other great resources are available from this site.

◆ *Investing in REITs* by Ralph Block (Book): If you own or are considering investing in REITs, you need to read this book! The author systematically explains how to spot excellent REITs, build a diversified portfolio, and factor in economic vulnerabilities and accounting considerations into your analysis.

◆ National Association of Real Estate Investment Trusts: NAREIT is a great source of cold, hard statistical data on the industry. (www.nareit.com)

Other Types of Real Estate Ownership

As you can see, a REIT is as far removed from the day-to-day management as you can get and still retain the basic benefits of real estate investing. More hands-on types of investment in real estate include:

◆ **Single ownership:** You and you alone.

◆ **Partnership:** A way to finance the purchase of larger, more expensive buildings. Partnerships don't always go smoothly, so be sure you have the right or option to buy a controlling interest.

◆ **Corporation:** Not a good move for the individual investor because you will end up paying taxes at both corporate and individual levels. Also, you lose the tax shelter benefit of deducting any depreciation on your property from your personal income.

◆ **Limited Partnership:** Basically, a limited partnership is comprised of a general partner and a number of limited partners (including you). This form was popular in the 1980s but has dropped in popularity because investors have realized how hard it can be to sell your share in the partnership and get your money back. Liquidity and marketability are drawbacks of limited partnerships. Limited partnerships are also used for energy (oil and gas) investments.

The Least You Need to Know

- By qualifying for REIT status, a corporation can avoid the double-taxation of profits.

- As an asset class, REITs have historically offered higher yields with lower volatility than common stocks.

- Mortgage REITs are essentially fixed-income securities; focus on equity and hybrids instead.

- "Funds from operations" is often a better metric of profitability than reported net income due to the specific economic characteristics of real estate.

Part 4 Basic Financial Statement Analysis

Past the glossy photographs of management and employees in the annual report, you can find the financial statements. Buried in the numbers are the secrets of the enterprise: clues to the efficiency of operations, liquidity, profitability, and cash flow.

You may feel like the figures are Greek now, but by the end of Part 4, you'll understand what to look for, what to avoid, and how you can uncover hidden value by diving below the surface. Prepare to begin your career as a budding security analyst!

Chapter 16

The Income Statement

In This Chapter

- Calculating gross and operating profit margins
- The cost, equity, and consolidation methods of accounting for investments
- Basic and diluted earnings per share
- The importance of other comprehensive income

To choose successful investments, you need to be able to evaluate profitability. To help you, we're going to spend this chapter walking through some of the items most commonly found on the profit and loss statement. We explain what you want to look for and teach you how to calculate a few handy financial ratios to evaluate a company's performance.

Sample Income Statement

Companies are required to disclose certain things on the income statement. Generally, however, there is some leeway with presentation; that's why almost no two income statements look alike. If you've already requested and received some annual reports using the info from Chapter 11, go grab them so you can see for yourself.

For those of you who don't have piles of 10K's and financial reports lying around ... (yet) ... we offer you this sample consolidated income statement for AutoZone.

AutoZone: Consolidated Statement of Income

In Thousands, Except Per Share Data	Aug. 28, 2004	Aug. 28, 2003	Aug. 28, 2002
	(52 Weeks)	*(52 Weeks)*	*(53 Weeks)*
Net Sales	$5,637,025	$5,457,123	$5,325,510
Cost of sales[1]	$2,880,446	$2,942,114	$2,950,123
Operating, selling, general and administrative	$1,757,873	$1,597,212	$1,604,379
Operating profit	$998,706	$917,797	$771,008
Interest expense, net	$92,804	$84,790	$79,860
Income before income taxes	$905,902	$833,007	$691,148
Income taxes	$339,700	$315,403	$263,000
Net income	$566,202	$517,604	$428,148
Weighted average shares for basic EPS	84,993	94,906	104,446
Basic EPS	$6.66	$5.45	$4.10
Diluted EPS	$6.56	$5.34	$4.00

(1)Includes cost of warehouse and delivery expense

Revenue

Revenue, or net sales as it is frequently called on Wall Street, represents the money that was brought into the business. If you are looking at the annual report of Wal-Mart, for example, this is the amount that was rung up at the company's cash registers throughout the world.

Although revenue itself isn't important—profits are—it can be a very important indicator as to the future direction of net income. Barring some sort of decrease in expenses, a company with declining revenue is likely to have a corresponding decline in profits, sooner or later.

Some considerations: for quarterly reports, how do revenues compare with the same quarter in the previous year? For annual reports, how do they compare to last year, five years ago, ten years ago? You are looking for changes or deviations in the normal patterns; both up or down. If you find any, scan the text for explanations. If you aren't satisfied with them, call the company, ask for the investor relations officer (IRO) and introduce yourself as a shareholder with questions. If there is no IRO, or you are still not satisfied, go progressively up the line: treasurer, financial vice president, president. Remember, you are a shareholder, an owner; act like one.

Cost of Goods Sold

Often shorthanded as COGS, this line shows you how much the actual product sold cost the company. For a book publisher, this is going to reflect the cost of paper and ink. At a furniture manufacturer, this would include the cost of wood and nails.

Gross Profit and Gross Profit Margin

Gross profit is equal to revenue minus cost of goods sold. Gross profit margin can be calculated by dividing gross profit into revenue. Both figures are a major indication of manufacturing efficiency.

Is the gross profit margin improving or deteriorating? Compare the most recent results with previous years and quarters. Unless a company has acquired an unrelated business or is changing its product mix, the gross profit margin should not fluctuate significantly. In fact, short of a viable explanation, substantial changes in the historical gross profit margin can be a sign of shady accounting.

Our sample income statement from AutoZone doesn't have gross profit broken out as a separate item. We can calculate it ourselves, though:

	2004	**2003**	**2002**
Net Sales	$5,637,025	$5,457,123	$5,325,510
Cost of Sales	$2,880,446	$2,942,114	$2,950,123
Gross Profit	$2,756,579	$2,515,009	$2,375,387
Gross Profit Margin	0.4890 (48.90%)	0.4609 (46.09%)	0.4460 (44.60%)

The gross profit margin is improving thanks to managerial efficiency. This is a very good sign.

SG&A Expenses

Selling, general, and administrative expenses represent all of the other costs it takes for a company to operate. This includes salaries, utility bills, office supplies, advertising costs, and more.

One thing you want to watch for is an increase in SGA expenses as a percentage of revenues. Such a trend line, spread out over several years, could be a sign that expenses are getting out of control, which does not bode well for future profits. It could also signal an inefficient, bloated management structure.

Research and Development (R&D)

Research and development expenditures are costs associated with new product creation. For some companies, such as an insurance group, this expense is nonexistent.

Fiscal Facts

Sometimes R&D expenses are rolled up into the SG&A expense line, in which case you would need to work your way through the 10K to uncover the details. Other times, it is broken out separately as a line-item on the income statement.

For others, such as technology and drug firms, the level of R&D spending is a critical indicator of future success.

Look to see if R&D is keeping pace with revenues. If it's not, the company may be shortchanging its future to boost current reported earnings. Also look at a company's competitors; if everyone else in the industry is spending 10 percent of sales on research and development while the company you are analyzing only spent 5 percent, the odds are good that, several years down the road, the other companies are going to be larger, more profitable, and have greater market share.

Operating Profit and Operating Profit Margin

Operating profit is calculated by subtracting SG&A expenses from gross profit. Operating profit margin is calculated by dividing operating profit into revenues. Comparing a company's operating profit margin to those of its competitors can give you an idea of how effectively management is controlling expenses. The questions you should ask are the same: how does operating margin compare with the same quarter in the previous year? The last five years? Ten years?

Going back to our sample income statement, you can see that AutoZone breaks out operating profit. We have to calculate operating margin, on the other hand, ourselves:

	2004	2003	2002
Net Sales	$5,637,025	$5,457,123	$5,325,510
Operating profit	$998,706	$917,797	$771,008
Operating Profit Margin	0.1772 (17.72%)	0.1682 (16.82%)	0.1448 (14.48%)

Looking at these numbers, AutoZone's operating margin is improving; very favorable.

Income from Continuing Operations

In the ordinary course of events, companies buy and sell subsidiaries, sometimes for strategic reasons, sometimes because they believe there is a more attractive use for the capital. Income from continuing operations is the amount of money a company generated from the businesses which it currently owns and expects to own for the near future.

Income from Discontinued Operations

Once a company has identified a business it is going to spin off, sell, or shut down, it will track the results separately. This is done so investors will know not to expect those profits (or losses) in future years. The figure displayed on the income statement is shown net of tax.

Nonrecurring vs. Extraordinary Gains and Losses

Nonrecurring events are those that are unusual, but can reasonably be expected to occur as a routine part of operation. For a company that handles volatile chemicals, an explosion or fire may be nonrecurring; it is a possibility, happens every once in a while, but isn't likely in any given year. Nonrecurring events are shown gross of tax, above the line.

Extraordinary items, on the other hand, are those that are highly unusual and not expected to occur again. This can include things like a monetary award from litigation or a manufacturing firm losing a factory due to a natural disaster such as earthquake or flood. Extraordinary items are shown net of tax on the income statement.

It is important to realize that an event that is classified as nonrecurring at one business—the explosion we discussed, for example—can be classified as extraordinary at another; for a company like The Gap or Wal-Mart, an explosion at one of its stores would be completely out of character with the operating nature of the business.

For the most part, extraordinary items should be excluded from your analysis of a company because they are not representative for the potential cash flows from the business. You should factor them in when calculating *average earnings*, which you'll learn about later. This will help you avoid businesses that use *"big bath"* accounting and take large extraordinary charges to clear the way for better earnings in the future.

Investor's Idiom

Sometimes, when management knows the current fiscal year is going to disappoint investors, it will purposefully make the results look *worse* by throwing in every conceivable write-off; clearing out the financial closets, so to speak. Management knows that investors will probably overlook one bad reporting period, but they are hesitant to forgive a string of bad news. By sweeping the deck, the way is cleared for higher earnings in the years immediately following. This unethical accounting maneuver is known as **big bath**.

Minority Interest

One item you're likely to see on the income statement is "minority interest." This occurs when a business accounts for an investment using the *consolidation method*. Don't know what that means? Let's dive, for a moment, into the arcane world of accounting rules. You may want to go get some caffeine to muster up your strength!

When one company invests in another company, there are three ways it can recognize its portion of the profits. Depending upon the operations of the acquiring business, this can have a dramatic influence on the level of reported earnings. The method utilized is determined by the degree of control the investor exercises over the investee.

- ◆ The Fair Value Method

    The fair value method is used when one company invests in another, yet post-transaction, controls less than 20 percent of the voting power. The investment is recorded on the balance sheet at cost. Only dividend income is reported on the acquirers' income statement.

Fiscal Facts _____

The fair value method does not represent economic reality. Imagine, for a moment, that General Electric purchased 4 percent of Coca-Cola's common stock. In 2004, Coke reported a net income of around $4.85 billion. That means that GE is entitled to around $194 million in the profit; because Coke only paid out $2.4 billion in dividends for fiscal 2004, however, GE is only going to be able to report $96 million in income on its income statement!

◆ The Equity Method

The equity method is used when the investor controls between 20 and 50 percent of the voting power of the investee. Under this method, the carrying amount of the investment is subsequently increased by the investor's proportionate share of the profits and decreased by all dividends received.

The result is far more accurate than the fair value method because it recognizes that the acquiring company has earned some sort of return on its investment even if the profits are not paid out as cash dividends.

◆ The Consolidation Method

The consolidation method is used when an investor controls over 50 percent of the investee's voting power. It requires the acquiring company to consolidate *all* of the income, expenses, assets, and liabilities of the acquired company. The portion not owned is subtracted out of the income statement and balance sheet under an item called "minority interest."

Here's an example: Imagine you own a chain of restaurants. McDonald's offers to purchase 80 percent of your common stock, but wants you to retain the other 20 percent personally to give you incentive to grow the business. After the acquisition, McDonald's income statement is going to fully incorporate all of your sales and expenses because the investment fits the criteria for consolidation. It would have a minority interest line to back out the profits that belong to you, the minority owner, because they have no right to those funds. The balance sheet would also contain a liability item that reflected your pro-rated portion of the business assets.

Operating Income Before Taxes

This line reflects a company's profit before Uncle Sam's cut.

For a variety of reasons, a business may have tax credits that will reduce its overall tax expense. Sometimes these arise due to past losses; other times, temporary laws that encourage repatriation of assets from foreign subsidiaries.

When attempting to estimate a company's profitability, it is very important that you examine the footnotes to see if such benefits are temporarily increasing reported earnings. If they are, realize that it is highly likely that earnings will be reduced at some point in the future. Factor it into your investment decision or you may face a rude wakeup call when profit growth fails to meet your expectations.

Net Income

This is the proverbial bottom-line. Net income represents a company's reported after-tax profit. It is the figure upon which earnings per share is based. In an ideal world, you want overall net income that is going to steadily rise in all economic environments.

Some management teams like to tout the fact that they have produced "record" earnings. You need to delve a little deeper to make sure that the claim is really something to be excited about. The reason? Unless all of the profits were paid out as cash dividends, the company had more capital with which to work; retained earnings used to build new factories or stores, hire additional employees, increase advertising, and more. In other words, if a business earning 15 percent on equity retains $10 million and the next year reports an increase in net income of $1.5 million, management has done nothing spectacular.

Earnings per Share

Ultimately, the total net income doesn't matter; rather, earnings per share do. There are two widely used EPS figures—basic and diluted.

Basic EPS

Simple and straight-forward, basic EPS is calculated as:

$$\text{Basic EPS} = \frac{\text{Net Income} - \text{Preferred Dividends}}{\text{Weighted Average Common Shares Outstanding}}$$

Notice that preferred dividends are subtracted from net income. You already know that, although equity, preferred stock has many of the characteristics of debt. Because the dividend payments are not available to the common stockholders, it makes sense to exclude them.

You should never have to do the calculation yourself. Businesses are required to disclose these figures on the face of the income statement.

Crash Alert _____

All of your estimates of profitability should be based upon diluted EPS, not basic EPS.

Diluted EPS

Stock options, convertible bonds, convertible preferred stock … these are all dilutive securities. That means that, if the owner opts to convert them, the corporation often creates new shares. The total number of shares outstanding increases, the reported net income is split among more shares, and you are left with a smaller piece of the pie. You need to somehow factor in the possibility that convertible securities may actually be converted … how do you do it?

The folks at the *FASB* come to the rescue by requiring a company to also disclose diluted EPS. The calculation is more complex so we won't get into it (nor will you ever need to know it); just realize that it is far more accurate than basic EPS because it assumes that all convertible securities that are currently eligible and would dilute EPS *are* converted.

Investor's Idiom _____

The Financial Accounting Standards Board, or **FASB**, is the independent agency responsible for establishing the rules that govern U.S. accounting. The Securities and Exchange Commission requires that these rules, known as Generally Accepted Accounting Principles, or GAAP, be adhered to when a company publishes its financial statements.

The Price to Earnings Ratio (P/E Ratio)

One of the oldest and simplest ways to estimate the relative expensiveness of a stock is to calculate its price to earnings ratio. This is done by dividing the current stock price by the earnings per share. Basically, it tells you how many years it will take for a company to "pay back" the cost of the stock assuming no growth.

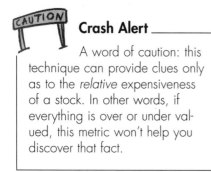

Crash Alert _____

A word of caution: this technique can provide clues only as to the *relative* expensiveness of a stock. In other words, if everything is over or under valued, this metric won't help you discover that fact.

Procter & Gamble, for example, has earnings of $2.60 and a stock price of $54.31. Dividing the latter number into the former, you find that the p/e is 20.88. To get an idea of how expensive P&G was, you would want to calculate the ratio for its competitors, as well.

Earnings Yield

The inverse of the price to earnings ratio is called the earnings yield. It tells you the implied return you are earning on your investment based upon the current stock price assuming no growth.

To calculate earning yield, simply take the number 1 and divide it by the p/e ratio. In Procter & Gamble's case, this works out to 4.789 percent (1 ÷ 20.88 = 0.04789).

Average Earnings

One technique you can utilize to avoid overestimating a company's profitability is to base your valuation on average earnings. Calculate the average earnings, including extraordinary items, for the past five to ten years. If the business is cyclical (e.g., a car manufacturer or an advertising firm) and trading significantly above that figure, this could be a warning sign.

Take a look at this ten-year chart of the Ford Motor Company's reported earnings per share taken from the most recent Standard and Poor's Stock Report for the company (July 30, 2005).

Ford Motor Company

Year	Reported EPS
1995	$3.58
1996	$3.72
1997	$5.62
1998	$17.76
1999	$5.86
2000	$3.59
2001	($3.02)
2002	$0.15
2003	$0.50
2004	$1.80

If you had been an investor in 1998, it looked like the company was trading between 2 and 4 times earnings; that's an implied earnings yield of 25 to 50 percent! Yet the average earnings of $3.96 would have shown you that this bargain wasn't so attractive.

Other Comprehensive Income

Some items bypass the income statement altogether and instead go into a special category called "other comprehensive income." There are three ways this can be displayed, so you're going to have to dig through the 10K:

◆ The company can create a second income statement.

◆ The company can add an "other comprehensive income" section to its standard income statement.

◆ The company can add "other comprehensive income" to the statement of stockholders' equity, which is eventually displayed on the balance sheet.

In the long-run, the items found in this section are just as important to the success of the company as the standard reported earnings. An excellent example is a company like Berkshire Hathaway that makes large investments in the common stock of other businesses. Looking at the most recent annual report, you can see that Berkshire acquired nearly $1.3 billion worth of Coca-Cola stock in the late 1980s. Today, the position is worth around $8.3 billion. That $7 billion gain is very, very real; yet, at no time did it show up on the income statement.

The reason: Until the stock is sold, the profit hasn't been "realized," in industry parlance. Instead, the unrealized gain is added to the other comprehensive income section of the statement of shareholder equity, and, in turn, the balance sheet. At the same time, a liability called "deferred taxes" is added to the balance sheet for the amount of tax that would be owed if the investment was sold.

The point is that if you had looked at Berkshire and attempted to value the business based on reported earnings, you would have ignored the very significant gains that were accruing in the corporate portfolio. At the end of fiscal year 2004, those gains, which included investments in companies such as Wells Fargo, American Express, and Gillette, amounted to over $28 billion!

Back in Chapter 11, you already saw how much value its position in Coca-Cola stock has added to SunTrust over the past 80 years—nearly $2 billion. Yet, once again, the gain would have gone unnoticed unless you had paid attention to the other comprehensive income section.

The Least You Need to Know

- Look for changes in gross and operating profit margins.

- The method used to account for one company's investment in another can affect reported net income.

- Diluted EPS is a more accurate estimate of profitability than basic EPS.

- Make sure earnings aren't being temporarily boosted by finite tax credits.

- Not all gains make it through the income statement; check the 10K for the other comprehensive income section.

Chapter 17

The Balance Sheet

In This Chapter

- ◆ Understanding accounts receivable and inventory turnover
- ◆ Measuring liquidity with the current and quick test ratios
- ◆ Calculating maximum sustainable growth rate
- ◆ Evaluating business economics with ROE and ROA

A balance sheet tells you two main things: what a company *owns*, and what a company *owes*. In this chapter, we teach you how to tell if a business is over-leveraged, evaluate management's use of the company's capital, make sure customers are paying their bills on time, and estimate the maximum sustainable growth rate.

Sample Balance Sheet

Here is a sample balance sheet from Steinway Musical Instruments, an actual company traded on the New York Stock Exchange.

Steinway Musical Instruments, Inc. and Subsidiaries

Consolidated Balance Sheets
(in thousands except share and per share data)

Assets **Current Assets:**	**Dec. 31, 2004**	**Dec. 31, 2003**
Cash	$27,372	$42,283
Accounts receivable	$88,059	$76,403
Inventories	$172,346	$152,029
Prepaid expenses	$5,937	$4,533
Deferred tax asset	$15,047	$13,022
Total Current Assets	$308,761	$288,270
Long Term Assets:		
Property, plant and equipment, net	$102,944	$98,937
Trademarks	$12,325	$10,319
Goodwill	$31,854	$31,665
Other intangibles, net	$5,290	$5,782
Other assets	$16,371	$10,692
Total Assets	**$477,545**	**$445,665**
Liabilities and Stockholders' Equity **Current Liabilities:**		
Current portion of long-term debt	$14,212	$10,638
Accounts payable	$14,789	$11,554
Other current liabilities	$43,892	$39,112
Total Current Liabilities	$72,893	$61,304
Long-Term Liabilities:		
Long-term debt	$208,580	$185,964
Deferred tax liabilities	$26,240	$25,565
Other noncurrent liabilities	$24,279	$20,197
Total Liabilities	**$331,992**	**$293,030**

Stockholders' Equity:		
Class A common stock, $.001 par value, 5,000,000 shares authorized, 477,952 shares issued and outstanding	–	–
Ordinary common stock, $.001 par value, 90,000,000 shares authorized, 7,550,295 and 8,521,392 shares outstanding in 2004 and 2003, respectively	10	10
Additional paid-in capital	$81,129	$74,626
Retained Earnings	$112,587	$74,626
Accumulated other comprehensive loss	(737)	(2,868)
Treasury stock, cost (2,045,450 and 774,000 shares of ordinary common stock in 2004 and 2003, respectively.	(47,436)	(15,853)
Total Stockholders' Equity	$145,553	$152,635
Total Liabilities and Stockholders' Equity	$447,545	$445,665

Current Assets

As you can see, the first group on a balance sheet consists of current assets. These are things that can be converted to cash within a short period of time (one year or less). Current assets are important because they can help you gauge a company's liquidity.

Cash and Cash Equivalents

You already know all about cash and cash equivalents. Corporations invest their excess cash in Treasuries, certificates of deposit, money market funds, commercial paper, and other highly liquid, safe securities to earn additional income. Generally, for an asset to count as a cash equivalent, it has to be virtually without risk and mature within 90 days or less.

High cash balances can drag down *return on equity (ROE)*. This can upset Wall Street analysts who will put pressure on a company to pay out large cash dividends, retire debt, and/or repurchase shares. Be wary of management that, despite constant entreaties, piles up cash and then blows it on over-priced acquisitions.

Short-Term Investments

Investments that do not qualify as cash and cash equivalents (for example, a certificate of deposit that matures in one year) are classified as short-term investments. Companies that want to hang onto excess funds, like Microsoft did several years ago when it amassed $30 billion before paying it out in the form of dividend and share repurchases, often turn to such securities in order to earn a slightly higher yield.

Accounts Receivable

Companies that sell to other businesses don't have cash registers where they ring up transactions. Instead, products are shipped to customers who, in turn, are given a certain number of days to pay the bill. In the interim, the balance that is owed is reflected on the seller's balance sheet on the accounts receivable line.

Things to look for: make sure that accounts receivable as a percentage of sales (on the income statement) is not increasing. Unless there has been a change in the type of business in which the corporation is engaged, this can be a sign that customers aren't paying their bills or that management is offering incentives in the form of more attractive terms to customers to try to shore up a weak pricing environment.

Accounts Receivable Turnover

One way you can measure a company's efficiency is to calculate the accounts receivable turnover, then compare it to competitors. The higher the ratio, the faster the business is converting its A/R to cold, hard cash. That's a good thing!

Let's calculate the accounts receivable turnover for Pepsi as practice. In 2003, the company had accounts receivable of $2.83 billion; in 2004, the number climbed to $2.999 billion. In 2004, net revenues equaled $29.261 billion.

Accounts Receivable Turnover = Sales[1] / (Beginning Receivables + Ending Receivables) ÷ 2

Step 1. Accounts Receivable Turnover = $29.261 billion / ($2.83 billion + $2.999 billion) ÷ 2

Step 2. Accounts Receivable Turnover = $29.261 billion / ($5.829 billion) ÷ 2

Step 3. Accounts Receivable Turnover = $29.261 billion / $2.9145 billion

Step 4. Accounts Receivable Turnover = 10.04

(1)For the most accurate figure, you would want to use credit sales, not total sales. Many corporations don't reveal the separation in their annual reports, however, so the investor is left to use this less accurate variable as a substitute.

Is a turnover of 10.04 good for Pepsi's industry? You can't know until you compare it to the company's major competitors.

Average Days Outstanding

Another handy trick you can use to see if a company's customers are paying it on time is to the divide 365 by the receivable turnover. This will give you the number of days it takes for the average customer to pay its bill.

Using our Pepsi example, you can calculate the average days outstanding as 36.35 (365 ÷ 10.04). If it is company policy for customers to pay within 30 days, this does not bode well; if policy is 45 days, on the other hand, this is a very favorable sign.

Inventory

Inventory levels can say a lot about a business. As an analyst, your primary task is to estimate the value of the inventory. For a business that manufacturers computer processors, $10 million in inventory is going to be worth about half that much in a year due to improvements in technology. In the world of construction, however, cement bags aren't as likely to become obsolete.

Inventory Turnover

Another great measurement of management efficiency is inventory turnover. It allows you to see how fast a company sells its inventory each year. Need the formula? We're happy to oblige!

> Inventory Turnover = Cost of Goods Sold / (Beginning Inventory + Ending Inventory) ÷ 2

Let's use Pepsi's data, once again. According to the most recent annual report, cost of sales in 2004 was $13.406 billion; inventories $1.412 in 2003 and $1.541 billion in 2004. Plug this data into our formula.

Step 1. Inventory Turnover = $13.406 Billion / ($1.412 Billion + $1.541 Billion) ÷ 2

Step 2. Inventory Turnover = $13.406 Billion/ ($2.953 Billion) ÷ 2

Step 3. Inventory Turnover = $13.406 Billion / $1.477 Billion

Inventory Turnover = 9.08

As with the other financial ratios, you can't tell if a company's turnover is good unless you compare it to its competitors.

Inventory Processing Period

Want to find out how many days it takes for the average item in industry to be sold? No problem! Simply divide 365 by the inventory turnover. Going with our previous example, Pepsi has a processing period of 40.198 days (365 ÷ 9.08).

Just like the average days outstanding, you can't know if the result is good or bad until you compare it to the company's competitors. The shorter the processing period, the less capital tied up in the business; products are selling well. A long processing period, on the other hand, can mean that sales are weak; this could portend a drop in income as management is forced to reduce prices to clear out old goods.

Prepaid Expenses

Have you ever cut your rent check early or, perhaps, paid your insurance in advance? Corporations sometimes do the same thing. Until the service is "earned," it is recorded as a current asset under the prepaid expense line of the balance sheet.

Current Liabilities

The current liability section represents all of the debts owed by the company and expected to be paid over the course of the next year.

Accounts Payable

Accounts payable is the opposite of accounts receivable. It is when the company owes another business money for a product it has purchased on credit.

Current Portion of Long-Term Debt

This entry is as straight-forward as it sounds; it is the portion of the long-term debt that is expected to be paid within the next year. Wall Street analysts are interested in this figure because it can help estimate the liquidity position of the business. This is very important for stockholders, who want to ensure that the business has the cash on hand to pay dividends, and for the bondholders, who want their interest payments.

Measuring Liquidity

We've talked about the importance of liquidity, ensuring that a business has cash on hand to carry on operations as usual. Investors, the clever creatures that they are, wanted a quick and easy way to measure this liquidity so they came up with two financial ratios: the current ratio and the quick test ratio.

Fiscal Facts

A rise in accounts payable is not necessarily a bad thing, especially in a retail business. Some businesses are so efficient that they actually sell a product before they have purchased it from their vendor, resulting in large accounts payable and, as you'll see later, negative working capital.

Current Ratio

The current ratio is the easier of the two tests. It is calculated by dividing current assets by current liabilities:

Current Ratio = Current Assets ÷ Current Liabilities

Like almost all financial metrics, a "passing score" depends upon industry. Remember this general rule of thumb: the more liquid the current assets, the less you need to be concerned if the quick ratio is a bit lower than a competitor. In other words, if

Company ABC has a quick ratio of 2, yet the current assets consist almost entirely of cash and cash equivalents, you should feel much more confident than purchasing Company XYZ, in the same industry, with an identical quick ratio but little cash and tons of inventory.

Generally speaking, a ratio of 1 or below is almost always a problem. It can signal the company doesn't have the resources necessary to pay its bills. The notable exceptions, however, are businesses that are so efficient they actually can operate with negative *working capital*. Wal-Mart is the perfect example of just such a company. The company sells the product to the consumer before paying its vendor for it—a huge competitive advantage.

Quick Test Ratio

The quick test (a.k.a. the "acid test") ratio is a more rigorous and intensive version of the current ratio. It is calculated by dividing current assets minus inventory by current liabilities.

Current Ratio = (Current Assets–Inventory) ÷ Current Liabilities

Why exclude the inventory? There is a risk of spoilage and obsolesce—for an ice cream company, the inventory can go bad; at a computer company, it may become obsolete. These risks are very real and, in the event of financial trouble, the company may have to have a fire-sale, offering products at a substantial discount to the recorded value. The quick test ratio protects the investor by building in a margin of safety.

Property, Plant, and Equipment

Large companies sometimes own thousands of acres of land, dozens of factories, and countless machines. The PP&E account, as it is known, reflects the total net *book value* of all of these assets. For a railroad company, for example, this would include real estate and boxcars. For a power utility, it would consist of massive generators.

Investor's Idiom _____

When a company purchases an asset, the cost is added to the PP&E account. Each year, a portion of the asset's value is written off as depreciation expense, which runs through the income statement (some companies tuck it away in the SG&A section, others break it out as a line item).

The cumulative depreciation expense is added to an account called "accumulated depreciation" on the balance sheet. It serves as an offset to the property, plant and equipment account. The difference between the PP&E account and the accumulated depreciation account is known as **book value.** Note that book value and market value—what the asset would be worth if it was sold on the market—can differ materially.

Long-Term Debt

Debts that are not expected to be paid within the next year are classified on the balance sheet as long-term debt. You want to keep an especially watchful eye on the total debt levels over time. Although some leverage can be good for shareholders, especially if a business is capable of generating high returns on capital employed, excessive debt can become so burdensome that it causes even the best businesses to go up in smoke.

Debt to Equity Ratio

There's a great way to evaluate the relative debt level of a company. It's called the debt to equity ratio and it's calculated by dividing a company's long-term debt by common stockholders' equity (we'll talk about shareholders' equity in just a moment).

A "safe" range depends entirely upon the dependability of a company's cash flows. Being a regulated monopoly, a power utility, for example, can count on a relatively stable base of earnings. As a result, utility companies can safely support much, much higher debt levels than could, say, a retailer or a movie studio which is at the mercy of public whim. When in doubt, you know the drill: check the S&P Guides or Value Line for safety recommendations and compare the debt to equity ratio to all of the company's close competitors.

Shareholders' Equity

The shareholders' equity section is calculated by taking total assets and subtracting total liabilities. It is literally the stated "net worth" of a company if everything the company owned could be liquidated at book value and the proceeds paid out to the stockholders.

In a successful business, a large component of shareholders' equity is retained earnings. This figure represents the profits from past years that have been reinvested in the enterprise.

Return on Equity (ROE)

Shareholders' equity is extremely important because it is used in the calculation of a key metric: return on equity. This figure is, perhaps, one of the single most important when analyzing the profitability, capital intensity, and future growth prospects of a company.

> **CAUTION**
>
> **Crash Alert**
>
> If a company routinely repurchases shares, this can result in a reduction in shareholders' equity due to the complexity of accounting rules. Do not automatically assume that decreases are due to losses!

In simplest term, return on equity tells you how much profit a company can generate each year for every $1 the owners have invested in the business. A company with a return on equity of 20 percent spits out $0.20 of profit for every $1 the owners have at work in the business. A business with a return on equity of 10 percent, on the other hand, generates only $0.10 for every $1 invested. An informed investor would rather own the first business because they wouldn't have to tie up so much money in the business; instead, they could pull it out and invest it in other enterprises, compounding their wealth faster.

Return on equity is calculated by taking a company's after-tax net income, subtracting any dividends paid to preferred stockholders, and dividing the resulting figure by the average shareholders' equity for the period.

Maximum Sustainable Growth Rate

A business that retained all of its profits would ultimately grow its book value at a rate equal to the return on equity. Using this fundamental relationship, you can actually gauge a company's maximum sustainable growth rate. Follow this checklist and you'll learn one of the secrets of Wall Street …

1. Check out the net income figure from the income statement. Write it on a sheet of paper. Now, flip through the annual report to the cash flow statement. Look for "dividends paid" under the "Cash Flow from Financing Activities" section (it should be toward the bottom—and don't worry ... we'll get into the cash flow statement in the next chapter). Divide the dividends paid figure by the net income figure to calculate the dividend payout ratio.

2. Take the number "1" and subtract the figure you just calculated in step 1 to calculate the retention ratio.

3. Multiply the company's return on equity (you can find this in the annual report) by the answer you just got in step 2.

Violà! The result is the maximum rate of growth the company can achieve if it continues to operate under similar conditions as the past (e.g., the payout and retention ratios stay the same, the product mix remains similar, and so on). To be safe, you may want to use average earnings and average shareholders' equity over a period of years to smooth out any year-to-year aberrations.

Let's do a practice calculation just to make sure you got it. Pearl Industries, a fictional company, reported a net income of $206 million last year. The business paid out total dividends of $100 million and has a ROE of 22 percent. Calculate the maximum sustainable growth rate.

1. $100 million dividends paid ÷ $206 million net income = 0.4854, or 48.54 percent dividend payout ratio.

2. 1 –0.4854 = 0.5146, or 51.46 percent retention ratio.

3. 0.22 percent ROE × 0.5146 retention ratio = 0.1132, or 11.32 percent maximum sustainable growth rate.

In other words, if you are attempting to value the company, you are going to have to have a really compelling reason to believe the business is going to generate more than 11.32 percent, such as a shift to more profitable product mixes, a decrease in working capital due to managerial efficiencies, or an increase in the retention ratio.

Return on Assets

Any time a company's return on equity is greater than its cost of borrowing, (this is true of a vast majority of businesses) return on equity can be artificially inflated by utilizing a large amount of leverage. For that reason, you want to do a secondary check called return on assets (ROA). Return on assets is calculated by dividing net income by total assets. Think of ROA as the ROE a business would earn if it was debt-free. Today, the average American corporation earns around 14 percent on equity; a stellar business may generate a return on equity of 25 percent. If, however, you found that the business had a ROE of 25 percent and a ROA of 14 percent, it is, inherently, mediocre.

The Least You Need to Know

- ◆ Accounts receivable and inventory turnover can give you an idea of how efficiently management is handling working capital.

- ◆ Exercise caution when investing in a company that has a current and quick test ratio noticeably below industry peers.

- ◆ The safer and more stable a company's profits, the higher the debt to equity ratio it can support.

- ◆ Return on equity tells you how much profit a company generates for every $1 of equity invested in a business.

Chapter 18

The Cash Flow Statement

In This Chapter

- Uncovering the sources of a company's cash
- Gauging management's plans through trends in capital expenditures
- The difference between CFO, CFI, and CFF
- The king of all: free cash flow
- A word on EBITDA

Many analysts believe that the statement of cash flows is the most important. The equivalent of a corporation's check register, it can reveal where the actual cash was generated and spent, both of which can often be buried through accounting maneuvers in the other financial statements. As a result, there is no question that the cash flow statement is the most accurate. Unlike the income statement and balance sheet, there are no estimates involved … you either received (spent) cash or you didn't.

Sample Cash Flow Statement

Of course, we wouldn't want you to begin without actually seeing a real-life example of a cash flow statement. Knock yourself out!

AMERICAN EAGLE OUTFITTERS, NC.
CONSOLIDATED STATEMENTS OF CASH FLOWS

(In thousands)	January 29, 2005	For the Years End January 31, 2004 (Restated)
Operating activities:		
Net income	$213,343	$59,622
Loss form discontinued operations	10,889	23,486
Income from continuing operations	224,232	83,108
Adjustments to reconcile income from continuing operations to net cash provided by operating activities:		
Depreciation an amortization	68,273	59,965
Stock compensation	25,166	1,192
Deferred income taxes	(17,087)	13,008
Tax benefit from exercise of stock options	28,800	674
Other adjustments	2,796	5,999
Changes in assets and liabilities:		
Merchandise inventory	(25,840)	6,681
Accounts and note receivable, including related party	3,878	(9,344)
Prepaid expenses and other	1,918	3,342
Accounts payable	4,466	21,124
Unredeemed stored value cards and gift certificates	7,373	2,725
Deferred lease credits	3,359	5,290
Accrue Liabilities	41,349	21,437
Total adjustments	144,451	132,093
Net cash provided by operating activities from continuing operations	368,683	215,201
Investing activities:		
Capital expenditures	(97,288)	(77,544)
Purchase of investments	(483,083)	(353,486)
Sale of investments	309,203	203,755
Other investing activities	(14)	(1,513)
Net cash used for investing activities from continuing operations	(217,182)	(228,788)
Financing activities:		
Payments on more payable and line of credit	(2,655)	(5,434)
Retirement of note payable and termination of swap agreement	(16,915)	-
Proceeds from borrowings from line of credit	-	-
Repurchase of common stock	-	(689)
Net proceeds from stock options exercised	57,533	1,139
Payment of cash dividend	(8,841)	-
Net cash provided by (used for) financing activities from continuing operations	29,122	(4,984)
Effect of exchange rates on cash	1,903	1,055
Net cash provided by (used for) discontinued operations	9,448	(11,618)
Net increase (decrease) in cash and cash equivalents	137,974	(29,134)
Cash and cash equivalents_beginning period	137,087	166,221
Cash and cash equivalents-end of period	$275,061	$137,087

The Sections of the Cash Flow Statement

There are three sections of the cash flow statement: Cash Flow from Operations, Cash Flow from Investing Activities, and Cash Flow from Financing Activities. Each has a different purpose and, as such, we examine them individually.

Cash Flows from Operations (CFO)

The first section of the cash flow statement is called cash flow from operations, or CFO. It is vitally important as it reveals the greenbacks generated by a company's core business. This is of paramount importance—even the wealthiest corporation can exist only on stored up capital for so long before the well runs dry!

The CFO section starts with the reported net income; the same one found on the income statement. It then adds back depreciation of property, plant, and equipment. Recall from the last chapter that an asset is acquired and the cost is then spread out and run through the income statement as depreciation expense over the course of several years. The result of this accounting treatment is that some analysts disregard the charge as they do not consider it a real capital outlay. Common sense tells you that the cash has already been spent; depreciation is merely the delayed recording of that outlay.

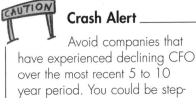

Crash Alert

Avoid companies that have experienced declining CFO over the most recent 5 to 10 year period. You could be stepping into a dying industry, such as the investor who bought shares of horse and buggy manufacturers a century ago.

You want to pay particular attention to depreciation as a percentage of net income and gross property, plant, and equipment. Sometimes, if a business is in trouble, it will take moves to reduce the level of depreciation expense. These tests will help you notice large changes in historical patterns.

Next, increases (decreases) in the asset accounts such as inventory, accounts receivable, and so on, are subtracted (added). The reason: if inventories increased, the increase was paid for out of cash. Therefore, it must be subtracted from the net income figure.

The result, after all of these changes, is the title-line, cash flow from operations. This figure represents the cold, hard, piles of cash that were generated by the business. In using this section to evaluate a company's health, there are two questions you should ask yourself:

1. Has cash flow from operations decreased noticeably over the past three to five years, while net income simultaneously increased? If so, there may be a problem. The quality of earnings could be suspect (note, if there have been large share repurchases, you need not be concerned; the rise in EPS would be the natural result of fewer shares outstanding).

2. Are inventory or accounts receivable levels decreasing, resulting in cash being added back into the calculation of CFO? If so, find out how and why the business is reducing its working capital.

Cash Flows from Investing Activities (CFI)

This section covers the purchase of property, plant, and equipment, the acquisition of other businesses, proceeds from the sale of subsidiaries, and other investing activities. Here's what you want to look for:

♦ What is the trend level for *capital expenditures*? Because this figure includes everything from the purchase of buildings to machinery, a falling line means that the management team reinvested fewer earnings into the core businesses. This can last for a while, but if it persists indefinitely, operating performance will eventually be affected.

Fiscal Facts

The trend in capital expenditures can give you an important insight into management's thinking. If you're investing in a hot retailer that is growing by opening new stores hand-over-fist, yet you notice that capital expenditures have nose-dived in the last two years, it probably means that the rate of new store openings is going to fall in the future.

♦ If acquisitions are broken out as a separate line, look for a trend. Pay particular attention to management's words in the letter to shareholders, press releases, and so on; if they tell you they are committed to returning capital to you in the form of dividends, share repurchases, or to strengthen the business by paying down debt yet you see large acquisitions, your executives may be more interested in enlarging their domain than your net worth.

♦ Do you notice unusually large sales or divestitures of investments or subsidiaries? Sometimes, when the cash flow from operations has weakened, management will sell off investments the business has accumulated in order to
generate funds necessary to carry out its mission. This is a problem because
asset sales are always finite in nature. Unless the executive team has made clear a
plan to restructure the business in its communication with shareholders, exercise
caution. At the very least, call the company and make an inquiry.

Cash Flows from Financing Activities (CFF)

The final section of the cash flow statement is dedicated to cash flows between a company and its creditors and shareholders. Once again, here is a handy list of things to
consider:

♦ **Proceeds from issuance of stock:**
Every time new shares are issued to
raise capital or to fund an acquisition,
your existing percentage ownership of the
business is reduced. This is almost always
bad for you. The lesson? Watch the line
like a hawk. Avoid companies that constantly issue new shares as precious little
of the reward is going to flow to your
bottom line.

Crash Alert

If you notice that a
large amount of cash is being
spent on the repurchase of shares
each year yet find that the actual
number of total outstanding
shares never seems to decline,
weep for fortune lost! The likely
cause? Management is issuing
itself stock options and then
repurchasing shares on the open
market to avoid dilution. Although
this is less of a sin than just issuing new shares willy-nilly, it is still
not ideal for you as a stockholder.

♦ **Proceeds from issuance of debt:** This
tells you how much cash was raised from
the issuance of fixed income securities
such as bonds. In most cases, you probably shouldn't be worried if you see a lot of
activity as long as the debt to equity ratio
on the balance sheet hasn't increased
drastically.

♦ **Repurchase of common stock:** Hallelujah! This is the line that holds special
meaning. As long as the company's common stock isn't overvalued, your portfolio would be well served if a lot of cash was spent here. Look for trends, particularly favorable ones (an increase in the dollar amount spent each year).

◆ **Repayment of debt:** Cash spent on paying down debt is almost always good. Check to see the relationship between debts repaid and proceeds from issuance of debt. If you notice the numbers are roughly similar, the company simply refinanced its existing liabilities—nothing wrong with, nor particularly exciting about, that.

◆ **Dividends paid:** This is the figure you need to calculate the dividend payout and retention ratios we've discussed throughout the book. For investors looking for current cash income, you want to see how the payout fluctuates as a percentage of net income. This can provide a clue as to the safety of the dividends.

Increase or Decrease in Cash and Cash Equivalents

The actual bottom line has very little meaning. Focus, instead, on the individual entries we've discussed thus far.

Free Cash Flow (FCF)

It may surprise you to discover that, despite all of the attention pundits and the nightly news give to reported earnings per share, a lot of financial professionals believe a different figure—free cash flow—is a better indicator of the true economic earnings of a business. Although everyone tends to have his or her favorite adjustments to FCF, most all agree on the basis:

Free Cash Flow = (CFO + Amortization and Depreciation) – Necessary Capital Expenditures

Ideally, you are looking for investments that generate large free cash flow in ever-increasing quantities. For those of you with a penchant for rapidly-expanding businesses that are going to change the world, you are likely going to find that most, at least during the initial phase, tend to be free cash flow negative! That's because sales growth often exceeds the growth in working capital.

A Word on EBITDA

Short for "earnings before interest, depreciation, and amortization," EBITDA became one of the mostly widely-toted financial metrics of the late 1990s. On the inside covers of many annual reports, charts with EBITDA marching skyward were featured. Investors grew excited. Management boasted of record performance. And all the while, there was just one problem … it doesn't represent reality.

Yep. That's right. Somewhere amid all the hoopla, investors forgot that corporations *do* pay interest on debt; they *do* pay for capital expenditures; and even though depreciation is a noncash charge, they *do* pay for items that are written up and subsequently amortized over a longer period of time. Infected with greed, the common and professional investor alike were all to happy to overlook this inconvenient fact, fueling the speculative orgy that resulted in ordinary people with no prior financial background quitting their day jobs to focus on day trading.

Crash Alert

Although EBITDA can be used to track specific trends in capital-intensive industries such as telecom, it should never be used as a substitute for free cash flow because it does not take into account changes in working capital.

Nor is EBITDA a substitute for free cash flow, as some would have you believe. Look at the formula for FCF again and you'll quickly see the reason. It factors in capital expenditures and changes in working capital, whereas the other does not. Any business owner will tell you that your fairy godmother doesn't pay for the stoves you need to operate your restaurant, or the computers you use to track your inventory.

The Least You Need to Know

♦ Examine trends in CFO to evaluate the underlying health of a company's core business.

♦ Pay attention to large acquisitions or changes in the historical level of capital expenditures.

♦ Avoid companies that continually issue new shares of common stock.

♦ Free cash flow is a better indicator of profitability than reported earnings.

♦ In virtually all cases, EBITDA is a useless metric for the average investor.

Chapter 19

The Footnotes

In This Chapter

- ◆ Knowing what your business does
- ◆ Avoid buying into a lawsuit
- ◆ Adding operating leases to long-term debt
- ◆ Relying upon key customers
- ◆ Pension obligations
- ◆ Uncovering stock option expense

Diving into the notes to the financial statements can be an eye-opening experience. There are number of things that the Securities and Exchange Commission (SEC) and Financial Accounting Standards Board (FASB) require companies to disclose here—often buried on page ninety in a tiny font—that you're not going to find anywhere else.

In this chapter, we show you some of the major things you need to research before you consider buying a company's stocks or bonds. We use real-life excerpts from 10K's and annual reports to illustrate each topic.

Prepare yourself. You may not like what you're going to see …

Description of Operations

It is absolutely vital that you know and understand your companies like the back of your hand—how they generate cash, strengths, weaknesses, sales figures, distribution systems, and more. Only by having a grasp on these items can you evaluate management's performance.

Take Coca-Cola, for example. Many people incorrectly assume that, when they go to the grocery store and pick up a pack of Coke, it was the Coca-Cola Company that manufactured and shipped the product there. In reality, Coke creates a concentrate and then sells it to both independent and affiliated bottlers around the world. These bottlers, in turn, mix the concentrate with carbonated water, bottle it, and truck it to your local grocery store. On the other hand, Coca-Cola does directly provide the fountain Coke you enjoy at McDonald's. This distinction may seem small but it is not. An investor thinking about the entire system would suddenly realize that there is a middleman between Coke and the product shelves; as a result, it is extremely important to monitor the relationship between the company and its bottlers.

Legal Proceedings

You want to pay particular attention to the legal proceedings section of the 10K. Most of the time, a corporation is subject to routine litigation that is not expected to have a material impact on operations. Wal-Mart, for example, is sued multiple times each day yet that is not likely to dent the retailing empire.

Other times, a legal entanglement can bring the entire business down (and your investment along with it!). USG Corp. (symbol: USG) is just such a company. At one point, USG traded for only 2 to 4 times earnings, giving it an earnings yield of 50 to 100 percent. Yet dive into the footnotes and you'll find there's a reason: The company is operating in Chapter 11 bankruptcy as a result of asbestos-related liabilities. Take a look at some selected excerpts for yourself:

> **Super Strategy**
>
> There's an old saying on Wall Street, "never buy into a lawsuit." For the average investor, this is prudent advice. Jury verdicts are often a wild card based upon human emotion, not logic.

On June 25, 2001, the Corporation and 10 of its United States subsidiaries (collectively, the "Debtors") filed voluntary petitions for reorganization (the "Filing") under Chapter 11 of the United States Bankruptcy Code in the United States Bankruptcy Court for the District of Delaware (the "Bankruptcy Court"). The Chapter 11 cases of the Debtors have been consolidated for purposes of joint administration as In re: USG Corporation et al. (Case No. 01-2094). This action was taken to resolve asbestos claims in a fair and equitable manner, to protect the long-term value of the Debtors' businesses, and to maintain the Debtors' leadership positions in their markets. The Debtors are operating their businesses as debtors-in-possession subject to the provisions of the United States Bankruptcy Code. These cases do not include any of the Corporation's non-U.S. subsidiaries.

And then later in the 10K:

One of the Corporation's subsidiaries, U.S. Gypsum, is among many defendants in more than 100,000 asbestos lawsuits alleging personal injury or property damage liability. Most of the asbestos lawsuits against U.S. Gypsum seek compensatory and, in many cases, punitive damages for personal injury allegedly resulting from exposure to asbestos-containing products (the "Personal Injury Cases"). Certain of the asbestos lawsuits seek to recover compensatory and, in many cases, punitive damages for costs associated with the maintenance or removal and replacement of asbestos-containing products in buildings (the "Property Damage Cases").

U.S. Gypsum's asbestos liability derives from its sale of certain asbestos-containing products beginning in the late 1920s. In most cases, the products were discontinued or asbestos was removed from the formula by 1972, and no asbestos-containing products were produced after 1978.

The amount of the Debtors' present and future asbestos liabilities is the subject of significant dispute in Debtors' Chapter 11 Cases. If the amount of the Debtors' asbestos liabilities is not resolved through negotiation in the Chapter 11 Cases or addressed by federal legislation, the amount of those liabilities may be determined through litigation proceedings in the Chapter 11 Cases, the outcome of which is speculative.

The result, of course, is that you cannot estimate the value of the company. If the asbestos liabilities are not capped by Congress or resolved in some other equitable fashion, the defendants will likely raid the entire company lock, stock, and barrel, rendering the enterprise worthless. If, on the other hand, a resolution is reached, the company could be worth many times the current share price. There is no certainty and, as a result, you could not include this in your investment operations; it is inherently speculative.

Operating Leases

A lease is an agreement that results in one party gaining access to an asset in exchange for rent payments. As a practical matter, leasing is an extremely popular form of financing. Retail stores lease space in malls across the country. Airlines lease planes.

Under GAAP accounting rules, if a lease effectively transfers ownership of an asset to the lessee, then it is capitalized. In practical terms, that means that the leased property is put on the balance sheet as an asset and subsequently depreciated, similar to if the lessee had purchased the property outright.

Other leases that don't meet the criteria for capitalization are known as "operating leases." The asset, although under the company's control, is not reflected on the balance sheet; the lease payments, although a legally enforceable contract, are not reflected as a liability on the balance sheet. The FASB, however, requires disclosure of operating leases, including the payments due by time period, in the notes to the financial statements.

Why should you care? Leases are very real expenses that, if defaulted upon, have the potential to hurl a company toward a path that ends squarely in bankruptcy court. As a measure of conservatism, you should add the leases to the short and long-term debt shown on the balance sheet, respectively, and then ask yourself if you believe the company can service the adjusted debt load.

Consider American Eagle Outfitters (symbol: AEOS). The specialty retailer has performed extremely well in the last few years. A glance at the balance sheet shows that the business has historically carried little or no long-term debt. A quick dive into the 10K, however, reveals the following:

Leases

The Company leases all store premises, some of our office and distribution facility space, and certain information technology and office equipment. The store leases generally have initial terms of ten years. Most of these store leases provide for base rentals and the payment of a percentage of sales as additional rent when sales exceed specified levels. Additionally, most leases contain construction allowances and/or rent holidays. In recognizing landlord incentives and minimum rent expense, the Company amortizes the charges on a straight line basis over the lease term (including the pre-opening build-out period). These leases are classified as operating leases.

The document goes onto to reveal the future minimum lease obligations:

Fiscal year (in thousands)	Future Minimum Lease Obligations
2005	$135,410
2006	$135,810
2007	$132,950
2008	$129,295
2009	$121,059
Thereafter	$327,896
Total	$982,420

The nearly $1 billion in minimum lease obligations should be added to the long-term debt figure on the balance sheet when you perform your analysis.

Reliance upon Key Customers

You always want to know if a single key customer generates a large percentage of sales and profits. In almost all cases, if such a relationship does exist, it is bad for the shareholders for a number of reasons:

♦ The key customer can put pressure on the company to sell its products at lower prices, hurting margins.

♦ In the event the key customer gets into financial trouble of its own, orders may fall significantly. If the business has utilized leverage in anticipation of the sales provided by this customer, it may be unable to pay its bills.

♦ If the company's smaller customers believe their needs are being put behind the large customer, they may take their business elsewhere, further exasperating the reliance upon the key customer.

 **Crash Alert**

In an ideal world, you wouldn't want a single customer to account for more than 5 percent of sales. A customer base, like your portfolio, should be diversified. Otherwise, the business (and your investment) could be one key contract away from bankruptcy court.

The American Locker Group (symbol: ALGIE) is the perfect example of why key dependence upon a single customer can wreck an otherwise viable enterprise. The company creates "coin-operated, key-only, and electronically controlled" lockers.

In 2004 and 2005, the U.S. Postal Service accounted for more than 50 percent of American Locker's sales. When the contract came up for renewal, the USPS chose to go elsewhere. Instantly, half of the company's cash flow was wiped out; management had to cut $3 million in annual operating expenses. As a result, it shut down its Jamestown, New York, facility and consolidated operations at the Grapevine, Texas, headquarters. Up to 37 positions are going to be eliminated (the company only employs around 154 people!). The stock price fell from a 52-week high of $16.37 to $3.62, destroying over 75 percent of market capitalization.

If you glance at the company's detailed quote data at Yahoo! Finance, it appears as if the business is trading at a price to earnings ratio of 2.34. You, however, know the whole story and would not be seduced into thinking that the business was necessarily undervalued.

Related-Party Transactions

Related-party transactions aren't necessarily bad. Going back to American Eagle Outfitters, it's clear the company has delivered tremendous value to long-term share-holders. Yet a glance at the proxy statement will tell you that Ari Deshe and Jon Diamond, both directors, are married to CEO Jay Schottenstein's daughters.

Some analysts get very concerned about apparent conflicts of interest such as this. We recommend you take each situation on a case-by-case basis and focus on the substance, not form, of things. Deshe and Diamond, for example, both own millions of shares of AEOS common stock, making them and their spouses independently wealthy. Human nature being what it is, it's unlikely that either would take action they believed was going to hurt the stock-holders just to protect their jobs; exactly the reason we suggested you look for companies with directors that own large amounts of the stock.

> **Crash Alert**
>
> If you can't understand a company's footnotes and explanations, they may not *want* you to. In such a case, steer clear.

Pension Obligations

When a company promises to pay a pension to its employees, it sets assets aside that, based upon its calculations, will one day be sufficient to pay the accumulated benefit obligation it has amassed over the years.

Accounting rules being what they are, pension funds can be "overfunded" or "underfunded." Unless you delved into the 10K, you would never know! An overfunded pension is one which has more than sufficient assets to pay all of the promises the company has made to its employees based upon key assumptions (e.g., how long those employees live, the return the assets will earn when invested). An underfunded pension is one that, were the company liquidated today, would not have sufficient assets in the plan to fulfill its obligation to employees. When a pension is underfunded, somewhere along the line the company is going to have to come up with the cash and contribute it to the plan instead of spending it on new stores or paying higher dividends. The perfect example is General Motors. The auto maker has set aside nearly $90 billion for pensions and around another $20 billion for healthcare costs, yet the entire market capitalization of business was $15 billion in May, 2005. These obligations, long ignored by traditional accounting, have effectively transferred all of the benefits of ownership to the employees.

You can't estimate the future cash flows of your business unless you know the status of the pension plan. To give you an idea of how bad things can get, take a look at the 10K of Northwest Airlines (symbol: NWAC) which is teetering on the edge of bankruptcy [emphasis added]:

> Our indebtedness and other obligations, including pension funding liabilities, are substantial.

> We have substantial levels of indebtedness. As of December 31, 2004, we had long-term debt and capital lease obligations, including current maturities, of $8.8 billion. … We also have significant obligations related to operating leases that do not appear on the consolidated balance sheets.

> We also have noncontributory pension plans covering our pilots, other contract employees and salaried employees. Funding obligations under these plans are governed by the Employee Retirement Income Security Act of 1974, as amended ("ERISA"). <u>As of December 31, 2004, our pension plans were underfunded by $3.82 billion, as calculated in accordance with SFAS No. 87, Employers' Accounting for Pensions ("SFAS No. 87").</u> Unless future asset returns exceed plan assumptions, we will have to satisfy the underfunded amounts of the plans through cash contributions over time. The timing and amount of funding requirements also depend upon a number of other factors, including interest rates, asset returns, potential changes in pension legislation, our decision to make voluntary prepayments, applications for and receipt of waivers to reschedule contributions, and changes to pension plan benefits.

These two paragraphs reveal several things:

♦ Not only is the company in debt by $8.8 billion, but it has substantially more in the form of operating leases that aren't reflected in the financial statements. After some more digging, we find that the company has $7.8 billion in operating leases related to aircraft, $1.9 billion in other, nonaircraft operating leases, and $2.6 billion in aircraft commitments.

♦ In addition to these approximately $21 billion obligations, it owes another $3.82 billion to its pension fund!

Would you want to invest in a company that had nearly $25 billion in debt equivalents and lost almost $900 million in fiscal 2004? No! If you had merely glanced at the financial statements, you wouldn't have realized the extent of the problems.

Fiscal Facts _____

Following the U.S. Airways court victory allowing it to eliminate its pension obligation, many airlines have renewed hope. Although this will remove a huge cost burden for the companies, the employees, many of whom worked for the company their entire career, are going to be left holding the bag. This makes it even more important for you to invest. Nothing is certain in this world, not even pensions.

Stock Option Expense

There has been a firestorm of controversy surrounding accounting of stock options. The good news is that the FASB, thanks to the support of Senator Shelby in the United States Congress, is requiring companies to expense stock options on the income statement beginning in 2005. Prior to this decree from on high, some companies voluntarily expensed option awards to employees; most, however, buried the cost in a footnote, far away from the eyes of the average investor.

First, some basics. A corporation gives an employee the right, but not the obligation, to purchase a specific number of company shares at a specified price. Those options become exercisable after a predetermined amount of time has passed. For example, imagine you work for The Walt Disney Company. As part of your compensation package, you are given the right to purchase 1,000 shares of stock at $30 per share. The current stock price is $15 per share. Your options are exercisable after three years.

If, three years later, the stock is trading at $40 per share, you could write the company a check for $30,000 (1,000 shares × $30 purchase price) and then turn around and sell those shares on the open market for $40,000 (1,000 shares x $40 selling price). (Note: In reality, you'd only have to write a check if you wanted to retain ownership of the stock. Otherwise, a financial institution would float you the cash to purchase the shares, immediately sell them, and just send you the proceeds of the difference—$10,000—less fees and commissions.)

Clearly, this transaction does make the owners of the business (that's you) poorer in two ways:

♦ Instead of selling the stock to the employee for $30, the company could have gone and issued those shares directly to the public for $40. The spread pocketed by the employee ($10,000) would have gone directly into the corporate coffers.

♦ If new shares are issued, your equity ownership has been diluted. You are now entitled to a smaller portion of the profit. This can actually make a good business an unattractive investment; there are some companies that have potential stock option dilution amounting to 20, 30, or 40+ percent of the business! Absolute absurdity! Run from such Machiavellian management.

You can learn a lot by examining the range of exercise prices and the weighted-average remaining contractual life of the options that have been awarded to employees. Make sure management isn't setting the bar too low; the exercise price should be above the current stock price.

The Least You Need to Know

♦ Know the sources of your investment's cash generators.

♦ Don't buy into a lawsuit that threatens to wipe out the firm.

♦ Add minimum payments due under operating leases to total debt when calculating liquidity and solvency.

♦ Avoid companies with large, underfunded pensions.

♦ Examine stock option activity to ensure management is being reasonable; it says a lot about how they view and treat you, the owner.

Part 5 — Fundamental Investing Strategies

In the 1989 Oscar-winning film *Wall Street*, Charlie Sheen's character, Bud, is told by co-worker Lou Mannheim, "Stick to the fundamentals, that's how IBM and Hilton were built … good things sometimes take time." Later, shortly before Bud's downfall, Lou gives him a final warning, "Remember there're no short cuts son, quick buck artists come and go with every bull market but the steady players make it through the bear markets." Hear, hear!

In this part of the book, we're going to get down to the fundamentals of constructing and measuring your portfolio so that you, too, can make it through bad times. You'll learn how to always incorporate Ben Graham's "margin of safety," the importance of diversification and asset allocation, how to calculate your investment performance, evaluate your financial advisor, and ways to reduce your tax bill.

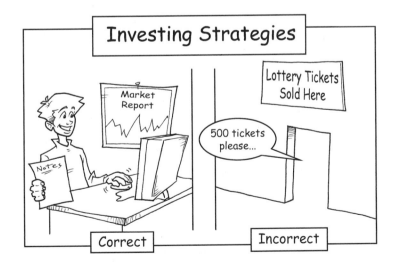

Chapter 20

Always Let Price Be Your Guide

In This Chapter

- ◆ Making price-based decisions
- ◆ Ben Graham's margin of safety
- ◆ Reducing risk through dollar cost averaging
- ◆ Increasing returns by reducing expenses
- ◆ How to think about a falling stock market

Investors often make the mistake of asking, "Is company XYZ a good investment?" Instead, the question should be, "Is company XYZ a good investment *at this price*?" That distinction can mean the difference between average results and a market-beating record.

Price Determines Results

Imagine you are the head of an investment group with $100 million in capital. One day, an investment banker walks into your office and presents you with the opportunity to purchase one of two hotels (assume for the sake of simplicity that both have comparable returns on equity and neither will grow):

♦ Hotel A is a premier property with an illustrious client base, five-star service, unparalleled accommodations, world-renowned chefs, and a stellar reputation. Each year, the business has a net income of $5 million. You have an opportunity to purchase the corporation for $62.5 million.

♦ Hotel B is a chain of large budget hotels that offer standard, comfortable accommodations to business travelers. The name is not recognized outside of the geographic region in which the company operates. Each year, the business has a net income of $1 million. You have the opportunity to purchase the corporation for $7 million.

Fiscal Facts

Legendary investor Peter Lynch managed the Fidelity Magellan Fund between 1977 and 1990. During this time, Lynch, who was more apt to invest in boring companies such as funeral homes or sewage treatment plants rather than high-tech, high-fliers, compiled a record that puts him squarely in the all-star ranks of money management by returning more than 2,700 percent to investors during his tenure. He retired at the young age of 46.

You quickly calculate that Hotel A will return 8 percent per annum, whereas Hotel B will return 14.28 percent. Although the second hotel has far less prestige—to paraphrase famed mutual fund manager *Peter Lynch*—"the money spends the same." Clearly, the better choice is Hotel B.

Yet on a daily basis, investors the world over make the mistake of immediately purchasing shares of the companies perceived to be "the best" regardless of price. It is true that you should pay up for an excellent business because the economics of the enterprise make it likely to generate cash flows at ever-increasing rates. The secret is not to pay an unlimited sum. It is simple math. If you pay too much for a business—even if it is growing at above-average rates—you are likely to have below-average performance because no asset can indefinitely grow faster than its internal rate of compounding—a basic law of economics.

Valuing a Business

How much should you pay for a business? That depends upon your required rate of return; your "hurdle rate." This should be determined by taking the current rate on the longest-term obligation of the U.S. government, adding an inflation premium based upon your outlook of prices in the future, and topping it off with a risk premium based upon the variability of the underlying cash flows.

You need to estimate how much profit a business is going to generate in the coming years and discount it back to the present using your hurdle rate. The thing is, as you figured out in Part 4, you can't accept the reported net income figure as economic truth. Some analysts believe free cash flow represents a more accurate measurement of earnings; others make their own adjustments to come up with an amount that they believe could be taken out of the business as dividends without affecting the health of the enterprise. The decision is ultimately your own.

Now, plug the formula into the following dividend discount model:

$$\frac{1}{K-G}$$

1 = Your adjusted earnings per share (EPS) figure

K = Your minimum acceptable required rate of return

G = The growth rate of EPS

Say you expect Company ABC to generate $2.00 EPS, grow at 8 percent per annum thereafter, and your required rate of return is 15 percent (based upon 4.22 percent Treasury, a 3 percent expected inflation premium, and a risk topper). Plug that data into the model to calculate the maximum price you could pay.

$$\frac{\$2.00}{.15 - .08}$$

or

$$\frac{\$2.00}{.07}$$

$$= \$28.57$$

The key to a successful valuation is to be conservative both in your calculation of true EPS as well as your estimate of the future growth rate. Very, very few businesses will be able to grow forever at a rate larger than the economy as a whole. Indeed, the bigger the firm, the more likely that the amount of capital at work is going to drag down returns. It is going to be much more difficult for General Electric, with a nearly $400 billion market capitalization, to grow at 15 percent than it is for a smaller firm like Starbucks. If you are overly optimistic in your estimates, you run the very real risk of overpaying and falling below your required rate of return, sometimes substantially so.

Crash Alert _____

Allow us to offer one caveat. From time to time, you may find a company that appears to be trading at an astronomical implied rate of return. You need to delve into the 10K to uncover the story. Take USG, for example. The company recently traded as low as $15.50 per share, or only 2x earnings. That's an implied rate (with no growth, mind you) of 50 percent per annum! Yet further study revealed that the company was facing bankruptcy due to asbestos litigation. The risk simply isn't worth it; if you lose everything, you have nothing to compound.

Spotting Speculative Bubbles

The lesson, of course, is that capital should be allocated based upon opportunity cost. For example, if you estimate a firm's intrinsic value at $10 and the current market price is $65, you are most likely going to earn higher ultimate profits by parking your money in Treasuries until you can find something more attractive. (On the other hand, remember to keep your expectations in check. Over long periods of time, the odds are substantially against you earning more than 12 percent in the stock market, yet many investors have expectations as high as 15 or 20 percent; total absurdity unless they have the education, rationality, discipline, and financial prowess necessary to achieve such a goal.)

When opportunities are scarce, you may find yourself tempted to simply throw money into an enterprise just to feel like you're "doing something." Whenever you pay more than your estimate of the net present value of the discounted cash flows, you engage in the greater-fool game. You are banking on your ability to unload the asset at a higher price to the next guy that comes along. Sooner or later, someone is going to realize that what they are purchasing has no root in the underlying value and want to sell. This can set of a chain reaction that leaves the last person holding the bag, in some cases suffering complete financial ruin.

The most famous example of such foolishness is the seventeenth-century Dutch Tulip Bubble. For an entire season, every man in Holland became a speculator in tulips (yes, the kind you see planted in your neighbor's yard). As the frenzy continued, more and more people quit their day jobs and devoted themselves entirely to trading. The frenzy reached such heights, it was reported that one rare specimen sold for 6,700 guilders, or nearly the equivalent of 45 years worth of wages for a commoner! As you can guess, the party ended with a spectacular bang, just like our own bubble of the late 1990s.

There are a few key tests you can apply in order to ascertain if you are operating in an inflated price environment:

◆ Are the purchasers of this asset class depending upon price appreciation as the primary driver of profit rather than cash generated from operations? For example, an investor who purchases a plot of land in an expanding township with the expectation of selling it for a higher price later is in a decidedly more speculative position than one who purchases a housing unit with a long-established history of cash flows out of which the mortgage will be serviced.

◆ Has there been above-average interest in the asset class by the average person? One of the tell-tale signs of a speculative bubble is a large number of ordinary people with no prior experience in a particular field quitting their day job to focus on that field (for example, the manager at your local department store and your dentist stopped going to work in order to trade stocks online or flip real estate elsewhere in the country).

◆ Has the asset class recently increased to a price that is historically unprecedented? Is it at or close to an all-time high?

Ben Graham's Margin of Safety

We've already introduced you to Ben Graham, the late "Dean of Wall Street," father of value investing, and author of treatises such as *The Intelligent Investor* and *Security Analysis*. Graham's record (as well as those of his students from Columbia University) stands in the top percentile of all money managers. The key to his success, in his own words, was his insistence upon a *margin of safety*. This prevented him from overpaying for an asset.

There are several ways you can incorporate a margin of safety into your own operations:

◆ **Only Purchase at a Discount to Your Estimate of Value**

If, for example, you calculate that you can pay $15 for a particular asset in order to earn your required rate of return, you wouldn't want to actually buy the asset unless it was trading at, perhaps, $11 per share. During ordinary economic times, a vast majority of financial securities are going to fail this test. All you need is a few, however, to build a stellar record.

- **Choose Defensively**

  Graham recommended an investor look for seven key traits in a stock: adequate size of the enterprise, a sufficiently strong financial condition, earnings stability, a long record of increasing dividends, earnings growth, moderate price to earnings ratio, and a moderate ratio of price to assets.

- **Diversify**

  Another way to incorporate the margin of safety concept into your life is to build a diversified portfolio that includes both stock and bond components. Graham suggested owning no less than 25 percent and no more than 75 in either asset class, overweighting the class you believed to be the most undervalued. In his own operations at the Graham-Newman Partnership, the Dean maintained widespread diversification and likened the practice to an insurance company that sought to spread out exposure to adverse events. Although there may be a few failures, the overall results will be quite satisfactory if the investor remains logical and rational. We discuss how to select an asset mix in the next chapter.

Using Dollar Cost Averaging to Lower Your Cost Basis

As you can tell, one of the biggest risks you face is overpaying for an investment. This can be reduced, however, by establishing a *dollar cost averaging* plan into an index fund or a diversified group of common stocks.

How does it work? Instead of valuing different assets, determining which ones are cheaper on a relative basis and investing a lump sum, you instead invest fixed, smaller sums over longer periods of time into a stock or mutual fund. This protects you from locking your cash into a single price which could, in the event of a crash, take years to recover. It works because as average market prices increase, your cash will purchase fewer shares; likewise, when prices decrease, your cash will purchase more shares.

 Investor's Idiom

Dollar cost averaging is the process of investing fixed sums of money at regular intervals. As the price of the stock or mutual fund fluctuates, your cash buys more shares when the market is undervalued, and fewer shares when it is overvalued. The result is a lower average cost basis and, in the long-run, higher profits. It's a time-proven technique to reduce the risk of investing all of your nest egg at the height of the market.

Let's work through an example using real data. Assume you inherited $125,000 in January of 2000. You have decided to invest in the Vanguard 500 fund (that grand-daddy of all index funds we discussed back in Chapter 14). You have two options:

- You could invest everything in a lump sum. At the then-price of $119.18 per share, this would buy you 1,048.83 shares of the fund.

- You could create a dollar cost averaging plan to reduce your overpayment risk.

You, being the prudent investor you are, choose to spread out your purchases over time. After some careful consideration, you decide you want to be fully invested after five years and you will invest an equal amount, each quarter, between now and then. At the end of the period, you own 1,268.32 shares at an average cost of $98.48. Here's what your purchases would have looked like:

Dollar Cost Averaging Purchases

Date of Purchase	Per-Share Purchase Price	Amount Invested	Shares Purchased
January 2000	$119.18	$6,250	52.44168
April 2000	$124.46	$6,250	50.21694
July 2000	$123.09	$6,250	50.77586
October 2000	$123.27	$6,250	50.70171
January 2001	$118.18	$6,250	52.88543
April 2001	$108.37	$6,250	57.67279
July 2001	$105.34	$6,250	59.33169
October 2001	$92.45	$6,250	67.60411
January 2002	$98.92	$6,250	63.18237
April 2002	$94.52	$6,250	66.12357
July 2002	$80.39	$6,250	77.74599
October 2002	$78.44	$6,250	79.67874
January 2003	$76.09	$6,250	82.13957
April 2003	$81.90	$6,250	76.31258
July 2003	$88.82	$6,250	70.36703
October 2003	$94.61	$6,250	66.06067
January 2004	$102.24	$6,250	61.13067

Dollar Cost Averaging Purchases (continued)

Date of Purchase	Per-Share Purchase Price	Amount Invested	Shares Purchased
April 2004	$100.47	$6,250	62.20762
July 2004	$100.36	$6,250	62.27581
October 2004	$103.36	$6,250	60.46827
	$98.48	$125,000	1269.3231

*Per share prices adjusted by Yahoo! Finance for Dividends and Splits

By June, 2005, the fund was trading at $110.77 per share. The lump-sum investor's portfolio was worth $116,178.90—five years of investing and you've suffered a loss of $8,821.10! Under the dollar cost averaging plan, however, your portfolio would have grown to $140,602.58, an increase of $15,602.58.

 Crash Alert _____

When you start a dollar cost averaging program, you must invest fixed amounts of money at regular intervals. If you increase or decrease your investments based upon your outlook for the market, you risk overweighting periods of high prices. The biggest mistake you can make is lowering or ceasing your contributions during market crashes. As you can see from the chart, as the prices decrease, the amount of shares you are able to acquire for the same amount of money increases. Later, when the market recovers, these turn out to be your most profitable purchases.

Reducing Trading Costs

If you purchase $500 worth of General Electric stock and pay a $20 brokerage commission, you've already lost 4 percent of your principal. That money comes directly out of your profits and, in fact, is going to exceed your entire dividend income for the year! Had you waited and invested $5,000, on the other hand, the fact that your trading expenses were spread out over a larger number of shares would have caused you to lose only 40 basis points.

"How, then, can I create a dollar cost averaging plan?" you ask. "I can't invest $5,000 at a time!" Don't worry! Here are some tips as to how you can reduce your trading costs and, in turn, the price you pay for your investments:

◆ **Consolidate Your Purchases**

As part of a dollar cost averaging plan, consider investing quarterly, in larger sums, rather than monthly. This will spread out commissions and lower your per-share cost basis.

◆ **Sign Up for DRIPs or Automatic Investing Options**

We've already discussed the benefit of low or no-cost DRIP programs for common stocks. Many mutual funds also offer a similar automatic investing option. You can have small amounts automatically withdrawn at regular intervals from your bank account and invested in additional shares of a mutual fund, all the while paying no commission. With some plans allowing you to contribute as little as $50, you would be wise to dollar cost average on a weekly basis. Just make sure you don't stop contributing before reaching the minimum required investment or they will liquidate your account!

◆ **Avoid After-Hours Purchases**

Some brokers will allow you to buy or sell certain securities after hours. Due to low volume, however, price fluctuations are much more drastic. In addition, you will likely pay extra commissions and fees. Except in the most unusual of circumstances, there is rarely justification for such trades.

How to Think About a Falling Stock Market

Throughout the chapter, you've seen how overpaying lowers your investing returns long-term because, ultimately, an asset is only worth the present value of its discounted cash flows. In the short term, however, prices can fluctuate wildly for any number of reasons—war, uncertainty as to the direction of interest rates, or economic slowdown, just to name a few.

Graham, creator of the price-as-your-guide philosophy, told his students in *The Intelligent Investor* that, "… the investor who permits himself to be stampeded or unduly worried by unjustified market declines in his holdings is perversely transforming his basic advantage into a basic disadvantage. That man would be better off if his stocks had no market quotation at all, for he would then be spared the mental anguish caused him by *other persons'* mistakes of judgment."

The nature of the financial markets is that in each and every transaction, someone is betting an asset's price will increase and someone is betting it will decrease. Say you purchase 100 shares of Exxon Mobile at $50. Another party had to sell you those shares; one of you is wrong. As long as your decision to purchase is based upon a rational, conservative estimation of future earnings drawn from cold hard facts, you should never allow yourself to be concerned if the price of a stock you recently started acquiring dropped by 50 percent.

Super Strategy

Graham taught his students to think of the stock market as a manic-depressive business partner who came to them every day, offering to buy their half of a business or sell them his. Some days, he was full of doom and gloom, fearing the end of the world. As a result, the prices which he quoted were depressingly low. Other days, he saw nothing but blue skies and sunny days ahead and, as a result, would only sell them his equity for a high premium.

The student, being the wiser capitalist, had no particular affinity for Mr. Market, realizing instead that he was there to "serve, not instruct" them. In fact, Graham taught them to take whole-hearted advantage of the chum because he had no sense of loyalty to them.

Such a scenario would be no different than if you purchased a prize home in an excellent neighborhood for an attractive price. The day after you close the deal, we come to you and offer to buy your residence for half of what you paid. You would tell us to take a hike! You are confident, thanks to your knowledge of property values, that you could eventually receive a much higher price than that which we are quoting you. Yet day in and day out, investors part with fractional shares in excellent businesses simply because other people are selling. Repeat after us: *fear-based decisions are almost always a mistake.*

The reason for fear often stems from a lack of confidence in your analysis. The answer to that problem is simple ... if you cannot estimate the value of a business, then any purchases you make of its shares is inherently speculative. Instead of selecting individual issues, you should develop a diversified portfolio of mutual or exchange traded funds. In this case, your confidence can stem from your belief that the economy will be stronger in 20 years than it is today; knowing that, in the meantime, you can build up a large equity position in it.

Market crashes should be viewed for what they are—excellent opportunities for you to increase your ownership of corporate America at a lower price.

The Least You Need to Know

- ◆ The surest way to earn low rates of return is to overpay for an asset.
- ◆ Always be conservative when estimating growth rates and future earnings per share.
- ◆ Be wary of investing in any asset class that appears to be operating under the sway of a speculative bubble.
- ◆ Incorporate a margin of safety into every investment.
- ◆ Dollar cost averaging can lower your overall cost basis.
- ◆ Keep trading costs low; every penny saved is another penny compounding.

Chapter 21

Asset Allocation

In This Chapter

- ◆ Sample asset allocation mixes for your portfolio
- ◆ When it is okay to concentrate your investments
- ◆ Rebalancing your assets
- ◆ Developing an emergency fund

Asset allocation is the process of dividing capital among different types of investments to generate the highest possible returns given a desired level of risk and stated objective. For those with extensive financial training, asset allocation doesn't make much sense because they would be better off putting their capital to work in the top few opportunities they believed offered the highest returns. For ordinary investors who don't know how to adjust inventory valuations, hedge foreign currency risk, value warrants, or estimate the impact of interest rates on profitability, prudence doesn't permit such concentration.

Instead, the average investor should construct a widely diversified portfolio, both in terms of asset class (stocks, bonds, real estate, and so on) and individual issue (for instance, owning 30 stocks instead of 5). As you learned in the previous chapter, this is one of the key ways Graham taught to incorporate the margin of safety principal into your financial affairs for three reasons:

◆ Diversification reduces individual *issue risk*. Had you owned 30 stocks in a portfolio, equally weighted, and one of them happened to be WorldCom, the loss, although unpleasant, would not have derailed your financial plans.

◆ Diversification among asset classes reduces *system-wide risk*. In the event of a stock market crash, such as the one that occurred in 1929, the investor that has his assets split among stocks, bonds, and real estate is not going to be as affected as the one that holds his entire net worth in equities.

◆ Diversification can improve your odds of overall success. To illustrate, imagine you placed $5,000 into four different investments. Five years later, here were your results …

Investment	Original	CAGR[1]	After 5 Years
Investment A	$5,000	30 percent	$18,565
Investment B	$5,000	12 percent	$8,812
Investment C	$5,000	8 percent	$7,347
Investment D	$5,000	n/a (total 30% loss)	$3,500
Total Investment	**$20,000**	**Market Value**	**$38,224**

(1)CAGR = Compound Annual Growth Rate. See Chapter 22 for calculation.

Your compound annual rate of return for the entire portfolio would be 13.83 percent, increasing the original investment of $20,000 to $38,224. Had you invested everything into Investment A you would have $74,259; Investment B, $35,247; Investment C, $29,387, and Investment D, $14,000. Spreading your assets out not only decreased your issue and system-wide risk, you actually compounded faster than three of the four "all-or-nothing" portfolios.

Remember Your Objectives? There's an Asset Mix to Achieve Them!

Now that you've gotten this far, you understand the time value of money, the way different asset classes function, and the importance of incorporating Graham's margin of safety. It's time to build some sample portfolios!

Think back to Chapter 4 when we discussed the four investing objectives: capital preservation, current income, capital appreciation, and speculation. There is an *asset allocation* mix to achieve the first three (as for speculation, anything goes). In this section, we work through scenarios, and then provide a solution for how you can construct a portfolio accordingly. Please note that this section is merely a starting point to give you an idea how the choice of assets can be determined by your objective; consult with your own financial advisor or planner to construct a portfolio that is appropriate for your needs and risk profile.

Investor's Idiom

Asset allocation is the process of dividing capital among different types of investments (stocks, bonds, real estate, etc.) to generate the highest possible returns given an investor's desired level of risk and stated objective.

Scenario 1

You have saved $10,000 for the first year of college. Although you want to earn some return on the cash, you absolutely cannot afford to take any risk.

Solution: Your objective is capital preservation. You are going to want to limit your investments to cash and cash equivalents such as Treasuries, certificates of deposits, money market funds, savings bonds, savings accounts, and, if your assets permit, highly liquid bonds maturing within the next year. Except in periods of high inflation, the reinvested interest should maintain your purchasing power until you can tap the capital for your needs.

The Result

The net result is a portfolio with little or no chance of principal loss with sufficient income generated to keep the inflation-adjusted value of the capital in tact.

Scenario 2

You are about to retire and have accumulated $500,000 in capital over the course of your career. Right now, the money is sitting in a bank account. You want to construct a portfolio that will generate cash for you to supplement your Social Security income. You never plan to take any of the principal out of the portfolio and would like it to continue to grow for your estate.

Solution:

Your objective is current income with the potential for some long-term growth.

Real Estate (15 percent, or $75,000):

With a low correlation to other asset classes, you want to include a real estate component. You could choose something like the Dow Jones Real Estate Index Fund (Symbol: IYR), currently yielding around 4 percent. With a low expense ratio, you can be sure that most of the fund's profits are flowing directly to your hands.

Fixed Income (40 percent, or $200,000):

The fixed income portion of the portfolio is largely going to be dictated by our outlook for interest rates. At the time of this writing, the Federal Reserve was raising short-term rates. Long-term rates, however, have actually declined in what Alan Greenspan appropriately deemed "a conundrum." In light of this, as well as the fact that interest rates are now in the low end of the historical range, it wouldn't be prudent to lock in large amounts of money at long maturities.

To keep balance in your portfolio, place 40 percent in short and medium-term maturities (no more than 5 to 8 year maturities, on average). Your choices, particularly concerning whether or not to invest in munis, will depend upon your tax bracket. At current rates, you could expect to earn around 4 percent pre-tax on this component.

If you wanted to invest a small portion into less conventional securities, you could choose something like the Vanguard Convertible Securities Fund (symbol: VCVSX) which is currently yielding 2.8 percent and has grown at nearly 10 percent annually over the last 15 years. Historically, the entire portfolio has consisted of widely diversified special-situation convertible fixed income securities.

High-Quality, Dividend-Paying Stocks (45 percent, or $225,000):

Given the current interest rate environment and your desire to grow over the long run, it may be wise to overweight the portion of the portfolio dedicated to high-quality, dividend-paying stocks. There are several banks, for example, that currently boast a dividend yield of 4.5 percent; the rate on 10-year Treasuries is only 4 percent! Volatility aside, the underlying value of a Treasury is not going to have the potential to appreciate like a well-run business can. Think back to our Coca-Cola example in Chapter 11. In 1997, the company was paying a $0.56 dividend. In 2005, it had grown to twice as much ($1.12 per share). The value of the checks you receive in the mail would have doubled, whether or not the underlying stock price increased or decreased. A Coke bond would not have done the same.

To achieve broad diversification, your best option may be the Dow Jones Select Dividend Index Fund (symbol: DVY), which is comprised of one hundred of the highest yielding common stocks, excluding REITs, in the Dow Jones United States Total Market Index. The current yield: just under 3 percent.

Super Strategy

If you're investing for current income and growth, check out Morningstar's *Dividend Investor*. The newsletter features model portfolios based upon high-quality, individual common stocks with long histories of safe, secure dividend payments.

If you believe certain industries are going to outperform, you may want to look into the respective HOLDRs. Regional Bank HOLDRs are currently yielding 3.37 percent. You wouldn't want to be exposed to just one sector of the market, though. Perhaps you could consider investing in the Utilities HOLDR, as well, which is currently yielding 3.97 percent.

The Result

The net result would be a portfolio that had the potential to appreciate (via the common stock component), pay out ever-increasing amounts of cash on an annual basis, retain market value due to a balance between asset classes, and avoid a meltdown from overexposure to a single company. On average, the pre-tax cash distributions on the portfolio would be $17,000 to $20,000 in the first year.

Scenario 3

You just graduated from college; degree-in-hand, you land your first job. You are 22 years old and want to retire with $10 million when you are 65. Assuming a 12 percent rate of return, you calculate that you would need to save $9,250 annually, or $177 per week, to reach your goal.

Solution:

Your objective is growth. You are far enough away from retirement that you can put up to 100 percent of your assets into equities, the highest returning class by far. The best way to ensure you reach your goal is to keep expenses low, dollar cost average into your positions, and avoid frequent trading.

Your largest investment should probably be in the S&P 500; the best option being the Vanguard 500 Index fund (symbol: VFINX). You may also want to set up automatic investment plans into four or five other mutual funds based upon your own individual tastes (for example, a value investor might look into firms such as Oakmont, Muhlenkamp, Third Avenue, and Royce). Remember to consider reinvesting all of your capital gains and dividend distributions!

You might include international equities, perhaps up to 10 or 20 percent of your portfolio. When the U.S. stock market is underperforming, these can provide an attractive boost to your returns. Look for a broad-based fund (avoid funds that invest in individual countries) with a relatively low expense ratio and a disciplined approach. One of the best options is the Tweedy Browne Global Value Fund (symbol: TBGVX) because, unlike virtually all of its competitors, it hedges foreign currency exposure, removing the biggest single risk.

As you get closer to retirement, you're going to slowly start shifting your assets to allocation models that reflect your increased need for capital preservation and current income.

If and when you get the desire to dabble in individual common stocks, set up a separate account and fund it out of your paycheck. That way, if it turns out you've found the next Starbucks or Wal-Mart, great! If it turns out you made a mistake and lose everything, your long-term investing goals will not be damaged in any way, shape, or form.

Concentrating Your Assets

You may wonder when (if) it is okay to concentrate your assets into the stock of a single company. Although everyone dreams of finding the next Microsoft, there are only a few cases where it is acceptable to concentrate your assets into the stock of an individual company, deviating from your ideal asset allocation mix.

- ◆ You have extraordinary faith in an individual person or group of managers.

- ◆ You have evaluated and understand the situation completely. You believe the commitment has a low probability of permanent loss with a large potential upside. An example would be a media analyst in the 1970s purchasing shares of the Washington Post or an oil executive in the 1990s investing in the industry because he knew $10 per barrel oil was not sustainable.

Realize, however, that you have placed a tremendous amount of your future into the hands of that single management team and business. If, after evaluating the chances of success, you are comfortable with this risk, so be it.

Note that we did not recommend holding a large portion of your net worth in the stock of your employer. The reason? You already have enough invested with the firm. If the business goes bust, you're out of a job. Why wipe out your portfolio, as well? The risk simply isn't worth the potential reward.

The Result

The net result is a portfolio that is selected for long-term growth potential. The volatility is high but you aren't concerned because you understand the different between market price and intrinsic value. The ride may be lumpy, but you ultimately expect to arrive with more capital.

A Word on Rebalancing

If you look at the investments you've purchased, they probably fall into a few different categories. For instance, of your equities, some might be "energy," such as oil and gas companies, or "technology," such as software manufacturers. As you learned in Part 3, these categories are called sectors.

Now, stick with us. Philosophically, the technique we are about to teach you is eschewed by a large constituency in the financial community (one the authors of this book being one of them). Yet, we would be remiss if we did not explain the practice and why so many financial professionals recommend it to their clients.

It's called rebalancing. The basic premise is this: if you plan to purchase more stocks, put more money into the equities that did poorly. Why? So that you maintain positions for each sector that are comparable.

Let's say you started with $10,000 and split it evenly, buying $2,500 worth of stock in each of four different sectors: technology, health care, energy, and finance. By the end of the first year, maybe your technology stocks are now worth $3,000, health care stocks dropped to $2,000, energy shot up to $4,000, and your finance stocks held steady at $2,500. Your portfolio is now worth $12,000, but you no longer own an even 25 percent in each sector:

$$
\begin{array}{ll}
\$3,000 & \text{(technology)} \\
+\ \$2,000 & \text{(health care)} \\
+\ \$4,500 & \text{(energy)} \\
+\ \$2,500 & \text{(finance)} \\
=\ \$12,000 &
\end{array}
$$

We're suggesting that you rebalance your portfolio so that you again own 25 percent in each sector. With a $12,000 portfolio, that would mean holding $12,000 × .25, or $3,000, in each sector. You'll have to sell off some of your energy stocks to beef up your holdings in health care and finance.

With taxable accounts, the goal is to generate as few capital gains as possible. That's why we recommend passive equity holdings and/or index funds, which minimize taxes—if nothing's being sold, no capital gains are being generated. You don't want to sell equities in a taxable account unless you are at a milestone year (your child might be approaching his or her first year of college, for example). If the equities in your taxable accounts have declined significantly, however, you might want to rebalance upward. Use the proceeds from bond or bond fund sales, which should generate minimal capital gains. That's all there is to it!

Professionals might disagree with this approach, arguing that you should pour money into your "winners" and less into your "losers." This is fine for professionals whose job it is to carefully research their holdings. Right now, you're a rookie and your one big asset is (yes, you guessed it) time. As long as you stick with top quality investments, the time you invest in them is more than likely to pay off. You may not have as many big winners, but, by the same token, you should have fewer (and maybe no) losers.

Just-in-Case Cash

Think of your asset allocation plan as a stroll down a beautiful trail in the woods. If you stay on the path, you'll eventually reach your destination, but if you chase every butterfly or every storm sends you running for shelter, you'll get lost and may never find your way back to your path.

Hospitalizations, funerals, weddings, auto or home repairs, gifts, taxes, and so on, don't show up programmed on a calendar. They occur with little or no advance warning, and you either have funds set aside to cover them or you go into debt. Selling off your investments is a huge mistake, triggering capital gains taxes and throwing your portfolio out of balance. Going into debt, both financially and psychologically, can take the fun out of a happy event or make a sad one even sadder.

Your umbrella for those times when life drenches you with unexpected expenses is your emergency fund. This should be roughly 10 percent of your annual income or $10,000, whichever is greater. Some experts recommend keeping half your annual salary in an emergency fund, but that's a bit extreme. If you're making $50,000 a year or less, it's awfully hard to save $25,000. These days, with low down payments available on homes and easy car financing, few emergencies require $25,000 (lack of health insurance being the notable exception). Ten percent, or $10,000, should cover you for most of life's hiccups. This is the single most important thing you can do to secure your financial future; an emergency fund ensures that you never have to touch your investments.

Super Strategy

Don't forget the 10 percent rule. Put aside 10 percent of every paycheck and you'll be able to painlessly create your emergency fund within a year's time. For those of you who make so little that this is difficult to do, figure out a way to consistently put something into the emergency fund. Even $50 a month (dinner out for two in most cities) is a start.

Mattresses Are for Sleeping, Not Stashing

It's important to save money for emergencies, but it's equally vital that you have immediate access to that money when a serious situation does arise. And, no, keeping your cash under the mattress is not the best place, even if it is immediately accessible!

What are your options? The same as for any capital preservation goal—Treasuries, certificates of deposit, money market funds, savings bonds, and savings accounts.

Crash Alert _____

Recall that although you can always cash Treasury bills within 24 hours, if you sell before maturity, you may receive less than the maturity value, and perhaps even less than the amount you invested due to changes in interest rates!

Also remember to keep certificate of deposit maturities short. If you cash in a CD early, you will be penalized. For example, the typical six-month $1,000 CD might incur a penalty of around $12 if you cashed it at three months. If the CD was paying 4 percent interest, you would have expected a return of $40 for the year, or $20 for six months, so that $12 penalty sucks up more than half of what you'd hoped to earn!

The Least You Need to Know

◆ Diversification reduces individual issue risk, system-wide risk, and increases your chances for success.

◆ Your ideal asset mix is dependent upon your investing objective.

◆ Unless you are selecting individual investments or you truly believe an area of the market is overpriced, rebalance your holdings annually.

◆ To develop an emergency fund, save 10 percent of your paycheck each month for one year.

Chapter 22

Evaluating Investment Performance

In This Chapter

- Understanding total return
- Measuring simple return
- Calculating compound annual growth rate
- Choosing a benchmark for comparison
- Absolute vs. relative performance
- Grading your financial advisor

In every endeavor, success is measured by some sort of scorecard. In baseball, it's RBIs. In the culinary arts, it's the number of stars awarded in the Zagat survey. In investing, there are several metrics that can be used to evaluate your performance. This chapter is dedicated to helping you do just that. Grab your financial records, take out a calculator, and prepare to find out where you fall on the totem pole.

Total Return

At the end of the year, some investors make the mistake of glancing at their portfolio and gauging their performance based upon the increase or decrease of the security prices. Back in Chapter 11, however, you learned there are *two* sources of profit for an investor: appreciation in the security, and dividend (interest) income.

Wall Street came up with a figure—*total return*—to measure both of these components. Often performed on an annual basis, this metric provides a more accurate picture of the underlying performance of the portfolio.

> Total Return = (Value of security at the end of year – Value of security at beginning of year) + Dividends Received / Value of a security at the beginning of the year

Here's an example. Kelsey Lea purchases 100 shares of Altria Group (symbol: MO) on January 5, 2004 at a total cost of $5,559. One year later, her stake was worth $6,040, giving her a gain from unrealized appreciation of $481. During that time period, she also collected $282 in dividends. What's her total return for the year? Glad you asked!

> Total Return = ($6,040 - $5,559) + $282 / $5,559
>
> Total Return = $481 + $282 / $5,559
>
> Total Return = $763 / $5,559
>
> Total Return = 0.1373, or 13.75 percent

Calculating Simple Return

Simple return tells you how much you earned on an investment once you've sold it, expressed as a percentage of cost basis. Here's the calculation:

> Simple Return = Net Proceeds from Sale of Investment + All Dividends Received / Cost Basis – 1

Say you purchase 100 shares of Pfizer for $22, paying a $15 commission; a cost basis of $2,215. Later, you sell the stock for $35 per share, again paying a $15 commission. Your net proceeds from the sale are $3,485. Assume you also received a total of $68 in dividend income during the time you held the stock.

Simple Return = $3,485 + $68 / $2,215 − 1

Simple Return = $3,553+ $68 / $2,215 − 1

Simple Return = 1.60 − 1

Simple Return = 0.60, or 60 percent

Your before-tax simple return on this investment was 60 percent. (If you wanted to calculate the after-tax return, change the first variable to "net after-tax proceeds from sale of investment" and add it to "after-tax dividends received."

Simple return has one major drawback. It doesn't take into account the length of time an investment was held. After all, 60 percent pre-tax may sound impressive, but if you held your stock for 20 years to generate that return, you haven't even kept pace with inflation!

Calculating Compound Annual Growth Rate

To solve this shortcoming, you need to calculate an investment's compound annual growth rate, or CAGR. As you discovered when you learned the time value of money formulas, the rate at which your capital compounds has a dramatic effect upon your wealth. The higher the rate, the more money you make. Over long periods of time, the difference can be many, many millions of dollars.

To calculate CAGR, you are going to begin with an adjusted version of simple return. The only difference is that the second-to-last step is omitted; you're not going to subtract "1". We'll call this factor "Part A".

Adjusted Simple Return = Net Proceeds from Sale of Investment + Dividends Received / Cost Basis

Then, you're going to take the number of years the investment was held and divide it by 1. For example, if you held the Pfizer stock for 5 years, you are going to take 1 divided by 5; the answer is .20; we'll call this factor "Part B." (Really, what you've done is calculate the "X Root" but if we had said that in the beginning, your eyes might have glazed over.)

 Fiscal Facts

CAGR is a way to quickly and easily compare the performance of any asset—stocks, bonds, mutual funds, real estate, oil, copper, corn, coffee, your grandma's china—over a period of time.

Now, all you do is take the solution for Part A and raise it to the power of Part B and subtract "1". The answer is your CAGR!

Here's the actual math in action so you can see it step-by-step ...

Part A

$$\text{Adjusted Simple Return} = \frac{\textbf{Net Proceeds from Sale of Investment + Dividends Received}}{\text{Cost Basis}}$$

$$\text{Simple Return} = \frac{\$3{,}485 + \$68}{\$2{,}215}$$

$$\text{Adjusted Simple Return} = \frac{\$3{,}553}{\$2{,}215}$$

Adjusted Simple Return = 1.60

Part B

X Root = 1÷Number of Years Investment Held

X Root = 1÷5

X Root = .20

Putting It Together

CAGR = {Adjusted Simple Return$^{(\text{Raised to the X Root})}$}–1

CAGR = {1.60$^{(.20)}$}–1

CAGR = 1.0986–1

CAGR = 0.0986, or 9.86 percent

The answer, 9.86 percent, is the rate of return you earned compounded annually. Now, in reality, there may be some years when the stock was down 30 percent, and then it was up 90 percent. CAGR smoothes out that volatility.

Absolute vs. Relative Performance

The main question, of course, remains, "Is 9.86 percent a good rate of return?" The answer: it depends. You can evaluate the performance of your portfolio in one of two ways:

◆ **Absolute Return:** The rate I earned on my entire portfolio sufficient to get me to my financial goals? If, using the time value of money formulas, I had based my entire future projected net worth on a CAGR of 5 percent and I earned 9.86 percent, it was a terrific year.

◆ **Relative Performance:** How did my portfolio perform compared to a benchmark with the same risk/reward profile? If, for example, my benchmark was the S&P 500 and it returned 10 percent for the year, I would consider my 9.86 percent return insufficient. If the S&P 500 returned 8 percent, on the other hand, I would consider it a good year.

There is considerable debate on Wall Street about which is the most appropriate.

Who's correct? As the saying goes, "you can't feed your family on relative returns." Whether your portfolio happens to outperform another portfolio (the benchmark) is completely inconsequential. Unless you own the exact same assets that are found in the benchmark, it is highly probable your results are going to deviate on a year-to-year basis. The only thing that matters is that you are on the correct path to your financial dreams. If you require an 8 percent CAGR to retire on time with the amount of money you desire and your portfolio generates 12 percent in a particular year, it is absolutely absurd for you to feel upset because the S&P may have generated 17 percent during the same period. Focus on how your assets are doing; not Wall Street's.

Choosing a Benchmark for Comparison

For those of you who insist upon comparing your portfolio to a benchmark, here's a list of some of the most famous.

S&P 500

A very broad indicator of the market, the S&P 500 accounts for a majority of the total U.S. stock market capitalization. Most managers attempt to beat the S&P on a long-term basis. Because the S&P is weighted for market cap, the top 40 or 50 stocks represent 50 percent of the index.

Dow Jones Indices

The Dow Jones Industrial, Transportation, and Utility Averages are the oldest indices in the United States. All three are maintained and reviewed by the editors of *The Wall Street Journal* (WSJ). Unquestionably, the most famous of the three is the Dow Jones Industrial Average (DJIA) (when you hear about "The Dow" on the nightly news, this is the one to which the anchor is most likely referring).

The 30 component stocks that make up the DJIA don't just come from the industrial sector—they cover everything from consumer staples to financial services firms. The only requirement for inclusion is that the firm be "a leader in its industry." You can rest assured the WSJ editors ensure that only the bluest of the blue chips gain access to this exclusive club.

Wilshire 5,000

By measuring the performance of all U.S.-domiciled equities, the Dow Jones Wilshire 5,000 index is the most comprehensive representation of American markets. The name reflects the approximately 5,000 individual stocks that were originally tracked; the figure stands much higher today, thanks to an increase in the amount of publicly traded companies.

Russell 2,000

The standard measure of small-cap stocks, the Russell 2000 index is reconfigured each year to exclude companies that have grown too large.

NASDAQ Composite

Weighted for market capitalization, the NASDAQ Composite Index measures all of the stocks traded on the NASDAQ; currently in the neighborhood of 3,000 equities. According to the exchange's website, this includes American Depositary Receipts, common stock, limited partnership interest, ordinary shares, real estate investment trusts, shares of beneficial interest, and tracking stocks.

NYSE Composite

The New York Stock Exchange, home to America's most illustrious companies, tracks the aggregate price of all stocks traded on its floor. After each transaction, the NYSE composite is automatically updated electronically. The composite index is broken out into four sub-indices: financial, industrial, transportation, and utility.

Morgan Stanley International Europe, Australia, and Far East Index (MSCI EAFE Index)

The gold standard for international investors, the MSCI EAFE is an unmanaged, unhedged index that represents the equity markets of 21 countries outside of the United States. According to the MSCI, as of May 2005 the index represented Australia, Austria, Belgium, Denmark, Finland, France, Germany, Greece, Hong Kong, Ireland, Italy, Japan, the Netherlands, New Zealand, Norway, Portugal, Singapore, Spain, Sweden, Switzerland, and the United Kingdom.

Grading Your Investment Advisor

How do you know if the person with whom you've entrusted your assets is doing a good job? Let us count the ways …

Honors Your Risk Profile

Your portfolio should always be a reflection of your objectives. If your primary concern is capital preservation and your advisor is putting part of your funds in unhedged foreign equities, you need to fire them even if your returns have been spectacular.

Ample Returns on a Multi-Year Basis

Do not grade your advisor on an annual basis. The best investor in the world may have two back-to-back down years; having the courage and conviction to stick to a strategy is a sign of strength, not weakness. Investors tend to foolishly scold their

Crash Alert

Remember to check the CRD database we discussed in Chapter 10 for complaints filed against your advisor! An ounce of prevention can save you a lot of time ... and even more money!

advisors when it looks like they are underperforming in the short run. Case in point: At the height of the Internet bubble, a major financial magazine ran a cover story asking if Warren Buffett was washed up. Many people thought so because, despite being trounced by the speculative market for several years, Buffett refused to invest in companies he considered overvalued, instead piling everything into fixed income securities. When the market finally crashed, he emerged not only unscathed, but loaded with cash to take advantage of opportunities. The moral: if your advisor is sticking to the initial plan (and it was sound and conservative at the time of implementation), don't screw it up by calling him every five minutes and screaming about your relative performance. The only person you're hurting is yourself.

Instead, money managers should be evaluated on a multi-year rolling basis—5 to 10 years is ideal—in order to separate market moves from their performance. If your CAGR (after taxes and expenses) is sufficient to get you to your financial goals and is within several percentage points of a similarly-invested benchmark, rejoice.

Fee-Based

Ideally, you want to look for someone who is paid a fee based upon the size of your assets. It may seem counterintuitive, but sometimes the most intelligent thing you can do is sit tight on what you already own. Intentionally or not, a commission-driven advisor is more likely to engage in more transactions, adding frictional expense that costs you money in the long-run.

Also, some financial advisors are rewarded for selling you certain products (specific mutual fund families, insurance ...). This is almost never good for you. Perhaps one of the worst transgressions is those folks who convince their clients to hold a tax-advantaged investment, such as a variable annuity, in a tax-advantaged account. Such a move does not make financial sense. Fire them immediately.

The Least You Need to Know

- ◆ Total return is calculated by adding dividend or interest income to the appreciation in the price of a security.

- ◆ CAGR is the most important financial performance metric.

- ◆ Most investors will be better off managing their portfolios for absolute, rather than relative, returns.

- ◆ For those who follow relative performance, choosing a benchmark with similar characteristics to your portfolio is important; otherwise, you're comparing apples to oranges.

- ◆ Evaluate your advisors on a 5- to 10-year rolling basis.

Chapter 23

Keeping Uncle Sam's Greedy Mitts Off of Your Assets

In This Chapter

- ◆ Capital gains tax rates
- ◆ Avoiding wash sales
- ◆ Why dividends have become more attractive
- ◆ Reducing your estate tax

You've spent the last twenty-two chapters learning how to invest your money and get your life on financial track. Now, we're going to discuss the various ways Uncle Sam can tax you, and what you can do to reduce the pain.

Capital Gains Tax

A capital gain is simply the profit from the appreciation of a security. Investments held for less than one year are taxed at your personal income tax rate—as high as 35 percent! Congress, however, wants to promote long-term investment in corporate America, so the rates for the exact same investment held more than one year are much lower; prior to the passage of The Jobs and Growth Tax Relief Reconciliation Act of 2003, 20 and 10 percent, respectively. Today, those rates have been lowered to 15 and 5 percent until 2009, when we'll return to the historical levels.

The result is that you can lower your tax bill by simply holding your investments longer. This is the reason that low-turnover portfolios, such as index funds that track major indices like the Dow or S&P 500, trounce most managed mutual funds year-in and year-out; investments are rarely sold, lowering the tax liability while increasing the amount of capital that is compounding for you.

The Wash Sale Rule

One way to lower your tax bite is to try to use your investment losses to offset your gains. Back in the day, intelligent Wall Street types would dump a stock with unrealized losses prior to the end of the year, then turn around and repurchase them on the first trading day in January.

Super Strategy

With securities, your decision should always be driven by investment merits, not tax considerations. All things being equal, however, take full advantage of the tax laws. Just apply these three rules:

◆ Try to hold securities longer than 12 months so you can take advantage of the lower tax rates.

◆ Offset gains with losses whenever possible.

◆ Beware the wash sale rule.

The government got wise to this and implemented the *wash sale rule*. Basically, it stipulates that if you sell an investment, you cannot deduct the loss from your taxes if you purchased "substantially identical" assets during the 30 calendar days prior or subsequent to the sale (that's a 61 day block of time, counting the day of sale).

Think you can cleverly dodge the wash sale rule? Think again. The IRS forbids taking losses if you sell the stock to your spouse or your own company. Likewise, you couldn't sell the stock and then turn around and purchase an option to acquire, locking in the current price.

Dividend Taxes

According to our good friends at the IRS, The Jobs and Growth Tax Relief Reconciliation Act of 2003 also provides that dividends are taxed at capital gains rates of 5 percent (0 percent in the year 2009) and 15 percent, provided that the investor has "own[ed] the stock for more than 60 days during the 120-day period beginning 60 days before the ex-dividend date." Prior to the act, these cash distributions were taxed at personal rates which were much, much higher.

As a result, dividends are going to be much more attractive over the next few years; the most likely result being a rise in the stock of dividend-paying companies as demand for these equities increases.

Big Changes in Estate Taxes!

The estate tax was among the most onerous in the U.S. tax system, starting at 37 percent and running up as high as 55 percent. It was a bummer to think that you might have a million dollars to leave to your kids, but the government could take half of it before the money even got to them.

Fortunately, what the government hath taken away, it hath slowly returneth. In 2002, it got a little easier to keep your hard-earned bucks in the family. A key section of the Tax Relief Act of 2001 creates a significant increase in the estate tax exemption, with a full repeal slated for 2010. Similarly, the highest estate (and gift) tax rates will gradually decline. Here are the details:

Year	Estate tax exemption	Highest estate/gift tax rates
2005	$1.5 million	47%
2006	$2.0 million	46%
2007	$2.0 million	45%
2008	$2.0 million	45%
2009	$3.5 million	45%
2010	–	–

On January 1, 2010, there will be a full repeal of all estate taxes. That's the good news. Now for the bad: The repeal will expire on December 31, 2010, and the law in effect prior to June 7, 2001 will be revived.

Fiscal Facts

The maximum rate for the estate tax and the gift tax is going down, down, down.

That means the maximum estate tax exemption will return to $1.0 million, and the highest rate will jump back up to 55 percent. This so-called "sunset provision" (which we are betting the Feds will invoke, citing "budgetary safeguards") has given rise to a rather sick joke among legal eagles:

Lawyer to aging client: "Try very hard to expire in 2010."

Only in America! Well, enjoy the respite while it lasts.

The Estate Tax Repeal ... Not So Appealing?

Turns out it depends upon your state of residence. Bear with us now, this is a bit confusing. In most states, for every dollar you pay in state estate taxes, you get a dollar in credit to apply to your federal death taxes. Under the 2002 Tax Relief Act, however, this credit will be phased out and replaced by a straight deduction which will be worth much less than the credit. About half the states plan to automatically reduce the tax as the credit is reduced, but in 23 states and Washington, D.C., the underlying tax will remain even as the credit disappears. The larger your estate, the more you could be hurt by the elimination of the credit. Estates in the millions could wind up paying more estate tax rather than less.

One more thing ... although supposedly the estate tax will be repealed altogether in 2010, no one is convinced that will really happen. If the Democrats get control of Congress, if the government decides it can't do without the revenue from estate taxes ... if, if, if! We wouldn't count on it. Our best advice: If you have a large estate, work with an expert in estate planning and prepare to be flexible.

They Can Tax *That?!*

Maybe you think you don't have to worry about estate planning because your estate isn't worth more than $1 million. But take a close look at what's included in the definition of estate. It adds up fast. Let's make a partial list:

Fiscal Facts

Federal Estate Tax Return Form 706 must generally be filed and taxes paid by the estate within nine months following the estate owner's death.

- ◆ Taxable investments (stocks, bonds, mutual funds, CDs, money market accounts, etc.)

- ◆ Employer-sponsored retirement plan benefits

- ◆ All IRAs

- ◆ Personal residences less associated mortgages

- Business/partnership interests

- Life insurance proceeds (at time of death)

- Automobiles and boats less associated loans

- Jewelry and collectibles (antique furniture, paintings, coins, stamps, etc.)

- Other items of value (clothing, furniture, etc.)

- Taxable lifetime gifts

Does any of this look familiar? It should mimic what's on your personal balance sheet. (Have you gotten that together since Chapter 5? Nag, nag!)

Are there any deductions? Precious few. We've indicated some in our partial list (mortgages and car loans). Others include funeral expenses, transfers to charities of your choice, and the cost of administering your estate (trust bank fees and the like).

Super Strategy

As you get older, the value of your estate is going to continue to increase. You may not be a millionaire now, but you may be in 2006 or 2016 or 2026. First, carefully estimate the value of your estate. Have jewelry, collectibles and other property appraised. Think about what gifts you want to make to charities and to family members. In short, use this chapter as inspiration to get organized—then, see your attorney!

Watch That Generation Gap

Ordinarily, assets you have upon your death in excess of the estate tax exemption are taxed at the rates we discussed earlier in the chapter. Patriarchs of wealthy families, however, got the brilliant idea that they would simply make bequests directly to their grandchildren, paying a single estate tax (instead of passing it onto their children who would later pass it onto the grandchildren, incurring two separate estate taxes).

Congress wised up to this in the 1980's and passed the Generation Skipping Tax, or GST. The law assesses a double estate tax on assets passed onto third-generation heirs directly. The result? Without proper planning, a $100 million fortune could be whittled down to around $30 million if left to your grandchildren!

Tax-Saving Alternatives

Meanwhile, we can at least make you aware of some useful tax-saving strategies.

Gimme Shelter

A smarter way to use the unlimited marital deduction is to divide your assets in half and will only half to your spouse. Use the other half to set up a credit shelter trust (CST). Your spouse gets all the income generated by the trust's investments during his or her lifetime. The principal goes to your children when your spouse dies. Ideally, the assets used to set up the CST will be no more than the exclusion amount in the year of your death. At the time of your death, assets equal to the exclusion amount for that year go to create the CST, and the balance goes directly to your spouse via the unlimited marital deduction. At the time of your spouse's death, the CST is excluded from his or her estate. Voilà! You've cut your and your spouse's estate tax bill in half.

QTIP: No, Not the Kind You Stick in Your Ear

In addition to the CST, you can also set up, via your will, a second trust that qualifies for the marital deduction. What kind of trust qualifies? The most popular choice is called the Qualified Terminable Interest Property Trust, or "QTIP" for short.

With a QTIP, your spouse receives the income during his/her lifetime. At the time of your spouse's death, the assets pass on to whomever you've named in your will. The assets are still included in your spouse's estate, but you retain control of the assets "from the grave." The QTIP is great for a second marriage, for example, because you can make sure some of your assets reach the children of your first marriage after your second spouse dies.

Charitable Trusts

There are two kinds of charitable trusts:

- ◆ Charitable Remainder Trusts (CRTs)
- ◆ Charitable Lead Trusts (CLTs)

With the CRT, you set up a trust for the charity of your choice, but you retain all rights to the income generated by the trust until you and/or your spouse dies. At that time, the assets go to the charity. You get a charitable gift deduction (Schedule A on IRS Form 1040) and the assets in the trust are excluded from your estate.

CRTs take one of two forms: either a Charitable Remainder Annuity Trust or a Charitable Remainder Unitrust. The former pays a fixed dollar sum to you each year; the latter pays you a fixed percentage of the assets.

Alternatively, the Charitable Lead Trust provides all income to the charity of your choice for a set period—20 years, for example. At the end of that period, the assets revert to whomever (son, granddaughters, etc.) you initially named as the remainder beneficiary.

You can establish a CRT or CLT:

♦ At the time of your death, via your will, protecting some of your estate from taxation.

♦ During your lifetime, improving both your income tax and estate tax situations.

Other Ways to Reduce Estate Taxes

There are several other ways to cut estate taxes and make sure more of your hard-earned money goes to the people you love, not to the IRS. Again, we recommend that you consult an attorney, but at least if you read this chapter, you'll walk into the law office reasonably well informed (always a plus, especially if you're paying by the hour). Consulting a licensed CPA wouldn't hurt, either.

Life (Saver!) Insurance

Life insurance can be used to pay any estate taxes, thereby nullifying the need for your heirs to sell estate assets to raise the cash for the tax bill. You can also create a life insurance trust to hold or purchase life insurance. At your death, the trustee would collect the proceeds and invest them for the benefit of whomever you named as beneficiaries. The proceeds won't be included in your estate as long as the policies are purchased at least three years before your death or transferred to the trust three years before death.

The Gift That Keeps on Giving

Gifting is another nifty way to lessen the burden of your pesky Uncle Sam. You can give $11,000 per person per year ($22,000 if you're making a joint gift with your spouse). This is an excellent way to reduce your estate, and thereby reduce your potential estate tax. Giving appreciated or potentially appreciating assets such as stock or real estate is a particularly good idea.

If you make medical or educational payments on behalf of your heirs, these payments are excluded from your estate—provided you make them directly to the source. Education is limited to tuition, and you must pay the college directly. Medical payments must be paid directly to the hospital, doctor, or clinic, or to the insurance company, if you are paying for medical insurance. These exclusions only apply when you make payment on behalf of others, not for yourself.

Just a Little Token—Gifts to Minors' Trusts

You can also set up a trust for a child or grandchild and appoint a trustee (a parent, usually) to oversee the use of the funds in the trust. The trustee can pay out necessary sums for the minor's needs—college tuition, for example. At age 21 the child or grandchild has full access to the trust, however.

Super Strategy

If it makes you nervous that your child or grandchild can get into a trust at age 21, you can set up a Crummy Powers trust. A Crummy Powers trust gives the child or grandchild access to the trust for only a few days each year to make withdrawals. Technically, the child or grandchild has access to the principal, but for a very limited number of days each year, making it more difficult for them to squander their inheritance.

Personal Residence Trust

You might also talk to your attorney about transferring your home to a trust, while retaining the right to use the home for a specified number of years.

For a personal residence trust, you make a member of your family the beneficiary. If you die before the specified number of years have passed, the residence stays in your estate (and you have lost nothing). If you live beyond the specified time, you get an exclusion for one of the biggest assets in your estate. The downside to this arrangement, of course, is that ownership reverts to the named beneficiary. If you want to continue to live in the residence, you must pay this named beneficiary a "competitive" rent. Let's hope you are on good terms with him or her at that time!

This is but a short list of some of the more popular measures to save on estate taxes. We urge you to seek professional assistance if you wish to pursue any of these options; individual state laws differ, federal law is subject to annual change and interpretation, and we can't possibly cover all of the nuances for each of these alternatives.

Above all, don't put off estate planning. As we've said throughout this book: it's your money!

The Least You Need to Know

- With the exception of tax-advantaged municipal bonds, dividend income is the most attractive thanks to the Bush tax cuts.

- Long-term capital gains are treated more favorably than short-term profits.

- Remember the wash sale rule: You cannot claim a loss on an investment if you repurchase the same investment within 30 days following the sale.

- You can reduce your estate taxes by giving $11,000 per person per year while you're still living.

Part 6 Advanced Investing Strategies

By now you've developed your own investment I.Q., and it's pretty darn high. You're capable of understanding some fairly complex investments and can decide whether or not to include them in your portfolio.

Most of us will never trade pork bellies or gold, but we can use the same tools that commodities traders use—such as options and futures contracts—to strengthen our own portfolios and protect them from volatile market swings. This section builds on everything you've learned so far and shows you how to apply advanced plays to your investments.

Take a look at the offerings in this part. It'll feel good to have a clue when you hear about hedge funds, or private equity funds at a party or on the news. You may even find that not only do you understand these investments, but they may also help you meet your goals.

Chapter 24

Hedging Your Options

In This Chapter

♦ All about options

♦ Protecting your portfolio with puts and calls

♦ Selling short vs. trading options

♦ Protecting stock positions

♦ Advanced hedging strategies

Well, we promised that at the end of this book we would get into some advanced investment plays, and here we are—about to tackle options. Can you believe you even know enough to get into this topic? But if you've been with us so far, you definitely do!

Weighing Your Options

Options are contracts that give you the option, but not the obligation, to buy or sell a specified quantity of a financial instrument such as common stock. Options have two purposes:

♦ To act as insurance for those who believe prices are going to fall and want to protect their portfolio.

♦ To enable you to profit from rises in stock prices.

Both options and futures contracts, which we discuss in the next chapter, are called *hedges*. You've no doubt heard the phrase, "He's hedging his bets." Options and futures contracts can be used to hedge your bets on the stock market. A caveat: the strategies we'll be discussing in this and the next few chapters are quite sophisticated and should not be undertaken without careful research and the support of a trusted pro.

Our goal is simply to give you enough background so you can ask that trusted pro intelligent questions. Toward that end, we've gone a bit deep on some topics; if you can get through it, great, but if you can't, don't sweat it now. Just keep us around as your personal reference. Should you find yourself considering any of these investments in the near future, we'll still be here right on your shelf.

Investor's Idiom

An **option** is a contract that is listed on an exchange just like a stock. The contract states what is to be delivered for what price and during what time period. At the end of the designated time period, the option loses all its value.

Puts and Calls

There are two kinds of option contracts: *puts* and *calls*. When you buy a call option, you are buying the right to purchase a stock at a set price, called the *strike price*, for a specified period of time—usually a few months.

Investor's Idiom

The **strike price**, also called the **exercise price**, is the price at which the holder of an option contract can buy (call) or sell (put) the underlying security. For example, a ComputerNerd, Inc., 50-call option means you can buy 100 shares of ComputerNerd, Inc. at $50 per share. A ComputerNerd, Inc., 50-put option means you can sell 100 shares of ComputerNerd, Inc., at $50 per share.

Here's a very simple example of how a call option contract works. Let's say you're thinking about buying 100 shares of ComputerNerd, Inc., stock, which is currently selling for $40 a share. You've heard that the company's coming out with an awesome new spreadsheet program and the stock price could rise sharply as a result. Hmmm ... what to do?

You could lay out the $4,000 now for the 100 shares and hold them, praying nightly that you were right about that software and looking forward to selling your stock for $6,000 when the share price rises to $60 for a tidy $2,000 profit. But what if ComputerNerd doesn't release the software on schedule due to an unanticipated glitch, causing the stock price to sink to $20? Oy! This could make for some very restless nights.

Hedge Your Bet with a Call

This is where an option comes in very handy. Instead of laying out $4,000 for 100 shares of ComputerNerd, Inc., contact your broker and buy a three-month call option on 100 shares of Computer Nerd stock at a strike price of $40. The option will only cost you, say, $400. Now, if the stock does rise to $60 before your three months are up, you have a contract entitling you to buy the stock for only $40. You'd pay only $4,000 for $6,000 worth of stock. You could turn around and sell the stock right away for a $2,000 profit. Pretty nifty!

If the stock price falls below $40, simply don't exercise the call option. Sure, you're out the $400 you spent on the option contract, but that's a lot easier to swallow than having spent $4,000 on the stock and watching its value shrink to $3,000 or $2,000 or less. With the call option, you've hedged your bet.

A put option is the opposite of a call option. A *put* is a contract that gives you the option to sell a security at a specified price until the contract's expiration date. With a call, you are hoping for the price of the security to rise, but with a put, you are protecting against a decline.

Prevent Portfolio Wipeout with a Put

Let's say you're bearish on ComputerNerd, Inc. You're convinced the company's spreadsheet software, which everyone else thinks is going to turn the industry on its ear, is destined for failure. Unfortunately, your spouse thinks differently and insisted on buying 100 shares of ComputerNerd at $40 a share. How do you protect yourself from disaster?

Call your broker and buy a three-month put option with a strike price of $36. This contract guarantees that for three months you can dump those 100 shares of ComputerNerd for at least $36 per share. If the stock tanks within the next three months, you can get out at $36, even if the share price drops to, say, $18. Instead of watching helplessly as your $4,000 stake in ComputerNerd drops to $1,800, you can exercise your option and get out with $3,600 intact. Because you've hedged your spouse's bet, you lose only $400, plus whatever you spent on the put option contract.

How Did This Get Started?

Options trading has been around about as long as securities trading, but until the 1970s, options traded in an informal, unregulated manner. Brokerage houses

Options trade in "round lot equivalents" of 100 shares. Each option contract covers 100 shares of the underlying security. Options are quoted in dollar terms, with the 100 shares underneath each option implied; a $2 option, for example, really costs $200—$2 for each share.

specializing in "puts and calls" would advertise their specials of the day in publications such as *The Wall Street Journal*. There was no regulated market.

After the 1973–1974 bear market for stocks took prices of popular indices like the Dow Jones and the S&P 500 down some 40 percent, it became clear that options could play an important role in stabilizing the market and protecting investors from severe drops. The government got involved in standardizing options trading. This led to the creation of the Chicago Board Options Exchange (CBOE). With the creation of the CBOE and its sister institution, the Options Clearing Corporation (OCC), trading in options grew phenomenally.

Risk-Loving Speculator Seeks Cautious Hedgehog

Options can be viewed in two ways: as rank speculation ("I bet you $200 that ComputerNerd, Inc., stock will go up 20 points in 90 days") or as a hedge ("I can protect myself against my ComputerNerd stock going down by buying put options with a $40 strike price for three months"). When you think about it, it takes both a speculator and a hedger to complete a contract.

An option's price is called a premium. The premium is the price the options buyer pays and the options writer receives for the option. The premium is like a commission, except that the premium diminishes in value steadily until the contract expires. A three-month contract offered June 1, 2005, to buy a ComputerNerd, Inc., 50-call option might sell for $3, for example, when it's first offered. The price will decline, however, over the course of the three months. Why? Because as time passes, the option is protecting the buyer for less and less time.

The option's price, or premium, is the maximum loss that the buyer of the contract can experience. An option for 200 shares at $3 costs $600. That's the premium. If the price of the stock doesn't go your way and you never exercise the option, you lose the $600. But that's all.

Investor's Idiom

An option **expires**—becomes worthless—on its expiration date. Options expire on the Saturday following the third Friday of the month in which they can be exercised. For example, ComputerNerd, Inc., December 50 options expire on December 16, 2006. Nine months is typically the maximum expiration date on an option.

An **option writer** (or "seller" or "issuer") creates the options contract, and must stand ready to honor the terms of the contract. If you write an option on 100 shares of ComputerNerd, Inc., common stock and the buyer of your options contract exercises his or her option, you must be prepared to deliver the requisite shares of ComputerNerd, Inc., to the buyer. The **option buyer** (or "holder") pays the options writer a premium for the right to buy the shares of ComputerNerd, Inc., in a call option or sell the shares of ComputerNerd, Inc., in a put option.

In the Money

Options are referred to as either:

◆ "In the money"

◆ "Out of the money"

◆ "At the money"

This swinging lingo simply defines the difference between the option strike price and the current price of the underlying stock.

If the strike price is less than the current market price, for example, a call option would be described as "in the money." You are already ahead by the difference (or spread) between the strike price and market price.

This same situation would be described as "out of the money" for a put option, however. Why? Because, you are behind by the same amount for the put. You are betting the stock will go down, but, darn, it's going the other way.

"At the money" means the stock price and strike price are equal.

Reading an Option Table

Let's take a look at a sample options table for The Coca-Cola Company taken from E*Trade. This chart is for options expiring on November 19, 2005.

Let's look at the first contract on the third line. This is the Coca-Cola $42.50 call option; you see it has its own ticker symbol (KOKV). The buyer of the contract has the right—but not the obligation—to purchase 100 shares of Coca-Cola at $42.50 per share, which is $1.77 less than the closing price of the common stock ($44.27) on May 11, 2005 (you'd need to look up the stock price). This is an example of a call option that is "in the money," because the buyer has the right to purchase the stock for a lower price than it is selling for on the open market.

Fiscal Facts

As the expiration date for an option approaches, the premium gets smaller.

The contract, like all of those in the table, expires on November 19, 2005. Recall that all contracts expire on the Saturday following the third Friday in the month. The volume was 19, or 19 contracts. Because each contract equals 100 shares, the Coca-Cola November 42.50 call options traded an equivalent of 1,900 shares of the underlying common stock.

The last (or closing premium) of $3.20 means that it would cost you $3.20 times 100 (everything being expressed in 100 share terms), or $320, to purchase this call option contract. And notice that your break-even point (strike price + premium – closing price of the underlying common stock) is $42.50 + $5.10 – $44.27, or $3.33. If the stock price goes up more than $3.33 the next trading day, you are ahead of the game. Of course, the stock price and the premium are subject to constant fluctuation (but that's the exciting part, right?).

Now, check out the put. Notice that there is a put option for the same $42.50 strike price. Here, the purchaser is wagering that the share price will decline. Because the strike price is less than the closing price, the put option contract is presently out of the money. The stock would have to decline by more than the difference, or more than $1.77, to be in the money. Notice that the break-even point is different: first, you have to get to at the money, which is the $42.50 strike price; then, you have to recover your premium, or $1.20, for a total stock price decline of $2.97.

	Calls				Strike	Puts				
Symbol	Open Interest	Volume	Net Change	Last	Price	Last	Net Change	Volume	Open Interest	Symbol
KOKU	499	0	0.00	7.60	37.5	.25	-.05	50	1,352	KOWU
KOKH	1,055	0	0.00	5.10	40.0	.55	-.05	10	1,934	KOWH
KOKV	4,538	19	0.10	3.20	42.5	1.20	0.00	0	4,056	KOWV
KOKH	1,055	0	0.00	5.10	40.0	0.55	-0.05	10	1,934	KOWH
KOKV	4,538	19	0.10	3.20	42.5	1.20	0.00	0	4,056	KOWV
KOKI	10,758	660	-0.05	1.50	45.0	2.20	0.00	5	902	KOWI
KOKW	3,894	215	0.05	0.65	47.5	4.00	0.00	0	268	KOWW
KOKJ	475	160	0.00	0.25	50.0	6.10	0.00	0	200	KOWJ
KOKK	0	0	0.00	0.00	55.0	10.90	0.00	0	52	KOWK

Options Galore

Although there are options traded for numerous months; this chart shows only options for expiring on November 19, 2005. Newspapers can't possibly show data on all of the months for all of the companies for which options are traded. Thanks to the Internet, however, you can quickly look up quotes for countless options.

Most Active Contracts

To illustrate the extreme risk involved in trading options, let's examine an actual historical example. Look at the "most active contracts" list in *The Wall Street Journal* for August 8, 2002. Under the most active contract list for that day, you would have found the following information for Cisco:

Option/Strike	Vol.	Exch	Last	Net Chg	Close
CISCO Aug 12.50 P	20,350	XC	0.35	-0.80	12.99

The P stands for Put; since August 7 was an "up" day in the market, the contracts with the biggest losses were put contracts. XC stands for the Exchange Composite. The net change of -0.80 means that the premium declined 0.80 from the August 6 close 1.15! In other words, had you purchased the put option (CISCO Aug 12.50) at the close on August 6 and sold it at the close on August 7, you would have lost 69.6 percent for the day (-0.80 / 1.15 = -69.60 percent)! In dollar terms, if you spent $115, you received $35, for a loss of $80.

Selling Short vs. Trading Options

Before the options market developed, speculators who wanted to bet that a stock's price was going to fall had only one play—to "short" the stock. When you short a stock, you don't actually buy the shares—you borrow them from a broker. You take the stock you've borrowed and sell it. Then you pray (fervently!) that the price of the stock will fall before you have to give the shares back to the broker.

What are you going to use to buy the shares to give back to the broker? That's right, the money you made selling the borrowed stock. What if you don't make any money selling the borrowed stock? You're in big trouble.

Let's say you borrowed 100 shares of ComputerNerd, Inc., agreeing to return them the next day. You go out and sell the 100 shares for $40 per share and make $4,000. If the stock price falls to $32, you'll only need to use $3,200 to buy the 100 shares to return to the broker. You can pocket $800 profit. Pretty nifty.

But what if the stock price shoots up to $50 per share. Uh oh, you're gonna need $5,000 to purchase those 100 shares. Well, you've got $4,000 from selling short. That other $1,000 is going to have to come out of your pocket. Big bummer.

Going back to our historical example of August, 2002: Because August 7 was a strong up day in the stock market, very few put instruments were profitable. But let's look at one that did work: The Verizon October 25 put contract. The contract closed August 7 at $1.50, v. $1.40 on August 6. So you made, for one day, .10/$1.40, or 7.1 percent. If you had simply "shorted" the stock at the close of August 6, at $29.87, and sold it at the close on August 7 at $29.47, you would have made a piddling 1.4 percent.

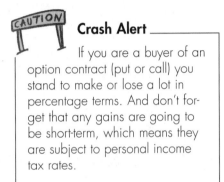

Crash Alert

If you are a buyer of an option contract (put or call) you stand to make or lose a lot in percentage terms. And don't forget that any gains are going to be short-term, which means they are subject to personal income tax rates.

Now you understand why the vast majority of option contracts are not exercised: The buyer of the put or call option is interested in trading the contract, not the underlying stock. The potential for profit is so much greater with option contracts.

Risky Business

Throughout this book, we've harped on the relationship between risk and return—and options are no exception. The very fact that you can reap such high returns with options should tip you off that they are extremely risky.

The day someone lost 69.6 percent on Cisco August 12.50 put contracts, for example, someone else could have made a bundle on Cisco October 15 call contracts. The contract closed at 0.65, up 0.10 for a day gain of 18.2 percent (+0.10/0.55)! The underlying common stock of Cisco gained only 7.6 percent that day. The option provided a much higher return.

> **Super Strategy**
>
> A variation of the covered call strategy is called a "buy-write" program, where you simultaneously buy, let's say, 100 shares of AT&T and write a call option on them. Some professional firms hire individuals specifically for their buy-write expertise to add value to the retirement accounts under their management.

Sellers of option contracts take on even more risk. As we said before, the buyer's maximum loss per contract is the amount of the premium. If, on May 12, 2005, you sold a call option for Coca-Cola November 19 with a $42.50 strike price, you would receive a premium of $320. But if Coke stock rose to $50 per share, you would have to spend $5,000 to be in a position to deliver if, by some chance, your contract was exercised. So, worst case scenario, you could suffer out-of-pocket costs of $4,680 ($5,000 – $320). Oh, the pain.

Option Strategies That Protect Your Stock Positions

In the previous example, we assumed that you, as the option writer, did not actually own the stock and would have to go buy it if the option you sold was exercised.

But suppose you did own the stock. You could write (sell) an option contract on the stock. This is called "covered call writing." When you own the underlying stock, writing a call is a conservative course of action. When you do so, you earn additional income minus the premium the option buyer pays you—which can help offset any minor price weakness in your stock. If the stock moves up in price, and for some reason the option is exercised, you already own the stock, so you won't take a hit on the price. Pretty much a win-win deal.

Using Puts for Downside Protection

An even more conservative step is to purchase a put option for a stock you already own. This gives you downside protection for simply the cost of the put. And, of course, you would fully benefit if the price of the stock went up.

You get unlimited upside, as well as protection on the downside, because the value of the put increases as the price of the stock decreases. This works especially well if the strike price is at or close to the market price, and you purchase the longest put contract, which has the lowest premium and provides more time for the strategy to pay off. This strategy works best if you are concerned about a significant correction in the stock market or your particular stock.

Again, remember that all these strategies involving put and call options trigger income tax events for taxable accounts. Repeat after us: "I will visit my trusted professional should I become intrigued."

Stock Index Options

Unlike individual stock options, stock index options give you a chance to hedge your entire equity portfolio—assuming it is diversified.

Stock index options dominate the options scene now due to the broad acceptance of the product by money managers. *The Wall Street Journal* lists 37 different indices upon which options can be written/purchased. These include well-known broad indices, such as the Dow Jones Industrials, S&P 500, S&P 100, NASDAQ 100, Russell 2000, sector or industry indices, and indices for foreign stock markets.

S&P Index Options

The contracts are listed under Index Options Trading in *The Wall Street Journal*. Let's take a look at the options contracts for two indices: the S&P 100 and the S&P 500 in the May 11, 2005 issue.

If we look under S&P 100 Index (OEX) and scan down to May 550c and May 550p (c standing for call and p for put), we can see the volume, last price, and net change for each:

Strike	Vol.	Last	Net Change
May 550c	2,313	7.90	-4.70
May 550p	4,655	3	1.55

We selected these two contracts because they are closest to the current price ($555.21). How do we know that? Because there is a table set into the Index Options Trading page called Underlying Indexes. And the fourth index down is the S&P 100. The value of the contract, the total exercise price, and the premium are each derived by multiplying each by 100:

$100 \times \$555.21 = \$55,521 = $ contract value

$100 \times 550c = \$55,000 = $ total exercise price

$100 \times 3 = \$3,000 = $ cost to purchase option

You can exercise the contract on any day, just like with individual stock options; however, the contract is settled with cash, not with the security.

The S&P 500 follows the same format and procedure as the S&P 100, with one important difference: the S&P 500 option can be exercised only on the expiration date. This is referred to as a European-style option. American-style options can be exercised on any given day.

Hedge Strategies for Index Options

Hedge strategies for index options are similar to those for individual stock options. Suppose you wanted to hedge your diversified stock portfolio by purchasing the correct number of put contracts. By "correct number" we mean that you would buy put contracts with values that approximate the decline in your equity portfolio that you are worried about experiencing.

Similar to purchasing insurance—which, in effect, this is—your premium is your maximum cost. Let's assume your equity portfolio is presently worth $1 million and is invested similarly to the S&P 100. Multiply $100 times the current value of the S&P 100 ($555.21) and you'll get $55,521. Divide this into $1 million and you'll get $18.01 (round down to 18). To hedge your portfolio, you'll need to buy 18 put contracts.

Pick the put contract closest to the current index price, or 560p, for the month you want. The premium for August 550 put options, for example, is $15.20. What's the maximum cost to you? $15.20 times $100 is the cost per contract, and you need 18 contracts. Your cost is $27,360, or 2.736 percent of your equity portfolio. As you can see, this is not cheap insurance. Equity index hedging is not for amateurs.

The Braveheart of Wall Street

Still with us? Good! If you're hankering for more, we've got two more aggressive strategies for you:

- ◆ **Straddles**. These are the simultaneous purchase of a put and call for the same stock or index at the same strike price and expiration date. The straddle buyer makes money if the price of the stock moves significantly up or down. The straddle writer makes money even if there is little or no stock price movement by capturing two premiums. This is a very hot strategy among professionals.

◆ **The spread**. This is the purchase and sale of options on the same stock, only the options have either a different strike price with same expiration date or the same strike price and different expiration dates.

A bull spread involves purchasing an option with a lower strike price (i.e., "in the money") and the sale of an option at a higher strike price (i.e., "out of the money").

With a bear spread, you sell the option at a lower strike price and purchase the option at a higher strike price.

These strategies can get quite esoteric and should not be tried in the comfort of your own home. And remember, again, that any success translates into short-term gains, which means you'll be paying income tax on them.

LEAPS

Finally, we have LEAPs, which stands for Long-Term Equity Anticipation Security. These are long-term option contracts that are very popular with individual investors. There are two main differences between LEAPs and regular options:

◆ LEAPS can be written for up to a three-year expiration date vs. a maximum of nine months for traditional options. If you are really convinced that the market is going to move strongly in a certain direction, a LEAP gives you more time than a traditional option to wait for that move to happen. All LEAPs expire in December on the Saturday following the third Friday.

◆ The price of a LEAP is one-tenth the price and size of a traditional option. This is much more manageable for individual investors than having to buy 100 round lots every time you want to buy a regular option.

The combination of a longer-term and lower contract size (one-tenth the size of standard contracts) make LEAPs attractive to individual investors. Just be sure you look before you leap—all the strategies in this chapter are from a very volatile and sophisticated game best left to experts.

The Least You Need to Know

- Options are contracts that give you the option, but not the obligation, to buy or sell a specified quantity of stocks or bonds.

- Options and futures contracts are called "hedges."

- When you purchase a "put", you acquire the right to sell a security at a predetermined price. When you purchase a call, you acquire the right to buy a security at a predetermined price.

- You can use options to protect your portfolio from stock market moves.

- Enlist the aid of an experienced broker if you want to get involved with options.

Chapter 25

Fancy Futures

In This Chapter

- How a future differs from an option
- Butter to zinc—the seven main types of commodities
- Buying on margin
- Using futures to offset uncertainty

Looking for a bright future? Well then, you've come to the right chapter. A futures contract is a legal agreement between two parties. One agrees to purchase from the other a specified asset at a specified price at a specified time in the future. Futures contracts are made on everything from commodities, like pork bellies or sugar, to stocks and indices.

There are also options on futures. Now, don't let this confuse you. Just remember that the purpose of these "advanced play" chapters is simply to give you some background in these complicated investments.

Both options and futures are called *derivatives* because they "derive" their value from the underlying security, index, or commodity they represent. Derivatives tend to be short-term "plays" dominated by large institutions. You participate at your own peril. If you do decide to play the game, be sure you work with a very experienced full-service broker specializing in options/futures.

What Is a Commodity?

A *commodity* is a basic food or raw material. If you turn once again to our old friend, *The Wall Street Journal*, you will see toward the back of Section C a subheading entitled Cash Prices. Listed here are cash prices for seven broad commodity categories, plus the London Metal Exchange Prices. The seven categories are:

◆ Grains and Feeds (barley, bran, corn, cottonseed meal, hominy, bonemeal, oats, sorghum, soybean meal, and wheat)

Investor's Idiom

A **commodity** is a basic food or raw material, such as cotton, gold, or pork bellies. There are seven main categories of commodities that trade on specialized exchanges.

◆ Foods (beef carcass, broilers, butter, cheddar cheese, cocoa, coffee, eggs, flour, hams, hogs, pork bellies and loins, steers, and sugar)

◆ Fats and Oils (coconut oil, corn oil, grease, lard, palm oil, soybean oil, and tallow)

◆ Fibers and Textiles (burlap, cotton, and wool)

◆ Metals (aluminum, antimony, copper, lead, steel scrap, tin, and zinc)

◆ Miscellaneous (rubber and steer hides)

◆ Precious Metals (gold, platinum, and silver)

Fiscal Facts

Futures trading is regulated by a federal agency, the Commodity Futures Trading Commission (CFTC). The CFTC, in turn, oversees the National Futures Association (NFA), which is the industry's self-regulating body.

For each of these items, the *Journal* reports the previous day's closing price. On May 11, 2005, the *Journal* reported that Top Quality Minneapolis Barley was priced at $2.45 per bushel. (Note: "Minneapolis" here refers to the exchange on which the barley is traded, not a type of barley.) The London Metal Exchange reports prices per metric ton for aluminum, tin, copper, lead, nickel, and zinc.

It All Began with Farmers

The first commodity exchange in the United States, and currently the largest futures exchange, is the Chicago Board of Trade (CBOT). The CBOT was formed some 150 years ago to serve as a medium of exchange for cash crops such as wheat and corn.

Futures trading began shortly after the end of the Civil War. Today, futures contracts are made not only for commodities but also for:

- Interest rates on all kinds of notes and bonds, including Treasury bills, notes, and bonds

- Indices like the Dow Jones Industrials, the S&P 500, and the NASDAQ 100

- Currency, from the Japanese yen to the Euro

How a Future Differs from an Option

An option is a right, but not an obligation, to buy or sell something at a specified price within a specified time. A *futures contract*, in contrast, is an obligation accepted by both the buyer and seller to make a specific trade at a specified time and price. Where an option buyer pays a premium, both parties in a futures contract put down a deposit, which is called *margin*.

The buyer of a future is "long" or has a "long position." A seller is "short" or has a "short position." Futures orders are entered with a broker just like stock orders.

Buying or selling futures is like trading stocks. "Long" means you own "it" (a stock, a bushel of wheat, whatever) and are betting that "it" will rise in price. "Short" means you do not intend to buy it and are betting that it will decline in price (and if it declines enough, you'll buy it then).

Investor's Idiom

A **future**, or **futures contract**, is an agreement between a buyer and seller to make a specific trade at a specified future date and price. Both parties put down a deposit, called a **margin**.

- "Market" means at the market price

- "Limit" means at or below the limit price to buy, at or above the limit price to sell

- "Stop loss" means execute the order if the contract declines to a predetermined price, at which point the order is executed on a "best price" basis

In the old days, a futures contract could literally result in 5,000 bushels of wheat being dumped on your front lawn! Today, few contracts go to the delivery date, and when they do, delivery is acknowledged by warehouse receipts. The reason delivery rarely takes place is because the buyer doesn't really want the commodity; he or she simply wants to make money by trading it. So, at some point before delivery date, the buyer will sell, and the seller will buy, canceling the contract.

It's like a stock trade: if you buy 100 shares of General Electric at 10 a.m. and sell those 100 GE shares at noon, you no longer have a position in the stock. You probably bought the stock because you thought the price was going to go up and you could sell it for more than you paid for it. Once you've sold the stock you have what we in the biz call "no position."

How Margins Work

When you buy a futures asset, you need to put down that deposit, called a margin. Before you can buy a future, your broker needs to be sure that you have sufficient money in your account to cover the margin.

Margin takes two forms:

♦ Initial or original—what you have to have in your account to initiate the purchase of the futures contract

Fiscal Facts _____

In the stock market, the Federal Reserve has ultimate authority over extension of credit by brokers to their customers (i.e., margin requirements) via "Regulation T." This power was given to the institution as a tool to implement fiscal policy.

♦ Maintenance—what you have to have in your account to maintain (keep) the futures contract

The initial margin is set by the exchange that trades the futures contract you are interested in purchasing. This amount will vary, depending on market conditions, but is usually around 10 percent. Your brokerage firm, however, may require a higher margin. Its decision is binding (unless you choose to take your business elsewhere).

Crash Alert _____

If your maintenance margin falls below the level required by your brokerage firm, you will receive a "margin call" warning you to put up sufficient cash to return your balance to the original margin level. If you fail to respond, your broker will liquidate your position by selling securities in your account. Maybe even the ones Grandma gave you. Yes, it's a cold, cruel world.

The maintenance margin is also determined by the exchange. Typically, the mainte-nance margin is 75 percent of the initial margin.

Here's an example: let's say you buy a $10,000 futures contract with an initial margin of $1,000. If the contract value declines to $9,750, your margin will drop, as a result, to the maintenance level, which is $750 (75 percent of $1,000).

Why? Well, your initial margin was $1,000, but the contract's value has since declined by $250 ($10,000 – $9,750 = $250). That decline comes out of your margin, reducing it from $1,000 to $750 ($1,000 – $250 = $750). At this point, you're still okay, because your margin hasn't fallen below the maintenance level. If the contract drops further, though—to $9,500, for example—your margin is cut to $500. You will be informed that you must deposit an additional $500 to bring your account back up to the initial margin of $1,000.

This simple example shows just how risky futures contracts can be. A small move in the price of the underlying commodity translates to a large dollar gain or loss for the contract holder.

Using Futures to Offset Uncertainty

Why do people mess with these risky investments? Because, just as with options, there are hedgers and there are speculators. Speculators are in the market to "make a killing" (or get killed). Hedgers are trying to offset a future unknown. Let's look at a couple of examples of how ordinary people use futures contracts as hedges against risk and uncertainty.

Suppose you're a cotton farmer. The current price of 40¢ per pound would provide you with a decent profit, but your crop won't be ready to go on the market for another six months. What if the price of cotton declines to 30¢ per pound by then? You could be wiped out. So you sell (go short) March '06 cotton futures. If cotton does drop to 30¢, you make money on your short—the premium for which you sold it. This money offsets the loss on your "cash" crop. If cotton stays at 40¢, you can cover your short position by purchasing a contract at 40¢. Now you have a loss, but you can offset it with the profitable sale of your cash crop.

Here's another example. Suppose you are a home builder about to open up a new development. You accept contracts for completion of new homes six to nine months from now. You've agreed to sell each house at a fixed price—but what if lumber prices go through the roof in the next six months and eat up all your profit?

Well, you could buy lumber futures at $288.70 per 1,000 board feet. If the price of lumber goes up, you have two choices:

- ◆ You could pay the higher price for the lumber and offset it by selling your lumber futures contract for a profit. Remember, if the price of lumber has gone up past $288.70 per 1,000 board feet, somebody out there will be happy to buy your contract.

- ◆ You could accept delivery of the lumber from your futures contract.

What if the price of lumber goes down? Well, the loss on the contract is offset with the lower price you actually pay for your lumber. Either way, you've hedged very nicely. This is a form of insurance, and that's what a hedger is looking for.

Financial Futures

Financial futures currently dominate the futures market. How would an investor use financial futures to hedge? Suppose you are the proud owner of a $1 million equity portfolio (taxable). You have a feeling that stock prices are going to start falling, but you're not absolutely sure; if you sell some of your existing stock positions and the share prices subsequently rises, you've lost an opportunity and incurred capital gains taxes. You look in *The Wall Street Journal* on May 11, 2005, and under the Future Prices heading you see the following:

DJ Industrial Average (CBT) – $10 x Index

	Open	High	Low	Settle	Chg	High(L)	Low(L)	Open Interest
June	10,367	10,371	10,242	10,274	-100	11,012	9,868	41,386

(L)=lifetime

These are futures contracts on the Dow Jones Industrial Average. *Open, high, low,* and *settle* are the prices for the previous day, May 10, 2005. *Chg* is the change in price for that day's trading. Here, it's -100 points. High and low are the lifetime high and low prices for the contracts, and open interest is the number of outstanding contracts.

If your portfolio is fairly similar to the Dow Jones Industrials, you could use these futures contracts to neutralize the negative effect a market decline would have on the value of your portfolio.

The June contract, for example, is valued at $10,274 × $10 = $102,740. Your $1 million equity portfolio divided by $102,740 per contract would require 9.733 contracts to neutralize a market decline. You could buy 10 contracts and plan to sell them for December 2005 delivery. If the market declines, your profit on the sale of the contract offsets your "paper" (unrealized loss) on your equity portfolio. If the market goes up, your equity portfolio appreciation offsets the loss on your contract.

Note, however, that if the market declines, and you close out your contracts at a profit, that profit will be taxed at ordinary income tax rates (you have to hold an investment for at least a year to get the lower capital gains tax rate). Hence, this hedging works much better for tax-advantaged accounts. The taxable investor fearing a market decline has three options:

♦ Use futures contracts, accepting the margin costs and tax consequences

♦ Sell stocks, incurring capital gains and commission dollar consequences

♦ Do nothing and ride out the potential storm

As we've noted throughout this book, over time the stock market has consistently recovered from even the most wrenching declines. Individual investors do best when they choose option three, and just ride it out. But we thought you should know a little about financial futures anyway, if only to impress somebody.

Options on Futures—Oy!

Options on futures contracts are about as risky as you can get. Like regular options, options on futures are a right, not an obligation, to buy or sell. As with regular options, you can either buy calls or puts. Interest rate options on futures, especially on Treasury bonds, are extra hot right now.

In *The Wall Street Journal*, under "Futures Options Prices," you will find "Interest Rate," and under that subheading the following:

T-Bonds (CBT)

$100,000; points and 64ths of 100 percent

If you wanted to purchase September call options with a strike price of 106, your premium would be 1-61. Because the option is quoted in 64ths, 1-61 means $^{161}\!/_{64}$, or 1.953125. Each premium point amounts to $1,000, so the premium would cost you

1.953125 times $1,000, or $1,953.13. You can also buy puts/calls on stock index futures.

The contracts are for specific months and can extend out to two years.

Spread Strategies for Speculators

Speculators toy with all these different futures contracts. Spreads are one of the more famous commodity futures strategies used by speculators. Typically, the speculator is looking for the price differential to widen or narrow between two different crops, like wheat and oats. He buys a futures contract on the commodity he expects to go up more in price, and sells a contract on the other. What happens to the spread in price between the two commodities is critical; not whether one or both increase or decrease.

If you expect oats to increase in price versus wheat, for example, you would buy an oats contract and sell a wheat contract. If you're right, you can make a lot of money. If you're wrong, you can lose a bundle. That's why it's called speculation.

Program Trading

"Program trading" is an expression you've probably heard on the news to describe why the stock market fluctuated sharply in the last hour or so of a trading day. Program traders work for large institutions and set up automated hedges that are triggered when the market hits certain key prices. In effect, they establish a spread—between the S&P 500 Index and a future contract on the index, for example.

When the spread widens because the future price rises, program traders automatically sell futures and buy the index. If the spread narrows via a lower futures price, they sell the index and buy the futures contract. Because the process tends to be highly automated, several institutions buying or selling large sums at any given time can have a dramatic impact on the stock market. In fact, program trading was blamed for the market crash of October 1987.

Fiscal Facts _____

Whether gold will ever regain even a vestige of its former allure is open to question. "Gold bugs" argue vociferously that the only long-term financial discipline for individual nations in a global economy is direct linkage of local currencies to gold. Fortunately or unfortunately (depending on your views), national leaders don't want to have their economic policies limited by a fixed amount of currency in circulation.

Super Strategy
How to hold gold (and other precious metals): you can buy and store gold bars or coins, but these provide no income return, and storage—even in a safe deposit box—costs money. A better strategy is to hold shares of precious metals companies or precious metals mutual funds.

Gold Nuggets

Earlier in this chapter, just for fun, we showed you where to find prices for all kinds of commodities in *The Wall Street Journal*. Unless you're a farmer or bridge builder, these markets should not concern you, with one possible exception: precious metals.

For centuries, the civilized (and sometimes not-so-civilized) world measured wealth in gold. Paper currencies were backed by it, dreams were spun from it, and wars were fought for it. It was, without exception, the one insurance policy against the ravages of inflation. In this country, some 25 years ago, President Richard Nixon severed the last direct tie between our currency and gold, freeing the dollar to seek its ultimate value. With the quadrupling of oil prices and double-digit inflation during Nixon's term, gold had soared from around $30 per ounce to over $800 per ounce. It currently trades for a little more than $300 per ounce.

As a result of the severance of gold's link with the dollar, investors no longer view gold as a monetary asset, but rather as a commodity. If this view is correct, gold will trade in the same wide cyclical ranges as other commodities, and will attract more speculators than investors. Will gold wrench back its historical role of inflation hedge from the current holder: the U.S. dollar? We think it's possible, having seen the dollar's value fluctuate over the years and the varying degree of respect shown to it by other nations. Right now the dollar is king, but we don't subscribe to those who think its reign will last forever.

The question for you, the investor, is whether you should own some or no gold. The answer depends entirely on how you feel about inflation and the dollar. There is compelling evidence that, in an inflationary environment, you would be better off investing in income-producing assets that can raise prices at a rate equal to or in excess of the inflation rate. This would include farm land, which could be leased out to tenant farmers, or an operating business such as Coca-Cola that can raise prices with little reduction in demand.

Precious Metal Companies and Funds

Because we're your pals, here's a list in alphabetical order of 5 precious metal companies, along with exchange list/ticker symbols:

- Barrick Gold Corp. NYSE [ABX]

- Coeur D'Alene Mines Corp. NYSE [CDE]

- Hecla Mining Co. NYSE [HL]

- Newmont Mining Corp. NYSE [NEM]

- Placer Dome Inc. NYSE [PDG]

If you prefer the diversification of mutual funds (and, as you know by now, we do), here are some of the largest no-load precious metal funds, listed alphabetically:

- American Century Global Gold 1-800-345-2021

- Midas Funds 1-800-400-6432

- Scudder Gold and Precious Metals Fund 1-800-225-2470

- Vanguard Special Gold and Precious Metals 1-800-662-7447

The Least You Need to Know

- A futures contract is a binding agreement between two parties. One agrees to purchase from the other a specified asset at a specified price at a specified time in the future.

- A commodity is a basic food or raw material.

- When you buy a futures asset, you need to put down a 10 percent deposit, called a margin.

- Futures can be used to hedge against anticipated changes in prices.

- If you want some precious metal in your portfolio, consider shares of mining companies or precious metal mutual funds.

Chapter 26

Alternative Investments

In This Chapter

- ◆ Investments once available only to the rich
- ◆ Exploring hedge, venture capital, and LBO funds
- ◆ Investing in business dealings via private equity funds and limited partnerships

"We're so glad we've had this time together …." Sorry, got caught up in a Carol Burnett moment. But seriously, we hope you've enjoyed this book. If you've read all (okay, most) of the chapters, you now have a solid grounding in investment basics that will help you sail through your financial life. You've also explored some fun stuff, like options, futures, and precious metals. In this, our final chapter, we'll zip through a few of the "alternative investments" that used to be discussed only in exclusive country clubs among millionaires but have, in the last decade, become available to the average investor.

How Regular Folk Discovered Alternative Investments

"Alternative investments" are equity products like *hedge funds* or venture capital funds that used to strictly be the province of very wealthy investors,

Investor's Idiom

A **hedge fund** is an unregistered investment fund whose managers can pretty much do whatever they want—invest in currencies or commodities, go short or long, use options and futures, etc. Some funds are very conservative whereas others are quite aggressive and make all kinds of risky currency and interest rate plays.

large public and private retirement plans, or universities with huge endowments like Harvard or Yale. These funds used to require $10–$20 million minimum investments, so they were only reasonable for people or institutions that had at least 10 times that much in their portfolios.

A few years back, however, two events occurred that introduced alternative investments to the rest of us. One was a bestselling book *Barbarians at the Gate: The Fall of RJR Nabisco* by Bryan Burrough and John Helyar. The book depicted, in an entertaining way, the efforts of firms like Kohlberg Kravis Roberts (KKR) to take over R. J. Reynolds via a "leveraged buyout."

In a *leveraged buyout* (LBO), one firm will offer to buy up any and all stock of another company at a price significantly higher than the current trading price of the stock. The idea is that the stockholders will be so excited by this higher price that they will sell all their stock to the takeover company. Once KKR owns all of R. J. Reynolds stock, for example, it owns R. J. Reynolds and can do with it what it will. And what it will do is send in a team to pare down debt and cut costs (meaning fire lots of people), making the revamped R. J. Reynolds lean and mean and very attractive to new potential stockholders. Then it will take the firm public again, selling its stock and making a fortune on the sale.

The second event was the media spotlight turned on investors like George Soros, whose hedge funds were blamed by several national leaders for adversely affecting and artificially manipulating currency values around the world.

Hedge Funds

Historically, hedge funds had limited the number of investors to fewer than 100 participants, which meant that they didn't have to register under the Investment Company Act of 1940 ("The '40 Act"). Due to the fact that they are unregistered, hedge funds can invest in currencies, commodities, public stocks and bonds, or whatever they like; they can do so by going long (buying), going short (selling borrowed shares), or using options and futures.

Venture Capital and LBO Funds

While hedge funds move in and out of markets quickly, basically speculating with options and futures and the like, other funds invest for the long haul in new or recently created businesses. These "private equity" funds are more like partnerships than traditional mutual funds. With a straightforward mutual fund, you own shares in whatever publicly traded stocks the mutual fund managers buy. Private equity funds invest in privately owned businesses that do not have stock trading in a public market.

Venture capital funds, for instance, provide the capital for start-up businesses. Investors in a venture capital fund are limited partners. The manager of the fund is the general partner.

Investor's Idiom

A **venture capital fund** invests in new businesses by providing start-up capital. The investors in a venture capital fund are limited partners in the businesses in which the fund invests and are entitled to a share of its profits. A **leveraged buyout fund**, on the other hand, borrows money to buy a company, revamp it, and take it public. Investors profit from what the LBO fund makes when it resells the company's stock.

Leveraged buyout funds are also proliferating. LBOs use primarily, if not entirely, borrowed money to purchase the outstanding stock of a publicly traded company by offering to purchase it from stockholders at a premium. This turns that company from a public to a private company, owned by the LBO's investors. Then the LBO team rigorously reduces the company's costs, pays down its debt, and takes it public once again—kind of like taking a race car with a blown engine off the track, rebuilding the engine, and putting it back on the track.

The rewards? Industry data is hard to come by because there are no reporting requirements for these funds, but they seek to do at least 150 percent better than the Standard & Poor's 500 Index.

Fiscal Facts

Unlike publicly traded funds, which are corporate entities owned by shareholders, private equity funds are partnerships. More specifically, there is a general partner who creates the fund, and limited partners who provide the capital. Typically, the general partner (GP) receives a 1–2 percent annual fee for managing the fund, and 20 percent of the profits realized. The limited partners (LP) receive the remaining 80 percent of the profits (after the return of their capital).

The Private Equity Fund of Funds

Historically, as we said, investment in hedge funds and private equity funds was limited to large institutional investors and wealthy individuals. In effect, Wall Street was servicing Park Avenue. In part, because of the voracious appetite for new capital, Wall Street, along with some major trust banks, have introduced a new concept: the private equity fund of funds. This doesn't mean Wall Street is serving Main Street USA, but it is a step in that direction.

A private equity fund of funds also has a general partner (GP) and investors who are limited partners (LPs). The GP receives typically a 1–2 percent annual fee, and a 5 percent share of the profits. What does the GP do? The GP selects other private equity funds (typically 10–15) in which to invest.

If you are a limited partner in a private equity fund of funds, you become, essentially, a limited partner in whatever funds your GP chooses to buy.

What You Need to Qualify for a Fund of Funds

How do you get to be an LP in a private equity fund of funds? Let's start with financial requirements. A limited partnership interest typically requires a minimum commitment of $500,000. This doesn't mean you write out a check for $500,000 and sit back to wait for the profits to roll in. (For one, who has an extra $500,000 just lying around?) It means that over the next three to six years you will receive "calls" to kick in as much as $500,000, typically in 5 percent pieces ($25,000), with the first 5 percent due when you sign the partnership papers. Obviously, this is a much easier check to write!

Because the partnership interests are not registered as securities under the Securities Act of 1933, you also have to qualify as an "accredited investor." This is defined as someone with more than $1 million of net worth or more than $200,000 ($300,000 if filed/filing a joint return) of adjusted gross income for the previous two years and expected for the current year.

On top of that, you are required to affirm that you are acquiring your LP interest as an investment and not for resale or distribution, and that you will not assign or transfer your interest without the consent of the GP. Got that? Now you can dazzle the cocktail crowd!

But wait, there's more! Congress also stated in a follow-up bill passed in 1940 that to participate in a limited partnership you must also be a "qualified purchaser." Today that's typically defined as meaning that you must have more than $5 million in investments (stocks, bonds, real estate held for investment purposes, commodities, and cash all qualify). How did Congress know back in 1933 and 1940 what current dollar worth would qualify someone as an "accredited investor" and a "qualified purchaser"? They didn't. What they did do was entrust the Securities and Exchange Commission (SEC) to establish and revise, from time to time, the definitions of an "accredited investor" and a "qualified purchaser." The General Partner (GP) of a limited partnership knows that if any of his limited partners is not qualified, the GP could lose his or her exclusion from the 1933 Act and 1940 Act. Therefore, the GP takes on the responsibility and ultimate authority to approve your application to be a limited partner.

How Limited Partnership Works

Assuming you are approved to invest as a limited partner in a fund of funds, what is the sequence of events?

1. You will honor the first capital call, which is 5 percent of your total commitment at the closing. So if you have agreed to a total commitment of $500,000, you will write out a check for $25,000 at the closing.

2. You will receive additional capital calls of, say, 5 percent over the first 6 years or so.

3. You may begin to receive distributions (moolah!) from the fund as early as the third year.

 **Crash Alert**

If you fail to honor a capital call from a limited partnership within 20 days you could face interest charges, and possibly even run the risk of having your interest sold for as little as 50 percent of book value. You definitely don't want to miss a call!

4. As a limited partner, you are entitled to a return of your "invested" capital, plus a pre-determined return (called the "preferred return").

5. After the LPs receive back their invested capital and the preferred return, the GP is entitled to a "carried interest amount" equal to 5 percent of the "carried interest account." The carried interest account is the difference between the aggregate portfolio distributions and the invested capital—in other words, 5 percent of the gain. This is called a "catch-up distribution."

6. After #4 and #5 have been honored, subsequent distributions are split (e.g., 5 percent GP, 95 percent LPs).

7. The fund will last for the number of years in the contract or until all assets are distributed, whichever occurs last.

Pros and Cons of LP Investments

There are several points to consider before getting involved with a fund of funds:

◆ You will receive an IRS Form K-1 to use to report partnership income each year. These are not usually available to meet the April 15 tax deadline, however. You can choose to either file an amended return or pay 110 percent of the previous year's taxes. We recommend that you choose the latter option.

◆ Because your fund has multiple fund holdings and multiple investment holdings in each fund, you will probably face state tax returns in at least several states other than your own.

◆ A fund of funds results in an additional layer of fees that makes it more difficult for you to beat the benchmarks on a long-term basis.

So if you are able to invest and decide that investing in an LP is for you, keep in mind the following advantages …

◆ Potentially superior returns to the public equity market

◆ A diversified portfolio of private equity investments

◆ An opportunity to participate in an equity class traditionally reserved for very wealthy individuals

… and disadvantages:

◆ These are risky and illiquid investments

◆ You have to make a very long-term commitment to the fund

◆ The tax filing requirements are a pain in the neck

The Least You Need to Know

◆ "Alternative investments" are equity products like hedge funds or venture capital funds that used to be strictly the province of very wealthy investors.

◆ A hedge fund is an unregistered investment fund whose managers can pretty much do whatever they want—invest in currencies or commodities, go short or long, use options and futures, and so on.

◆ Private equity funds invest in privately owned businesses that do not have stock trading on the stock market.

◆ Venture capital funds provide the capital for start-up businesses.

Useful Investing Information

Whether you need to contact the Federal Reserve, get a copy of your credit report, or open a brokerage account, this information can help you get in touch with the appropriate people.

Government and Regulatory Contacts

Federal Reserve Board's website:
www.federalreserve.gov

Federal Trade Commission, Consumer Response Center:
www.ftc.gov.

Internal Revenue Service:
www.irs.gov

Securities and Exchange Commission (SEC):
www.sec.gov

The Office of Consumer Affairs:
Securities and Exchange Commission
450 5th Street NW
Washington, D.C. 20549

Social Security Administration:
www.ssa.gov

U.S. Treasury:
You may purchase T-bills directly from the U.S. Government via the Treasury Direct Program or via banks or brokers, usually for a service fee. If you buy direct from the Treasury, you can do so in person, by mail, by phone (1-800-722-2678), or via the Internet at www.publicdebt.treas.gov. To utilize the latter two alternatives, you will need to provide a signature to open your account.

Financial Exchanges

Most exchanges will let you come in and check out their pits full of screaming traders. It's a sight (and sound) worth experiencing at least once in your life!

New York Stock Exchange (NYSE)
11 Wall Street
New York, NY 10005
212-656-3000
www.nyse.com

American Stock Exchange (AMEX)
86 Trinity Place
New York, NY 10006
212-306-1000
www.amex.com

Other exchanges include the Chicago Mercantile Exchange, Boston Stock Exchange, Montreal Stock Exchange, and the Philadelphia Stock Exchange.

Credit Reporting Agencies

For personal credit histories, contact:

Trans Union National
760 W. Sproul Road
Springfield, PA 19064-0390
www.tuc.com

Experian (formerly TRW)
National Consumer Assistance Center
PO Box 2002
Allen, TX 75013
www.experian.com

Equifax
PO Box 740241
Atlanta, GA 30374-0241
www.equifax.com

If you own a business, you'll want to run a credit check on it periodically, too. The three top credit-reporting agencies in this field are the following:

Dun & Bradstreet
One Diamond Hill Road
Murray Hill, N.J. 07974-1218
www.dnb.com

NCR Corp.
1700 S. Patterson Blvd.
Dayton, Ohio 45479
www.ncr.com

Experian (formerly TRW) Business Credit Services
National Consumer Assistance Center
PO Box 2002
Allen, TX 75013
www.experian.com

Consumer Information

Consumer Reports:
www.ConsumerReports.org.

Edmund's Automobile Buyer's Guide:
www.edmund.com

Kelley Blue Book (indispensable when selling or trading cars):
www.kbb.com

Investment Research

Value Line:
1-800-634-3583. A one-year subscription costs $598.

Standard & Poor's Stock Guides:
Annual subscription prices are $220 for the Stock Guide and $370 for the Bond Guide. You can order by calling 1-800-221-5277 or visiting the S&P website at www.standardpoors.com.

The Wall Street Journal:
www.wsj.com.

Amazing Online Articles, Tutorials, and Research Sites

There are some amazing research sites on the web that you can access yourself, such as the following:

- ◆ beginnersinvest.about.com (investing lessons and articles)

- ◆ www.briefing.com (analysts's upgrades and downgrades)

- ◆ www.hoovers.com (company profiles and financial data)

- ◆ www.marketguide.com (earnings estimates from First Call, insider trading from Vickers, and stock screening from Stock Quest)

- ◆ www.personalwealth.com (Standard & Poor's information, including Wall Street analysts's recommendations and consensus earnings estimates)

- ◆ www.sec.gov (essentially all Securities & Exchange Commission filings by companies)

- ◆ www.zacks.com (consensus earnings estimates, broker recommendations, and insider trading)

Internet Brokers

Ameritrade	www.ameritrade.com	1-800-454-9272
E*TRADE	www.etrade.com	1-800-387-2331
Fidelity	www.fidelity.com	1-800-544-5555
Harris Direct	www.harrisdirect.com	1-800-825-5723
TD Waterhouse	www.waterhouse.com	1-800-934-4448
Muriel Siebert & Co.	www.siebertnet.com	1-800-872-0444
Brown	www.brownco.com	1-800-822-2021
Schwab	www.schwab.com	1-800-435-4000
Scottrade	www.scottrade.com	1-800-619-SAVE

Mortgages

Want to use the Internet for online mortgage quotes? Here are three websites:

◆ E-loan at www.eloan.com

◆ Lending Tree at www.lendingtree.com

◆ Quicken Home and Mortgage at www.quicken.com/mortgage

Glossary

12b-1   Servicing fee charged on mutual fund.

401(k)   Retirement savings plan that allows employees who are eligible to choose how much of their pay is to be deducted for investment purposes and how the dollars are to be invested.

403(b)   A version of the 401(k) used by public employers, such as schools, hospitals, and other not-for-profit organizations.

adjustable-rate mortgage (ARM)   A mortgage with an interest rate priced off the yield for the 10-year Treasury note. Since the yield on the note changes every six months, so will the interest rate on the ARM.

adjusted gross income   AGI is gross income from your W-2 form, plus interest income, rents, royalties, etc., minus medical account deductions, alimony payments, and other adjustments.

alternative investment   An equity-based investment, such as a hedge fund or venture capital fund. Alternative investments used to be available only to very wealthy investors.

amortize   To write off a debt or fee over time.

annual report   Report, prepared by a corporation, that includes full disclosure of its financial statements.

annuity   An investment that yields fixed payments during the investment holder's lifetime or for a stated number of years.

ask price   The lowest price that a seller of a security is willing to accept for it in the market.

assets   Any item of value—from baseball cards to stocks—that you own.

back-end load   Fee charged when you redeem (sell) your shares in a mutual fund. Also referred to as "back-end," "back-door load," or "deferred sales charges."

balance sheet   A financial statement that shows what you own (your assets) and what you owe (your liabilities) at a given point in time.

bid price   The maximum price a buyer is willing to pay for a security in the market.

bill   An IOU that the U.S. government issues when it wants to borrow money for one year or less. The government agrees to pay back the lender at a specified maturity date, with interest.

bond   An IOU that a corporation or government agency issues when it wants to borrow money for more than 10 years. The issuer agrees to pay back the lender at a specified maturity date, with interest.

broker   A generic name for middlemen who facilitate trades between buyers and sellers.

business plan   Document prepared by entrepreneurs to show exactly how a new business will be operated; includes projections for sales and profits.

call option   Contract giving the contract holder the right to purchase a stock at a set price, called the strike price, for a specified period of time, usually a few months.

capital   A fancy word for money that is used for business purposes. Corporations issue stock to raise capital, for example.

capital gain   Profit arising from the appreciation of a security.

cash equivalent   Investment that possess little or no risk and can be converted into cash within 90 days.

certificates of deposit   Money market instruments typically sold by banks in three-month, six-month, or one-year maturities. CDs are very safe investments because they are fully insured by the FDIC, up to $100,000.

collateral   Something you own that can be pledged against a loan.

commission   A percentage fee paid to a broker for executing a trade.

commodity   Any product sold in the financial markets that can actually be weighed, such as gold, silver, pork bellies, sugar, or grain.

compound interest   The money you earn on interest (or dividends or capital gains) that you earned in a previous period. Compound interest enables your money to grow exponentially.

corporation   A legal entity that is separate from the owners of the business. This provides limited liability for the stockholders, ensuring they will not be personally sued for the conduct of the business.

credit card   An account that enables you to carry a debt indefinitely, as long as you pay interest.

credit report   Report created by private credit reporting agency (CRA) that is based on what creditors have said about you.

current ratio   A test of liquidity. Calculated by dividing current assets by current liabilities.

debit card   Card that enables you to make purchases with a direct deduction from your checking account.

deductible   The amount of expense you agree to cover before your insurance kicks in.

defined benefit plan   An employer-financed retirement plan that pays you an annual sum upon retirement.

depreciation   The loss in value of an item over time, due to wear and tear.

discount   The amount a bond is trading below par (100).

discount broker   Broker who simply executes trades, for a lower commission and without the additional services provided by a full-service broker.

diversification   A method of decreasing risk by increasing the variety of assets in a portfolio. If you own lots of different stocks, for example, your whole portfolio won't tank if one company goes bankrupt.

dividend   A cash distribution to the shareholders of a corporation represents the owner's pro-rated portion of the profits.

Dow Jones Industrial Average (DJIA)   An average of thirty well-known companies, such as AT&T or McDonald's, chosen by the editors of *The Wall Street Journal* to represent trends in the stock market.

Education IRA   Introduced in 1998, and now called "Coverdell ESA," this is an IRA to which you can make tax-deferred contributions of up to $2,000 per year, per beneficiary, until your kids are 18. Withdrawals for qualified educational purposes are tax-free.

equity   Ownership of property, such as stock or a house.

executor   Person who makes sure that the provisions of a will are carried out.

expiration date   Date by which an option contract must be exercised or lose its value.

fiduciary   A person or entity responsible for investing money on behalf of another person or entity.

fixed-income   Investment that provides income that remains constant and doesn't fluctuate (like stock prices do, for example). Bonds are fixed-income investments because when you buy a bond you are promised regular, steady interest payments.

fixed annuity   An annuity that promises to provide a fixed (predetermined) sum in an annual or other regular (e.g., monthly) interval.

front-end load   Sales charge deducted from the principal invested in a mutual fund.

future or **futures contract**   An agreement between a buyer and seller to make a specific trade at a specified future date and price.

general obligation bond   A bond backed by the tax-raising ability of the issuing state or municipality.

hedge fund   An unregistered investment fund whose managers can pretty much do whatever they want—invest in currencies or commodities, go short or long, use options and futures, etc.

income statement   A financial statement that delineates income and expenses.

index fund   A mutual fund designed to mimic the performance of an established benchmark such as the S&P 500.

inflation   A general rise in prices.

initial public offering (IPO)   A corporation's first stock sale.

institutional investor   A corporation, hospital, city government, or other large entity that has a portfolio.

interest   Payment you receive for lending someone your money. Interest is also the fee you pay when you borrow money.

IRA   An Individual Retirement Account, which is basically a shell that protects money you put in it from taxation until you start to take money out.

Keogh   Pension plan that allows business owners to shelter more income than SEPs or SIMPLEs do and to create vesting schedules for employees.

leveraged buyout fund   Fund that borrows money to buy a company, revamp it, and take it public. Investors profit from what the LBO fund makes when it resells the company's stock.

liability   A debt you owe. The opposite of an asset, which is something you own.

lien   A legal right to take someone's property and hold it until the owner pays a debt.

liquidity   The ease with which an investment can be converted to cash.

living trust   Legal document that names someone to manage your assets if you die or are incapacitated.

load   Sales fees and commissions charged to investors in a mutual fund.

long bond   The 30-year Treasury bond.

Long-Term Equity Anticipation Security (LEAPS)   Long-term option contracts that are very popular with individual investors.

lump sum   The entire value of an investment taken in cash at once.

margin   Deposit put down by both parties in a futures contract.

marginal tax rate   The tax rate you pay on the last few dollars you earn.

money market   Highly liquid financial instruments with rates that vary from day to day, week to week, or month to month.

municipal bond   A bond issued by a municipality like your city, town, or county. The interest paid by municipal bonds is, with a few exceptions, not taxed by the federal government.

mutual fund   A company that collects money from investors and invests on their behalf, usually in diversified securities.

net asset value (NAV)   The dollar value of all the marketable securities (stocks, for example) owned by a mutual fund, less expenses and divided by the number of the fund's shares outstanding.

net earnings from self-employment   The amount of income on which you pay self-employment tax, minus the tax itself.

note   An IOU that a corporation or government agency issues when it wants to borrow money for between one and ten years. The issuer agrees to pay back the lender at a specified maturity date, with interest.

option   A contract that states what is to be delivered for what price and what time period. The option is a right, but not an obligation, to exercise the rights stated in the options contract. At the end of the designated time period, the option loses all its value.

options buyer or **"holder"**   Pays an options writer a premium for the right to exercise the option contract created by the options writer.

options writer or **"seller"** or **"issuer"**   Creates an options contract, and must stand ready to honor the terms of the contract.

par   The original price of a bond, note, or bill. It is also the amount that the security will pay back at maturity and is referred to as "100."

penny stock   Stock trading at a low price, usually a few dollars.

pension   A regular payment made to you (or your family, if you pass away) by your employer that reflects how much you earned and how many years you worked at your job.

portfolio   A collection of assets such as stocks, bonds, mutual funds, real estate, fine arts, baseball cards, and so on.

premium   The amount that a bond is trading above par (over 100).

pre-tax   Describes dollars that are deducted from your pay before taxes are applied. Pre-tax contributions to a 401(k) or 403(b), for example, are deducted from your pay before it is taxed.

principal   The original dollar amount of a fixed-income investment; the amount received upon maturity.

probate   State court that decides how an estate will be distributed when the deceased person's will is nonexistent or unclear.

prospectus   A legal document prepared by a mutual fund and sent out to potential investors that describes the fund and its operations.

put option   A contract that gives you the option to sell a security at a specified price until the contract's expiration date.

quick ratio   A measure of liquidity. Calculated by dividing current assets less inventory by current liabilities.

return on assets (ROA)   Net income divided by total assets.

return equity (ROE)   Net income divided by book value; an indication of profitability.

return on investment (ROI)   The amount you expect to earn from an investment over a given period of time. ROI is also called rate of return (ROR) and is expressed as a percentage of your original investment.

revenue bond   A bond issued by an agency of a city, county, or state for a specific purpose. Revenues from that agency pay the interest on bonds that are outstanding.

revolving line of credit   Credit that puts an upper limit on what you can borrow. You can borrow up to that amount, and you pay interest only on what you actually draw down.

rollover IRA   Used to shelter money that's in a 401(k) if you change jobs and can't put the money in your new job's retirement plan.

Roth IRA   A new type of IRA that is more flexible than the traditional IRA but is only available to families earning under $100,000 a year. As long as your Roth IRA has been open for at least five years, you can withdraw up to $10,000 to buy a first home.

round lot   One hundred shares of stock.

Savings Incentive Match Plan for Employees (SIMPLE) IRA   A new option for self-employed people and small businesses with few employees, growing in popularity because it's very easy to use.

Securities and Exchange Commission (SEC)   Regulatory agency started in 1933 by Congress to protect investors.

self-employment tax   A tax self-employed people have to pay into Social Security because they don't have an employer contributing on their behalf.

Simplified Employee Pension (SEP) IRA   Essentially an IRA for someone who is self-employed, and small businesses with few employees. A SEP is like a 401(k), but contributions are limited to 15 percent of pretax earnings or $30,000, whichever is less. A good retirement plan for a sole proprietor who doesn't have employees.

Social Security   A system managed by the federal government, which provides money to people who are retired or are not able to work because of disability.

sole proprietor   Someone who owns a business alone, without partners.

spread   The difference between the ask and the bid price of a security or between interest rates.

stock market   The stock market doesn't exist as a physical place—stocks are traded at various stock exchanges, such as the New York Stock Exchange or The American Stock Exchange. All the exchanges together, along with the over-the-counter market, are considered the stock market.

stock option   The right, but not the obligation, to buy a stock at a fixed price after a fixed period of time (usually 12 months) for a fixed period of time (10 years).

stock split   A division of stock that increases the number of shares outstanding and decreases share price of the stock.

strike price   Also called the exercise price; the price at which the holder of an option contract can buy (call) or sell (put) the underlying security.

trade   To buy or sell securities on the financial markets.

Treasury bill securities   Securities issued by the U.S. Treasury that mature in one year or less. Treasury securities are fully guaranteed by the government and can be sold within 24 hours.

Treasury bonds   Long-term securities issued by the U.S. Treasury with maturities over 10 years. Historically, the Treasury has issued 20- or 30-year bonds.

Treasury notes   Securities issued by the U.S. Treasury that offer maturities from 2 years to 10 years.

Treasury strip   A piece of a Treasury security, such as a coupon or principal payment, that has been stripped from the original security.

Unit Investment Trust (UITS)   Hybrid mutual funds that invest like mutual funds but, unlike them, have a fixed termination date.

variable annuity   An annuity that provides an undetermined amount that depends upon the return of the annuity's underlying mutual fund; basically a mutual fund wrapped around an insurance contract.

venture capital fund   Fund that invests in new businesses by providing start-up capital. The investors in a venture capital fund are limited partners in the businesses in which the fund invests and are entitled to a share of its profits.

vested   Eligible to receive a pension. An employee is typically considered vested after five years at a company.

will   A legal document, signed by you and witnessed, that gives explicit directions as to who or what is to get whatever specific assets of yours you choose to list.

yield   The return on an investment expressed as a percentage.

How to Avoid Turning the Stock Market into Your Own Personal Emotional Roller Coaster

We all have friends who freak out over the stock market constantly. Guess what? Freaking out doesn't make your investments grow one bit faster.

Admittedly, buying and selling stock can be a very emotional game. It's like betting at the racetrack or rooting for your home team(s). At the end of the trading day, the race, or the game, you know whether you were a winner or a loser. You experience either instant gratification or instant remorse.

What's wrong with that? Nothing, if you can keep a single day or event in perspective. But most of us can't. When we turn to the next trading day, race, or game, our decision-making process is influenced strongly by the previous day's wins or losses. Winners get elated (and reckless); losers get depressed (and overly cautious).

These dramatic ups and downs are what make sports and the racetrack such glorious entertainment. But this is not the way to approach the stock market, unless you are investing merely for entertainment. If you are investing to meet your financial goals, however, you need to avoid using the stock market as your own personal emotional roller coaster.

How to do this? First, recognize that emotion comes from the heart and logic from the brain. In games of chance, emotion usually overcomes logic. So you need to come up with ways to block your emotions from affecting your logical decisions. Start by becoming an investor, not a trader. Traders live and die on the gains and losses they experience in the stock market each day; you don't have to do that, and you shouldn't. You are (or should be!) a long-term investor. Forget about day trading—that's an emotional game. If you need some drama in your life, go to the racetrack; it's a lot cheaper!

Market Timing Doesn't Pay

The best way to short-circuit an emotional response to the ups and downs of the stock market is with cold, hard facts. If you're going to invest in the stock market, start thinking in 10-year time chunks. Don't even pay attention to what the market is doing day to day.

Still don't believe us? Okay, assume that on December 31, 1990, you invested $5,000 in an S&P 500 Index Fund. Ten years later, on December 31, 2000, that $5,000 would have grown to approximately $25,000, assuming you did nothing more than reinvest the cash dividends in additional fund shares. Now, 10 years equates to about 2,500 trading days. If you were out of the market for the 20 best trading days, your $25,000 would have only grown to $12,500—that's right, less than 1 percent of the trading days during that decade accounted for half of the stock market return! Do you think you (or anyone else) could have picked those 20 days in advance? Do you think you can pick the 20 best trading days for this decade? Don't kid yourself, kid!

Here's the best part. Sure, there are a lot of pros out there who have access to better immediate information than you do. They could possibly beat you on day-to-day trading. Over 10 years, however, you and the pros are pretty much on equal footing. So stay calm, cool, and collected, no matter what the market does from day to day.

Here's the best piece of advice we can give you: don't even bother to look at the price of your stocks and/or mutual funds every day. If you're a long-term investor, why do you care what happened yesterday? If you're at a cocktail party and somebody asks you how your stocks are doing, just say, "I don't know; I'll check at the end of the month." Won't that get their attention!

Stick to the Plan, Stan!

In this book we taught you two strategies to control that 'ol devil emotion. The first is dollar cost averaging. You invest a fixed sum of money on a regular basis (every month, every paycheck, and so on). When prices are low, your fixed sum will buy more shares; when they are high, you buy fewer shares. This technique is a time-proven variation of the Holy Grail of investing: buy low, sell high. Second, rebalance your portfolio back to your initial asset allocation target levels every few years. Once again, you're cutting back on recent winners and adding to recent losers. It's like buy low, sell high. In both cases, you don't have to think about what you're doing, thereby keeping the emotion locked up. You just do it. Your 401(k) (or 403[b] or 457 plan) is the easiest example of these concepts. You automatically have a fixed sum deducted from your paycheck each payday (dollar cost averaging), and it is invested according to your standing instructions. And once per year, you rebalance and inform the plan administrator of your decisions.

Diversify!

Finally, don't put all your eggs in one basket. That's really exposing yourself to emotional highs and lows. Owning just one or a few stocks leaves you vulnerable to bad news that is company-specific, rather than stock market specific. During the year 2002, many employees lost a lot of money because they were heavily invested in their company's stock. So be a savvy investor: invest long term (10-year timeframe), dollar cost average, rebalance on a predetermined schedule, and stay diversified. All that logic will override any emotional reactions to stock market news that could derail your steady ride toward achieving your investment goals.

Index

F

G

J–K–L

M

Q

R

X–Y–Z

Check Out These
Best-Sellers

STANDARD & POOR'S

Standards & Poor's is pleased to offer the first 100 responders each month during 2005-2006, a complimentary copy of the S&P Stock Guide. To obtain your free S&P Stock Guide, return this card **(originals only)** and include your name and address below. All requests should be forwarded to: Philip Gentile Vice President Investment Services, Standard & Poor's, 55 Water Street, 43rd floor, New York, NY 10041.

This free offer is for purchasers of *The Complete Idiots Guide® to Investing, 3rd Edition by Alpha Books* **with a shipping address in the United States.**

Name _____

Address 1 _____

Address 2 _____

City _____

State _____ Zip Code _____

Standard & Poor's Privacy Notice

Contacting us reveals your address and any other information you include. We will use this information to help us fulfill your order or respond to your inquiry. Occasionally, Standard & Poor's shares data collected about customers and prospects with other units of The McGraw-Hill Companies and with respectable third parties, whose products or services we feel may be of interest to you. Many of our customers find these promotions valuable, whether they are shopping for merchandise, taking advantage of a special offer, or purchasing unique services. All of your personal information will be stored in a secure database in the United States, access to this database is limited to authorized persons.

If you would like to confirm the accuracy of the information we have collected from you, or if you have questions about the uses of this information, please mail a written request to Philip Gentile Vice President Investment Services, Standard & Poor's, 55 Water Street, 43rd floor, New York, NY 10041.

For more information about The McGraw-Hill Companies' Customer Privacy Policy or a complete listing of The McGraw-Hill Companies' premium brands, visit our website: www.mcgraw-hill.com.